eric
parry architects

Artifice

e
pa

volume 4

Introduction

Joseph Rykwert

Philip Guston, *Painter*, 1980 (cat. no. 40), lithograph.

Introducing this fourth volume of the work of Eric Parry Architects, I am aware that I do so after a hiatus: after all, every single one thing is made up of three parts, Aristotle taught us (*Poet* VII 2): A fourth volume to present the architects' continuing output is therefore – necessarily – a new beginning.

But there is another, and a truly melancholy reason for the sense that we have to start anew – since the first three volumes of this series were each one prefaced by Eric's – and mine – dear friend and collaborator, Dalibor Vesely. His death in 2015 has been mourned by his many friends and associates – as it has by the many students who were inspired by his teaching. What he and Eric Parry – and I – had and have in common is the conviction that architecture is as much a cultural activity as it is a social, a technical and economic one; as Dalibor put it: 'architecture is the praxis of culture'. A sense, too, that any building, particularly any new building, must challenge – even the most casual spectator or visitor – to demand some response; perhaps even interpretation and – whenever it can command it – some admiration from them.

In all EPA's work such a hermeneutic expectation has always been implicit. That is also why, I would suggest, the work now presented in this fourth volume – as had that in the earlier publications – offers a range of sensory (as it does of intellectual) experience to engage a visitor or spectator; even, occasionally, the casual passer-by; and I will try – for my part – to examine the implications of such an approach as I consider it in relation to some of EPA's recent buildings.

A token of this expectation is that Eric has been among the very few architects of his generation who have regarded collaboration with painters, sculptors or other artists a normal part of the design process. Characteristically, the very first project published in the first volume of the survey of EPA's work is for the workshops they had arranged for two artists – the sculptor Antony Gormley and his colleague and friend, the painter Tom Phillips.

Most of the buildings illustrated in this volume are urban; and the urban condition, even the very nature of urban fabric – impose some operation on building types. For London, the most diffuse type has long been the two-up, two-down terrace house, whose outlines were fixed by the fire regulations after the 1666 disaster. The one radical development of it early in the eighteenth century, was the running of terraces made up of such houses together into a quasi-palace. But permutations of it were infinite, and the one London housing development which attempted to defy it – the Adam brothers' Adelphi estate – was a signal failure. Perhaps John Nash's terraces lining Regent's Park offer the most extravagant and extensive exploitation of it. Another type was created by the end of eighteenth and beginning of the nineteenth century: the office block: a building on several levels, its one or two ground floors given to retail trade, all the floors above more or less unencumbered rentable space.

A different approach, independent of any types, *demands* and *involves* the architect in operating within a context, often a richly historical context which may involve ritual – or least, ceremonial action that needs to be acknowledged, respected – and occasionally and knowingly defied. Inevitably, consciousness of that second condition makes EPA the preferred architect when the design of buildings which shelter ceremonial – even liturgical – activities are in demand; so that when the renewal of St Martin-in-the-Fields was being planned they were called on; it also allowed them to deal most convincingly with the ceremonial space of a City Livery Company – The Leathersellers' Hall. Livery companies are an odd feature of the City of London – originally trade sodalities – almost unions and they have become part of the City's governance and many have been constituted as charitable foundations as well as dining associations, whose occasions are attended with much ceremony. The accommodation therefore includes a council chamber and a library all splendidly furnished with leather-upholstered furniture as befits the trade which it commemorates, but the true centre is the dining-banqueting Hall (the seventh since the Company was 'chartered' in 1444) the high walls of which are encircled by a tapestry frieze, the work of the Scottish artist Victoria Crowe which recounts the Company's doings.

The Livery Company had bought the site of St Helen's nunnery in the sixteenth century and the abbey church, now the parish church of St Helen's Bishopsgate can be seen through clerestory windows; while the south wall of the St Helen's Place building over the hall has been refaced in dark, purplish terracotta – and all that happens in the shadow of the Gherkin.

It was about this time that the neglected (and war-damaged) buildings of the London Charterhouse had to be restored and adapted to new conditions – particularly to an influx of visitors. What had been a black-death mass-grave on the edge of the City round 1350, had a strictly enclosed, semi-eremitic, Carthusian priory built over it half a century later; that monastery, (savagely suppressed by Henry VIII) was being turned into a Tudor mansion when the buildings were bought by a philanthropic privateer, Thomas Sutton. He established his double charity in the revamped old buildings: a school for pensioned boys (they were moved to Sussex in the 1870's where boys – and now girls, of course – pay a flat fee; but also a home for (now) forty poor brothers – single or widowed indigents who are provided with service rooms and a small income for the privilege of praying for the founders' repose: which makes the whole a semi-ceremonial but historically rich, complex establishment – easily identified as Thackeray's Grey Friars (not that he had liked his own schooldays there) to which he has the worthy Colonel Newcome retire after his bankruptcy. Its fabric is therefore an overlay of the many levels which had to be organized to welcome visitors through a new entrance court, leading them past the remains of the original priory church (some of it incorporated in the chapel) and the recovered tomb of Sir Walter de Manny, the priory's founder. The very complexity of the site seemed to provide an ideal occasion to engage EPA's approach.

EPA have only dealt with that two-up, two-down type when they have adapted such houses – most elegantly – for individual clients; but recently they have undertaken to deal with the now much more pervasive type, flatted housing. Towards the end of the eighteenth century, the type developed from the break-up of the palace in Europe, and from the up-grading of the urban slum in Britain. The large square block in East Village is their contribution to the complex reoccupation of Olympic competitors' housing; it shows EPA's almost uncanny ability to innovate while working on what is now almost the most common of building types.

Like much of the East Village building, the lower two floors are constituted as houses with street-level gardens, and a mix of social and free-market housing above. The travails of that project are no concern here – nor are all the severe planning and budget restrictions – not all of them unwelcome. But the character of the project is EPA's own – notably the avoidance of the besetting fault of the type: the constricting rigidities of a grid. That quickening is due in part to the way blocks are articulated, partly to the placing of balconies, but also to the staccato, Italianate design of the frame and its relation to the panelling. Budget restrictions notwithstanding, EPA have supplied their own art: brightly coloured silk-screened panels, in a style not unlike Corbusier's later paintings which become the balustrades of some balconies.

But EPA have much explored a different and later type of building; one which was formulated in the nineteenth century, the office building, with commercial space on the ground floors, rentable space indefinitely extending above. EPA first registered a notable success

opposite: Detail of the table and carpet designed by Eric Parry for The Leathersellers' Company.

Volumus quod sint unum corpus et una communitas perpetua et corporata et quod habeant successionem perpetuam · Henricus VI Rex 1444 ·

opposite: The Charterhouse's Entrance Court with the recovered tomb of Sir Walter de Manny.

above: Joseph Emberton's Simpson's of Piccadilly, now Waterstone's.

in dealing with it early in their work at 30 Finsbury Square in Islington – just beyond the edge of the City of London – which was a much applauded as a highly successful and very handsome variant on it. The rectilineal exterior limestone structure was rhythmically calibrated in counterpoint to the regular steel-and-glass transparent inner skin. In another early example, in the office block at the top of Savile Row, EPA invited the New York artist, Joel Shapiro to contribute a metal constructive sculpture which is arrestingly suspended over the recessed entrance of the building. And they have, in a sense, achieved the acme of the type in designing a home for the London Stock Exchange, which occupies the north side of Paternoster Square and in which they had also invited the contribution of some 'figurative' collaborators: the sundial expert Frank King and the letter designer and letter-cutter Lida Cardozo Kindersley.

Being able to play a more extreme variation on the type in his latest work must stand as another witness to the vitality of the office – and indeed these early essays led them to involve artists ever more vitally into their projects so that they have taken an increasing prominent part in the configuration of the work.

When working on One Eagle Place – to exemplify the most prominent recent example, and one of the first buildings shown in this volume – it has three faces: one to Piccadilly, another to the very narrow Eagle Place and a third to Jermyn Street; the fourth side being 'built in' to the corner building of Piccadilly and Lower Regent Street. The main entrance is from Piccadilly – a few doors away from Joseph Emberton's emphatically horizontal thirties-modern Simpson (now Waterstone's) building; and it stands in polychromatic opposition to Norman Shaw's dun, Portland-stone Piccadilly/Regent Street buildings, diagonally across from the Piccadilly Hotel – which had been conceived as backing into the Regent Street Quadrant; though that had later been neutered by Reginald Blomfield. Only that Piccadilly side of the hotel with its splendid 'giant' colonnade remains intact of Norman Shaw's Imperial gestures.

That prominent Piccadilly front of Eagle Place conforms to the type, being articulated by the usual shop-fronted ground floor, with a mezzanine and a duplex floor over; its tall, red-speckled gently coloured main windows announce the crowning polychromy; since EPA have invited the sculptor Richard Deacon to 'implant' a vigorously coloured faïence cornice to dominate the Piccadilly, that northern 'face' of the building – its impact enhanced by a recessed attic above it. That façade makes for a dramatic intervention at the heart of London – that harshly plastic but splendidly floral garland provides a challenging but harmonious contrast to the jarring, purse-grabbing lights of the neighbouring Circus, (with its aluminium Eros-Anteros shooting an arrow down Shaftesbury Avenue to commemorate an altruistic Earl, from whom it is named by a far-fetched pun – shaft-bury – on his title); nor is the Jermyn Street face forgotten, where a broach-like gold plaque by Stephen Cox dominates the oblique corner of that building. So a prime example of a building type which is an urban commonplace also establishes a striking, even a demanding presence at the heart of London.

A much more close-fitting variant on the type is the St Pancras Square building at King's Cross, which forms a part of the most important current planning development in Central London that occupies the abandoned shunting yards and the site of the disused cylindrical gasometers at the back of King's Cross Station. EPA's building occupies a central position at its northern edge. The site is trapezoidal – front and back parallel, (front about half the length of the back), sides oblique. The structure and much of the exterior cladding is in weathering steel (commonly known as Cor-ten) whose rusty colour and strictly orthogonal structure marks its contrast with its neighbours, all examples of less felicitous (or so it seems to me) adaptations of that same type.

The southward short side, spanned by a deep Vierendeel truss takes up the insistent orthogonality of the structure; but also opens the ground floor onto the new public space to be occupied by commercial users southward, as the type demands, but also inviting participation in the open space (which I am tempted to call a common) on its southern face – while irregularities of the site allow for the vagaries of access and parking on the north. More than in some of his other buildings, the configuration and the neighbourhood invite the landscaping of the flat roof – on which they worked with the landscape architect Todd Longstaffe-Gowan – as an almost wild marshland-park. Its material and configuration make this building the effective climax of the whole development; and it offers a standard by which its neighbours will inevitably be assessed.

Eagle Place and King's Cross offer two almost opposite examples of EPA operating the gamut of possibilities offered by the same building type in very different circumstances and on contrasting sites. A number of other examples show them considering different possibilities: as in the Savile Row example I mentioned earlier and in other instances in Bond Street where the minimal, typically thin late-twentieth-century face of recent buildings has to reconcile it with its thick stone or stucco neighbours.

Between St James's Square and Apple Tree Yard, a building facing onto Duke of York Street is largely occupied by office use; yet it is articulated – or rather conditioned – by a complex site and by a number of historical precedents, giving the type some of the allure of the historically qualified buildings I described earlier. The southern face, to St James's Square, was the location of Josiah Wedgwood's original showroom which is commemorated by a ceramic display in the generously open entrance hall – while on the north face, to Apple Tree Yard, a monumental inscription at ground level records Edwin Lutyens' working in that building during and after World War I (which meant that it was where he designed the Cenotaph and much of his Indian work). That Indian connection is also commemorated by a life-size relief figure carved in Indian diorite by Stephen Cox. The two bounding elements which had been largely gutted and used to install rather luxurious – mostly underground appointments – are articulated by a linking element which is marked by a shallow colonnade along Duke of York Street which offers a quasi-promenade to the bland street face.

The office building type underwent yet another transformation soon after the last war, when it moved outside the urban context into the 'Business' – or the 'Science' Park. Again EPA's earliest major buildings happened to be a variant of that adapted type – an impeccably detailed office building in Stockley Park, an early – and brilliantly successful – contribution to such developments set in the western reaches of London. It is one of the very first buildings illustrated in the first of these four volumes. More ambitiously, EPA organised the siting of another, more scientifically orientated development, the Granta Science Park at Great Abington, south of Cambridge, where EPA were co-responsible for the general plan of the estate (working with the Munich landscape architects, Latz + Partner). It is organised round a splendid cricket pitch – and the initial building is a modest if welcoming – and beautifully detailed amenities pavilion. In fact, the layout of the park followed the purchase of nearby Abington Hall, a late Georgian building (Pevsner is rather patronising) in a Repton landscape park: so it was The Welding Institute that initiated that development. Much more recently, EPA have given The Welding Institute a new headquarters – consisting of a complex of metal testing 'hangars' and their attendant offices. EPA persuaded the Institute to shelter within a fine exterior by 'coating' the complex in a skin of faïence battens – a material they had used so successfully – if rather differently – at the Holburne Museum in Bath – and which here gives the complex of offices and workshops a unity and a rich, distinctive surface.

The shallow colonnade along Duke of York Street, which connects Apple Tree Yard to the main entrance to 7 & 8 St James's Square.

As chance determined, two buildings, very similar in purpose and scale were designed about the same time; effectively they were both concert venues for schools where music is an important part of their activities. Both buildings were blessed with idyllic settings: the Cathedral School of Wells (which can claim to be the very oldest school in Britain) overlooks splendid lawns and has the eighteenth-century Cedars Hall as its headquarters while the cathedral is a powerful presence in the background; while the Music School for Brighton College is set in the unusually sympathetic Victorian Gothic setting of the College enclosure and has rather different requirements which the inclusion of a heavily insulated percussion room indicates.

Effectively orthogonal, the Wells music school commission accommodates the concerts which are an essential part of the school's life and the commission was won in a limited, invited competition. I was moved to learn that what convinced the Jury finally were Parry's enchanting drawings which conveyed the buildings' quality but also those of the wooded environment which the very name of the building suggests. In fact – if I may add a personal note here – I first met Eric Parry himself, still a student – as a draughtsman – more than forty years ago when he produced a brilliant and wholly convincing version of a project in Jerusalem with which I was struggling. This quality of sensitive and very accomplished draughtsmanship seems to extend to all the drawings which issue from the office.

One of the most recent projects to figure in this volume is the terrace restaurants set on the first floor of the Covent Garden market building's eastern face – and so backing on the Opera House. It has a – necessarily – light, but inflected structure, the front gently curving up towards the centre, the sides therefore lower and moving forward, giving the shell a decided sinuosity to contrast vividly with the granite rigidities of Charles Fowler's original structure and offer a spectacularly inviting addition to the Covent Garden complex.

If I have been so insistent on EPA's crucial skill in the manipulating of type that is because it must be so for any substantial practice nowadays, however innovative, however original. Nevertheless EPA are not hemmed by any such procedures. The enormous care they lavish on the smallest commissions, and on the smallest details within them, has made them excellent designers of smaller objects: furniture and even textiles are obvious by-products of their work. The approach which has also made them masters of body-hugging interior spaces as witnessed by their superlative designs of spas (Mandarin Hotel, Hyde Park Hotel) in which again they involve a sculptor, the same Stephen Cox who contributed to several of their other buildings.

However impressive these achievements, they will be inevitably overshadowed by the sheer bulk of EPA's further involvement in the development and manipulation of the office building type at which they have become uniquely adept. Earlier, at 60 Threadneedle they had given the usual office accommodation a gently curved façade and allowed window shading to let that sinuosity fully command of the situation, and so make that building one of the handsomest additions to the city. As the fame of the EPA offices has grown, so the work has also grown in scale; and the last – as yet uncompleted – project illustrated in this volume, the offices at 10 Fenchurch Avenue, the largest building they have designed so far. The project has gone through a number of permutations, some demanded by the owners, more by the planning authorities. Yet at the end of that tortuous process EPA emerge victors and the project now under construction shows the virtues of their approach – and of their tenacity. Vertically it has four effective levels; retail takes the two street levels. Nine rentable floors above that is office space; then the plan is retraced and further inflected to accommodate four more floors of office space: the whole crowned with a landscape which I am tempted to think of as a forest-park. At ground level, a passage through the building follows an ancient right-of-way and is interrupted by a large square two-storey hall – called banking hall; though its notable feature is a screen allowing the display of mobile works contributed by visual artists.

Though it occupies so prominent a 'face' on a city thoroughfare, the bulk of it is carefully faceted. The break at the eleventh floor, and the change of material and of glazing makes it almost seem that there are two buildings, one set above each other though the nature of the glazing and of the harmonising facing material provide the strong unifying surface – and the whole is crowned by a generous, and wild-seeming but in fact a carefully landscaped roof-park.

EPA are fortunate to operate at a time that seems to have worked free of the wretched stylistic squabbles which troubled much recent architecture: 'post-modern', 'high-tech', 'rationalist' (a misnomer, surely), 'classical', 'deconstructive' (more misnomers) are some terms bandied about, sometimes judgementally. No such label would fit at all comfortably any of the work presented in this volume – nor any they have done in the past.

Here is an architecture which is clearly, explicitly, proudly of their time. Yet always equally clearly, equally securely anchored in a past whose rich and fertile ground always nourished their projects as well as their speculations. Theirs is an architecture which requires to be judged and to be appreciated on its own terms.

View from the south façade of 4 Pancras Square, showing the extent of the triangular space of Pancras Square with the German Gym, the Great Northern Hotel and one of the towers of the former Midland Grand Hotel designed by Sir George Gilbert Scott in the background.

The northern side of St James's Square, London, with Eric Parry Architects' 7–8 St James's Square (mid frame) alongside Duke of York Street leading to Sir Christopher Wren's St James's Church.

Timely and Enduring Architecture

Jay Merrick

> For the first time I feel somehow
> That it isn't going to last,
> That before I snuff it, the whole boiling
> Will be bricked in
> Except for the tourist parts ...
>
> Philip Larkin, 'Going, Going', 1972

What is it about our cities and their architecture at the beginning of the twenty-first century that could be said to be both grounded and uplifted by tradition? It's not enough to point out, for example, that there are 600 listed buildings in the City of London alone, or that Bradford has one of the highest concentrations of listed buildings in Britain per capita. As for contemporary architecture designed as historic pastiche, I believe it is an insult to the past, and detrimental to the way the continuity of architectural tradition should be perceived. Buildings of this type belong in the satirical pages of Evelyn Waugh's *The Loved One*, as if they were bodies embalmed by Mr Joyboy in his necropolitan oasis, Whispering Glades.

Evelyn Waugh, *The Loved One* (1948), passim.

The tradition of architecture and place, thoughtfully pursued, is not about static perfections or dutiful representations of tradition or history; it a quest to achieve a living form of engagement.

Eric Parry Architects was established in 1983, and by now it is probably unremarkable to suggest that its work arises from an unusually sophisticated consideration of context, and a degree of meticulously crafted resolution that is unsurpassed in British contemporary architecture. The phenomena of history, place, and tradition are obviously evident in the architecture, as is the great influence of the idea of the European city as an agent of civility and creativity.

But one also encounters architectural improvisations – sometimes quite radical – that decisively transcend this content. The design vibrations produced by the practice's temporal and cultural tuning forks are not always predictable, and this aspect is, I think, particularly significant.

In the past, we have encountered the architecturally legible punctuated by the architecturally unexpected in projects such as St Martin-in-the-Fields and the Holburne Museum, Bath. And, of the works shown in this book, it is hardly hagiographic to suggest that designs such as those for 4 Pancras Square and 7–8 St James's Square are outstanding in the way they are intensely place-specific, yet architecturally original interventions in two utterly different London settings. In both cases, incidentally, the commercial performance has been impressive. This is an established outcome of EPA's commercial architecture, an earlier benchmark being

1 Aldermanbury Square, which achieved the City's highest space-rental rates when completed in 2007. The practice has always possessed the rare ability to convince clients to support unusually high qualities of materiality, detailing and fit-outs.

Indeed, this produces one of the challenges in describing their work: the use of certain words and phrases are unavoidable. They include: *refined, precise, rich materiality, finesse, exquisite, superb detailing.* Some, or all, of these terms have appeared in every commentary on the practice's projects that I've read; and they are salutary in relation to the way the same words and phrases are used by rather too many architects, and their clients, to accentuate little more than the specifically superficial qualities of their buildings.

In general day-to-day movement through London, and other British cities and large towns, one finds it difficult to walk past most substantial architectural schemes without imagining that giant hands had, in a matter of moments, simply attached vast prefabricated fascias directly onto the concrete or steel structures of yet another obligatory 'stunning landmark building'; no significant human skill required; and the soundtrack would be a series of loudly echoing grunts and clicks as the integral studs on the backs of the fascias are pushed into the structure's receiving sockets.

These buildings have architectural characteristics – articulations of plan, for example, or perhaps elevations in the now fashionably 'historically contextual' New London Vernacular manner endorsed by the Greater London Assembly for housing, which has become a default, planning-friendly approach to the design of substantial buildings. But they often come across only as default-mode urban products. Many new, nominally significant buildings have the strangely insubstantial aura of props that support the dramas of commerce, consumption and other kinds of monetised bunkering.

There is nothing objectionable about these quotidian dramas, of course – unless the buildings that serve them erode, rather than add to, contextual significance. It's notable that even in a situation of extreme design restraint and potential contextual banality – the creation of the East Village on London's Olympic site – Eric Parry and his team designed its residential blocks in the distinct manner of Berlin's twentieth-century *Plattenbau* housing developments; a customs union, so to speak.

There is a remark in Eddie Heathcoate's engrossingly metropolitan introduction to *Eric Parry Architects Volume 3* that seems even more relevant now than when it was published in 2015: "Whatever the architectural and structural change, the three centres [the City, Westminster and Southwark] have maintained a certain psychogeography, enough of the traces of history and use to preserve at least a spirit of the particular – the place." And if the traces of history become less than traces? What, then, can be particular, even in spirit?

"All continuity of history means is, after all, perpetual change," William Morris told the 12th annual meeting of the Society for the Protection of Ancient Buildings in 1889, "and it is not hard to see that we have changed with a vengeance.... Surely the vile and disgraceful heaps of misery and fatuity that should not be called buildings, which curse our towns and curse the history of the country, are truly and properly the expression of our life."

That uncomfortable diagnosis might be tested against the acceleration of what is, in both physical and financial senses, the urban turnover since the 1980s. In the twenty-first century, supercharged real-estate values and redevelopment have eroded or hollowed out portions of the majority of our towns and cities, and this is particularly the case in London.

Is it fanciful to think about the *enduring* character and tradition of cities, and the buildings and settings in them, when the evidence of their urban histories now compete with the super-abundant traces of other kinds of information that has no physical or temporal depth, and very little civic or ethical content? The existential realities generated by pixelated imagery, and the fugues associated with personal digital communication, have become culturally and psychologically significant components of most lives. Our sense, and fields, of perception are becoming simultaneously more concentrated, and more fragmentary.

Digital images can only be remembered in significant detail for a few days, and neuroscience also tells us that analogue images are more fully recalled, and convey emotion in a way that on-off photons can't. A digital image of Hawksmoor's St Mary Woolnoth won't produce the experience of approaching the church as it approaches you; nor can it prompt anything like Ian Nairn's uncanny reaction to it: "You don't remember until afterwards just how odd the building is... it transcends originality." The unbroken analogue wavelengths of light that emanate from the early eighteenth-century stone are themselves analogous to the survival of architectural tradition which, in Hawksmoor's case, was expressed in particularly novel, if not relatively surreal, ways.

Duke of York Street with St James's Square in the background, and Eric Parry Architects' designed 7–8 St James's Square on the left; also on the left a brief view of Stephen Cox's sculpture *Relief Figure Emerging* (2015) commissioned for the corner with Apple Tree Yard.

Ian Nairn, 'St Mary Woolnoth' in *London* (1966).

FULLER'S
THE RED LION
EAT.
AL DUCA
97
Harvie
GEO. F. TRUMPER

opposite: 4 Pancras Square's east façade from across Regent's Canal in London.

right: 5 Aldermanbury Square, north façade seen from the main square with Brewers' Hall on the right.

How do we understand – and particularly in cities – which phenomena around us seem meaningful, beyond the fact that they exist? What buildings or places or settings possess qualities that engage us in a resonantly particular, rather than superficially general, way? How many of these simultaneously pregnant states of being (or, indeed, states of building) can we absorb and understand in any single moment through what Kenneth Frampton describes as a "cultivated perceptual process"?

In a collection of essays by various authors in memory of Dalibor Vesely, see Kenneth Frampton, 'Towards an Ontological Architecture' in José de Paiva (ed.), *The Living Tradition of Architecture* Routledge, (2017), p. 155.

Nevertheless, aspects of our surroundings do sometimes spring into a heightened condition of presence that is initially wordless and uncritical – though, of course, even this apparently naked reaction must be triggered by an indissoluble core of established memories and emotions. I would offer Four Pancras Square in the King's Cross Central development as an example. It is something of a visual, spatial and tactile shock to encounter this building's composition of massive weathered steel Vierendeel trusses, external framing, and counterpointing recessions; and then to feel, unexpectedly, like a human figure in a palpable, spatially situated tableau.

In a quite different way, something similar is experienced at Granta science park in the Cambridgeshire countryside, though this time it's about the relationship of buildings and figures in a rural landscape. Here, the practice's extension of The Welding Institute is the first of the buildings in the science park whose architecture is a direct response to the surrounding landscape composed by Humphry Repton in 1803, and sensitively extended by Latz + Partner in the late 1990s.

Eric Parry refers to the subtly coloured patterns of panels on the elevations of the three big wings of the extension as a kind of camouflage. The patterns do illustrate a very suitable land-rising-to-sky conceit, but their gradations – particularly in the case of the three huge conjoined 'barns' of the testing wing – are also a distinct kind of art, accentuated rather than diminished by the practice's characteristically precise detailing.

The question of landscape in relation to site or architecture is less commonly a significant issue in Central London, but was central to the initial narrative aspect of EPA's assiduously restrained internal interventions at London's ancient Charterhouse. The entrance sequence effectively begins in the re-landscaped Charterhouse Square and leads to a new, beautifully crafted wrought-iron threshold pergola at the historic railings of Chapel Court. As a result, the once cloistered religious Charterhouse complex, which dates back to the fourteenth century, is now expected to attract at least 80,000 visitors a year; they will find that the interventions have left the resonances of faith and time, and the Charterhouse's fundamental aura of mystery, intact.

The Charterhouse scheme reminded me of a conversation with Eric Parry in 2008 which touched on architecture's relation to space. He confessed to a fascination with the polar environments faced by explorers: "Nothingness and hallucination, the recurring dream. No horizons in a white-out. What does it do to you?" This sensitivity about potential nothingness led, quite logically, to another sensitivity: "If I'm thinking about a building in a square, I'm also thinking about the street and what the street needs, and what a wall is to a square... the different lines that make up a civilised city. Metaphor, narrative and juxtapositions. And one other thing: the surrealism of cities."

The relatively few architects interested in reacting to, and expressing, phenomenal communions of time, place, and facets of culture in their work would not regard those remarks as surprising. However, the way the practice combines, with an almost forensic care, four aspects of design is remarkable. The first is a commitment to the tradition of architecture; the second is the intensely detail-conscious, Epicurean care taken to convey the highly crafted *making* of the practice's buildings, inside and out – the *homo faber* factor, as it were; the third is Parry's profound interest in the relationship between art and architecture; and the fourth, as already inferred, is the incidence of surreality in his work.

Of the buildings described in this book, the confluence of history, art and surreality is most vividly orchestrated at One Eagle Place. Not far away at 7–8 St James's Square, we encounter what is arguably the practice's most impressive and perfectly finished low-rise commercial scheme to date. It's a masterfully contrived, unexpectedly poetic evolution of formal manners, materiality and sculpture engendered by the historic signifiers of the locale – but also by what comes across as an untrammelled act of architectural imagination.

In the practice's hands, these ingredients can produce unusual architectural (if not intellectual) tensions. Leaving aside past projects in highly distinct, if not dominating settings – St Martin-in-the-Fields is the most obvious example – designs are generated by the imprecise auras of history and place; and yet they are often expressed in architecture of exquisite precision, great physical richness and unexpected modulations, such as the cantilevered, stylistically curious pavilion that projects from the rear of 7–8 St James's Square.

A 1919 essay by TS Eliot, "Tradition and the Individual Talent", discusses the tradition of poetry, but his ideas seem equally relevant to Eric Parry's architecture, which might be said to create three-dimensional harmonics (but not frozen music; see page 136) prompted by the history of places, and their architectural traditions. Eliot questions the general tendency to identify and celebrate individual differences in poetic creativity: something apparently new, isolated and unexpected is too often singled out. And then – you need to replace his words *poet* and *write* with *architect* and *design* – he says this:

"Whereas if we approach a poet without this prejudice we shall often find that not only the best, but the most individual parts of his work may be those in which the dead poets, his ancestors, assert their immortality most vigorously. And I do not mean the impressionable period of adolescence, but the period of full maturity.

"Yet if the only form of tradition, of handing down, consisted in following the ways of the immediate generation before us in a blind or timid adherence to its successes, 'tradition' should positively be discouraged. We have seen many such simple currents soon lost in the sand; and novelty is better than repetition. Tradition is a matter of much wider significance. It cannot be inherited, and if you want it you must obtain it by great labour. It involves, in the first place, the historical sense... and the historical sense involves a perception, not only of the pastness of the past, but of its presence; the historical sense compels a man to write not merely with his own generation in his bones, but with a feeling that the whole of the literature of Europe from Homer, and within it the whole of the literature of his own country, has a simultaneous existence and composes a simultaneous order. This historical sense, which is a sense of the timeless as well as of the temporal, and of the timeless and of the temporal together, is what makes a writer traditional. And it is at the same time what makes a writer most acutely conscious of his place in time, of his own contemporaneity."

We see exactly this tradition-charged contemporaneity in projects such as One Eagle Place and 7–8 St James's Square, and perhaps in the most virtuosically phenomenal way at the new Leathersellers' Hall, in the heart of the City of London, which is an *haute cuisine* feast of referential, beautifully made improvisations of space, furnishings and markedly different atmospheres.

Though less gripping in terms of architectural staging, the equipoise of tradition and contemporaneity is just as evident in relatively straightforward projects such as the addition to the Opera Terrace which overlooks the northeastern portion of Covent Garden. The new structure is keyed into the Victorian colonnade grid beneath, and the articulations of the pleated glazing of the envelope simultaneously suggest 1970s High Tech and Paxton's nineteenth-century glasshouses.

Detail of the new canopy over the entrance of The Leathersellers' Hall, where one of the scrolls (right of the frame) displays the heraldic outline of a demi ram in reference to the livery company's coat of arms.

TS Eliot, "Tradition and the Individual Talent", I, *The Egoist* (Sept. 1919), p. 55.

This is, strictly speaking, a radical addition to the terrace, yet it does not in any way insult the architecture of its neoclassicist host.

Relative to their scales, there is as much artfully conceived craft in this small intervention as there is at One Eagle Place. The *making* of architecture, and its aesthetic effects, is perfectly evident in both schemes. They recall a genial little essay by WR Lethaby titled *Art and Workmanship*, written in January 1913, the same year that Adolf Loos published *Ornament and Crime*. Lethaby was certainly not endorsing Loos's idea of a true and appropriate craft to be appreciated by an exclusive (and in his case, egregiously snobbish) cultural elect.

"If I were asked for some simple test by which we might hope to know a work of art when we saw one," wrote Lethaby, "I should suggest something like this: EVERY WORK OF ART SHOWS THAT IT WAS MADE BY A HUMAN BEING FOR A HUMAN BEING. Art is the humanity put into workmanship, the rest is slavery. The difference between a man-made work and a commercially-made work is like the difference between a gem and paste." Though Lethaby was not addressing commercial architecture, his words are apposite.

We can certainly understand the architecture shown in these pages in those terms, and in the various ensembles of furniture and fittings designed by Eric Parry. But I think what makes many of the buildings remarkable is the way they seem simultaneously familiar – contextually coherent, to put it very plainly – yet also quite other. The music pavilion at Wells Cathedral School has a calm, classically simple external form which nevertheless suggests, at least to this observer, a quite mysteriously archaic temple in the Somerset landscape, something singular, timeless and unexpectedly *found*. It's equally clear what the art and craft of the literally sensational Piccadilly façade of One Eagle Place references or abstracts, but one does not experience it as an elevation covered in historical and architectural footnotes.

In the case of 10 Fenchurch Avenue, the formal inspiration of the design is the magnificently Expressionist Chilehaus in Hamburg, the finest example of the city's pre-war *Kontorhaus* office building type. However, 10 Fenchurch Avenue's plan, central passage segment, and the design of its remarkable summit structure completely transcends this original inspiration and introduces something unique and substantial to the streetscape and arcane grain of what the City of London's past director of planning, Peter Rees, describes as the "foothills" of the Eastern Cluster of towers.

The original edition of Bernhard und Hilla Becher, *Anonyme Skulpturen: A Typology of technical Construction*, which was published in New York by Wittenborn and Co. in 1970, here in James Stirling's copy.

Ultimately, in Eric Parry's most ambitious buildings, there is always a strongly individual sense of what might be thought of as the art and imagination of time and place. Although he was writing about art, music and poetry, perhaps this remark in Hans-Georg Gadamer's essay, "The relevance of the beautiful", captures something of this dynamic in the practice's architecture: "Once again it is a question of articulating that space between identity and difference with which we are already familiar. One has to discover the autonomous time proper to a piece of music, the autonomous time proper to a poetic text, and this can only happen in one's 'inner ear'. Every reproduction, every poetic recitation, every theatrical performance – however great the performers may be – only succeeds in communicating a genuine artistic experience of the work itself if with our inner ear we hear something quite different from what actually takes place in front of us."

Lethaby's capital letters, see WR Lethaby, 'Art and Workmanship', *The Imprint* (Jan. 1913).

The architecture described in these pages is therefore not part of "the whole boiling" deplored by Philip Larkin; and it is evidently proof against the fibrillating opinions and expectations that currently render many lives and places doubtful, or strangely insubstantial in different ways. As this monograph hopes to show, the practice's architecture is very particularly of, and for, places in a way that much contemporary architecture is not. It continues history without a vengeance. It rejects sentimental inertia. It is timely, and lasting.

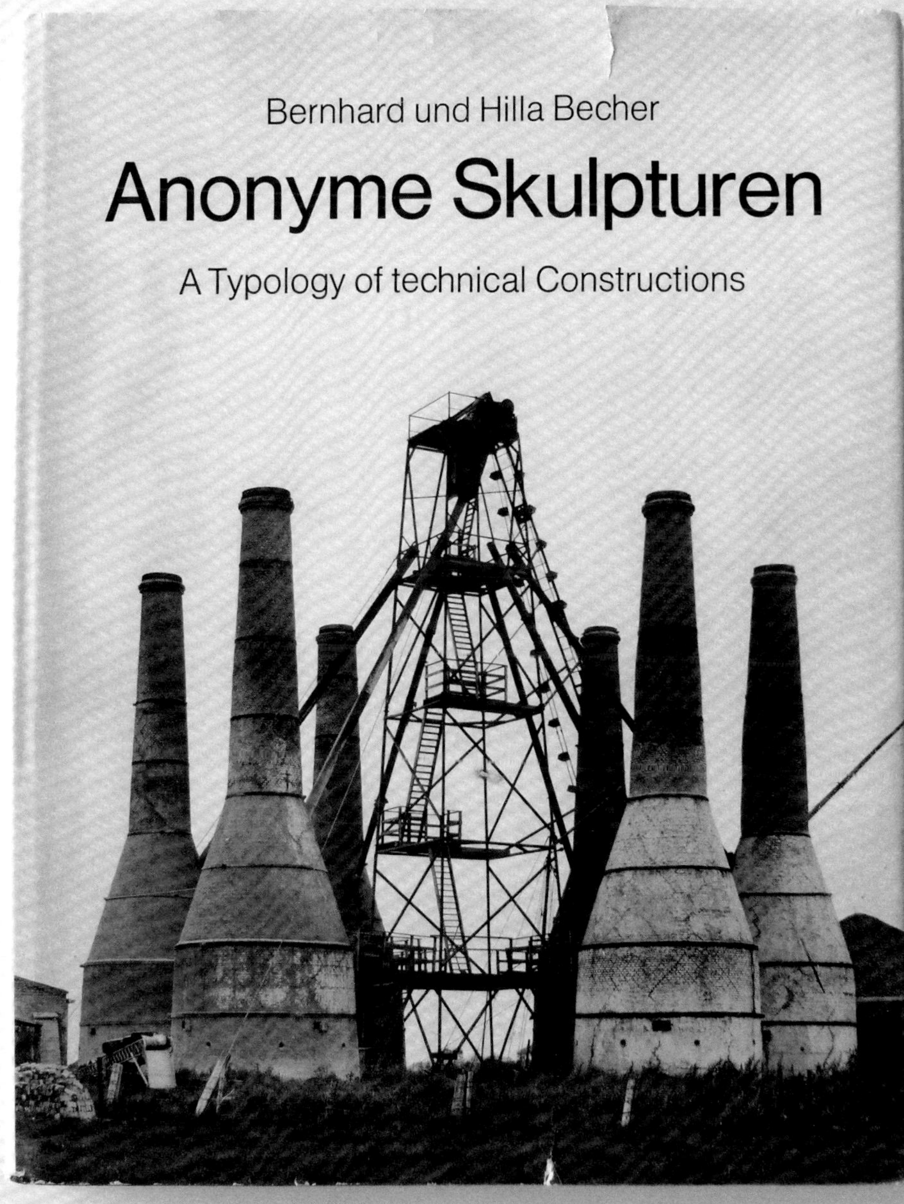
Bernhard und Hilla Becher
Anonyme Skulpturen
A Typology of technical Constructions

epa

volume 4

Contents

NOT FOR SELF BUT FOR ALL

4 Pancras Square

The design of the south-facing façade is masterful in the way it balances the striking presence of the truss-and-steel frame with the modulation of the setback balconies, which have an in-out rhythm accentuated by their white ceramic fascias and vitreous enamel handrails, and by the matching ceramic gleam of the *brise-soleils* on the higher-level glazing.

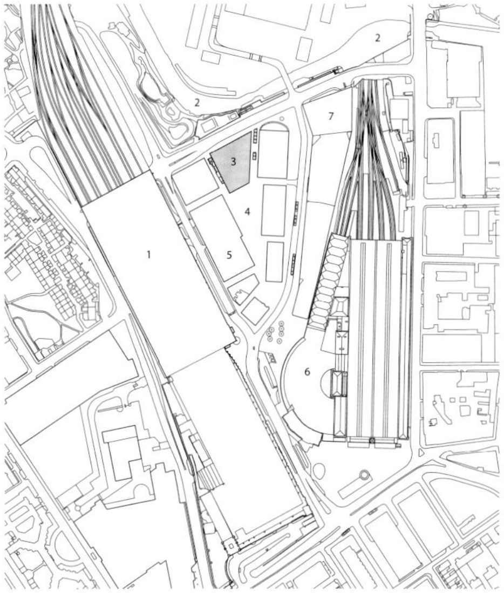

1 St Pancras Station
2 Regent's Canal
3 4 Pancras Square
4 St Pancras Square
5 Zone B
6 King's Cross Station
7 Zone A

N

0 200m

1:10,000

As this book goes to press, 4 Pancras Square is the only one of the 32 completed buildings and schemes under construction in Argent's development of the 67 acre swathe of once-degraded ex-railway lands between King's Cross station and Canal Reach whose structure dominates any consideration of its architecture as a whole.

The photographs of Bernd and Hilla Becher were a significant influence on the design. In the 1960s, following the Bechers' first exhibition at the Galerie Ruth Nohl in Siegen, Germany, their ostensibly laconic images of rugged industrial structures introduced a visual art that conveyed studiedly disinterested, and repetitive, moments of truth.

In a *Time* magazine article in 1969, headed "Beauty in the Awful", Bernd Becher said that the industrial structures he and his wife photographed "are so full of fantasy there is absolutely no sense in trying to paint them; I realised that no artist could have made them better. This is purely economic architecture. They throw it up, they use it, they misuse it, they throw it away".

Today, the opposite is much more likely: the idea of architecture as disposable fantasy objects applies not to industrial buildings but to superficially flashy, cheapjack commercial architecture. The other buildings in Pancras Square, apart from one whose exposed, iron-wrapped columns are not integrally structural, have forms that are clad in various familiar ways; which means that despite their considerable size and surface detail, the architecture of these Grade A office buildings – and particularly their envelopes – rarely conveys a sense of depth or weighty substance; they manage to seem substantially superficial, as it were.

The architecture of 4 Pancras Square – a 12-level, 170,000ft^2 building – is certainly a celebration of exposed steel structure, and its progressively weathering steel posts, beams and bridge-scale trusses are a powerful reference to the industrial character of London's King's Cross area in the second half of the nineteenth century; powerful, but highly refined in their rhythms, key details, and effects of depth and perspective. In a broad sense, something of the Bechers' "moment of truth" is evident in 4 Pancras Square.

It's obvious that 4 Pancras Square has been designed and built to last, and it projects a powerful sense of physical and commercial endurance in a part of the city that has been subject to a turmoil of change since the nineteenth century. According to Booth's 1892 London poverty survey map, a clump of nine gasholders intruded on what is now the roughly wedge-shaped Pancras Square site, and there was a big coal depot immediately to the north. Before that, EH Dixon's 1837

Eric Parry, *Elevation study for an office building at the proposed St Pancras Square, King's Cross London* (October 2003).

Elevation study for an office building at the proposed St Pancras Square, Kings Cross London

October 2003
(+ base May 2014) [illegible]

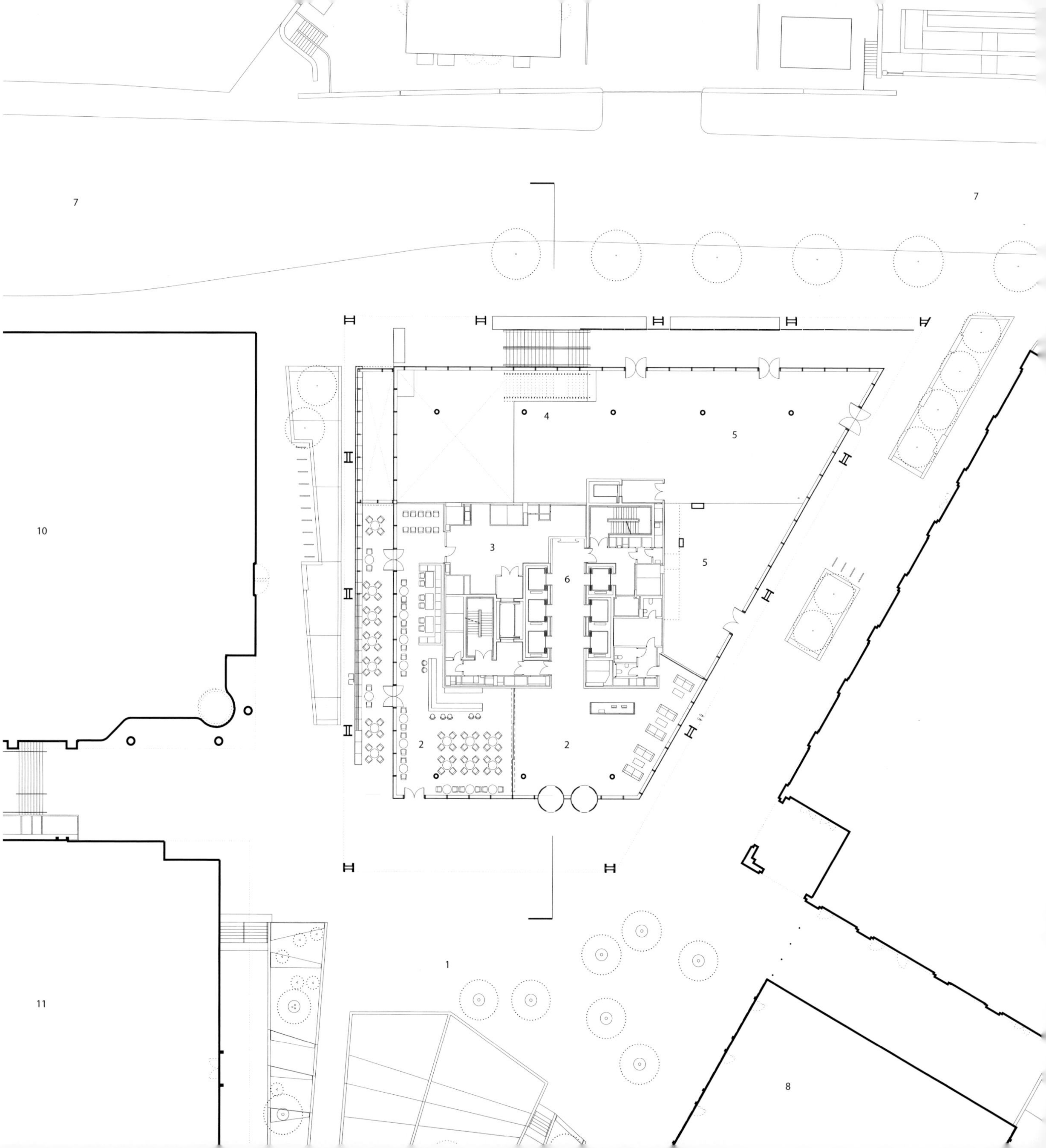

ground floor plan

1 Pancras Square
2 office reception with café area
3 café WC and preparation area
4 possible future stair (fit-out)
5 retail unit
6 lift lobby
7 Goods Way
8 2 Pancras Square
9 3 Pancras Square
10 5 Pancras Square
11 6 Pancras Square

N

0 10m

1:500

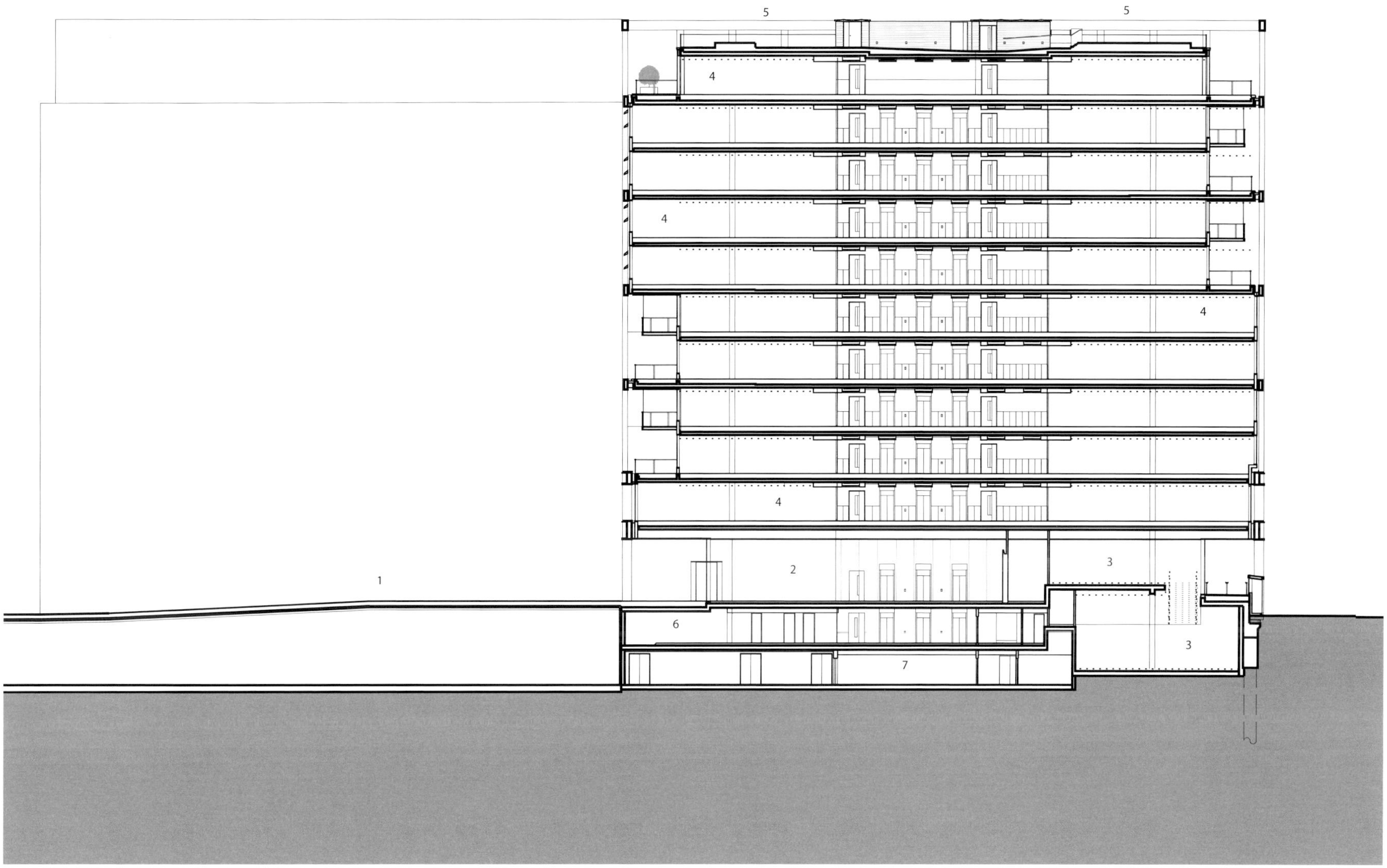

section

1 Pancras Square
2 reception
3 retail
4 office floors
5 roof garden
6 lower ground
7 basement

0 10m

1:500

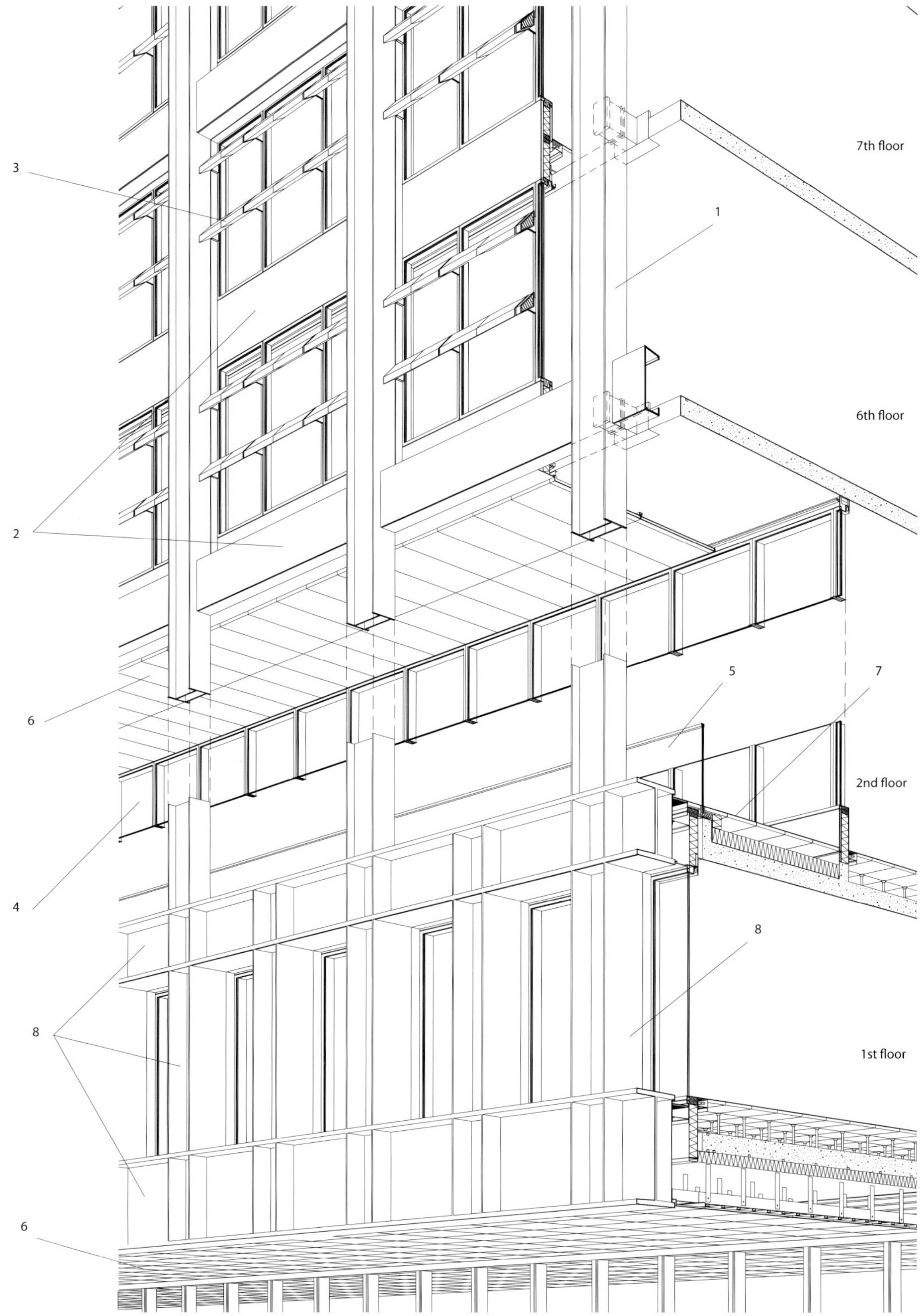

perspectival section

1 weathered steel structural pier
2 weathered steel panel
3 extruded glazed terracotta brise-soleil panel
4 full-height glazing
5 structural glazed parapet with vitreous enamel handrail
6 aluminium ceiling cladding
7 inverted roof system
8 weathered steel Vierendeel truss

Forming the structural belt of 4 Pancras Square, the sections of Vierendeel truss produced by Severfield in Bolton, where they were loaded onto a low-loader before being carried to the construction site in London to be installed. This particular stage of construction was documented by Eric Parry Architects in a short film entitled *4 Pancras Square on site* (2016).

watercolour painting, *The Great Dust-Heap, next to Battle Bridge and the Smallpox Hospital*, shows that this 200ft-high mountain of ashes, cinders and dead animals (and even, as found in 1847, an uncashed banker's cheque) reached the southern edge of today's Pancras Square. And once the King's Cross and St Pancras railway terminals were completed in 1852 and 1868, respectively, the development of the land north of them became a macaroni of mainline tracks and sidings.

The relatively few historical buildings that remain in, or near, Pancras Square include the 1865 German Gymnasium ("Serving Mittel-European inspired dishes all day long", which sounds gastronomically industrial), the listed Gasholder No. 8, the Great Northern Hotel, the 1851 Fish and Coal Building on the canal, and the Granary complex north of it. At the southern end of Pancras Square is the Stanley Building, constructed in 1865 by the Improved Dwellings Company to house railway workers.

Pancras Square is set on ground which rises to the north, and just beyond the site's top edge is Goods Way and a tight loop of the Regent's Canal. There are three buildings on the west edge of Pancras Square, and three on the east. Because of its position, 4 Pancras Square is the dominating architectural presence here, and the rather tightly packed eastern and western buildings create what looks and feels like a commercial close around the landscaped core of the site.

Two major asymmetries determined the design of 4 Pancras Square. The building's trapezoidal plan, established by the site masterplan rather than EPA, meant that the southern frontage facing Pancras Square is 27m wide, with the width of the building increasing to 59.5m at the north end; thus, the front and back façades are parallel, but the building's flank walls are not. The square rises to meet the relatively narrow frontage, and then declines to Goods Way and the three secondary entrances to the building, which are about one storey lower than the main entrance. The east-to-west slope of Goods Way adds to the complexity of the topography around the building.

The building, whose commercial space was pre-let, has a double structure, an outer weathering steel load-bearing frame linked to an internal concrete frame, and floor slabs whose exposed concrete soffits add to thermal mass and ensure increased ceiling heights. There are ten office floors, through which a central core rises, plus lower ground and basement levels which reveal themselves on the falling ground at the north end of the site. The south-facing levels 2 to 5 and north-facing levels 6 to 9 have balconies which are recessed from the outer structural frame. The south-facing glazing line, on levels 2 to 5, is set well back from the weathering steel; from levels 6 to 9, the glazing carries *brise-soleils*.

The north façade, facing Goods Way, seen from across Regent's Canal, at the time 4 Pancras Square was just being completed; also within frame, one of the old nineteenth-century office buildings that once belonged to the Great Northern Railway Company.

The north, east and south edges of the tenth floor are set well back behind a two-storey weathering steel-framed loggia to create substantial terraces on the north, east and south façades at this penthouse level. The deep reveals of the outer steel structure and the variations in façade depth reduce the wind tunnel effects around the building, control solar gain, and helped to deliver the building's BREEAM Outstanding energy rating.

The ground floor is double height, with the glazed reception volume and a retail space well behind the line of the huge Vierendeel truss and corner posts; it is also set off-centre to the east to make shelter under the west flank of the structure for a café terrace-cum-plinth which continues to the southwest corner of the structure; a ramp descends alongside the plinth so that cyclists travel down the slope to the southwest corner of the building and put their bikes in one of the 186 lockable racks in the secure storage room. There's a crisply designed shower and locker facility next to the cycle storage space in the car park in the lower ground plan.

At the northwest corner of the building, the porticoed structure is effectively three storeys high because the levels fall away; and as the ground floor retail layer is public-facing, most of the base of the building is transparently active and visually connected to the public realm on all four sides.

At roof level, the garden designed by Todd Longstaffe-Gowan was conceived as a 'found' wetland landscape whose planting would maximise ecological variety, and produce a deliberately imprecise user experience compared to the precisely demarcated landscape of Pancras Square. The various elements – water, long grasses, gravel, stones, and a relatively small number of cultivated feature plants – creates an abstracted, spatially informal patch of 'moorland', across which one walks on thick pre-weathered wooden planks of irregular size. The excellent views across the city from this faux Grimpen Mire lacks Sherlock Holmes and a savage hound, but invites an artist to produce a necessarily ironic twenty-first century equivalent of John O'Connor's imperially sentimental 1884 oil painting, *From Pentonville Road looking west: evening*.

If the elements of 4 Pancras Square are admirable in their arrangement and functional planning, it is the structural whole that determines the architecture's contextual and civic values. Everything about the visible structure, and its effects of depth, light and shadow, demonstrates an attention to detail that, according to Eric Parry, owes considerably to the meticulous set of RIBA Stage Three drawings produced by EPA

Main entrance on the south façade of 4 Pancras Square. The monumental Vierendeel truss, sustained only by two piers, allows the public space of the Square to flow visually (and physically) into the ground floor of the building and through the office reception and café areas.

director, Robert Kennett, and associate director, Robert Dawson. The combination of the frame's scale and its detailing has given the building a remarkable object-quality that, from the square in particular, seems to tremble between the industrial and the super-graphic.

The frame required careful detailing to prevent water pooling on horizontal surfaces, which would produce structural weak spots over time; run-off from the façades is captured to stop uneven patination, and to minimise stained water dripping onto the public realm. The horizonal surfaces of the frame's upper levels are slightly canted so that water flows back towards slots near the glazing line, which carry it into the building's internal drainage system. At ground floor, a slot drain around the edge of the site stops rusty drip-water running onto the public realm and staining it; and the bases of the piers are girdled with grilles to drain run-off from the steel surfaces.

The steel structural pieces, and the Vierendeel trusses in particular, are massive. The truss wraps around the building in 14 segments, with four bolted corner sections. The sheer scale of the truss elements can be summarised by the two segments forming the truss facing Pancras Square: it weighs 72 tonnes, the equivalent of five London buses, and its beams and posts took two weeks to weld together. Each truss section on the remaining façades was assembled using 280 bolts to join the beams, and 322 to join the tie beams; the 205mm weathering-steel bolts are the largest of their type available in Britain. The inner post-tensioned concrete floorplates join the steel framing with four-point concrete connections to flanges, to allow for differential movement.

The design of the south-facing façade is masterful in the way it balances the striking presence of the truss-and-steel frame with the modulation of the setback balconies, which have an in-out rhythm accentuated by their white ceramic fascias and vitreous enamel handrails and by the matching ceramic gleam of the *brise-soleils* on the higher-level glazing. The balconies appear to float in the air between the horizontal steel beams – an adroit piece of design, with the balconies hanging from the oversailing floor slabs on not very noticeable 25 mm stainless steel rods.

The contrast between the brute strength of the frame and the delicate poise of the balconies gives the main façade a tantalisingly ambiguous quality. One critic has associated the loadbearing frame with Mies van der Rohe's phrase "almost nothing", in relation to his design of an apartment tower in Chicago; he also mentions the flutes of a classical column. But it's equally possible to experience the steel frame as evidently almost everything, with

left: East corner of
4 Pancras Square.

opposite: View of the roof
garden landscaped by
Todd Longstaffe-Gowan and
designed by Eric Parry Architects.

Views of the roof garden landscaped by Todd Longstaffe-Gowan and designed by Eric Parry Architects.

as much in common with the matter-of-fact Victorian structure of Lewis Cubitt's King's Cross train shed as with phantom columns that have danced through time.

The massive base truss, whose beam-and-post composition recalls the Vierendeel bridge in Berlin named after Gustav Heinemann, is the first of two horizons created by the frame of 4 Pancras Square. The second is the loggia that crowns the building, which frames and emphasises the sky. Because of the rich colour, surface texture and graphic precision of the steel, we experience the building, for a moment, as two-dimensional; but then its three-dimensional depth sinks in – not just of the structure, but in the variations of flatness and recession, light and shadow, which are emphasised by the slim white ceramic fascias and *brise-soleils*. The structure also asks to be touched, in the same way that it's difficult to walk past the superb exposed outer steel structure of the Hancock Tower in Chicago without reaching out and stroking the metal.

All of these effects – human, haptic, historically related – are the result of intense concentrations of design concerning the relationships between form, articulation and the qualities of presence – the *isness* of the architecture which transcends so-called object-quality. The design of 4 Pancras Square recalls something said by Arthur Vierendeel: "When constructing in metal the dimensions must be determined *a priori* by aesthetic considerations and only afterwards should mathematical formulas be used."

And to that we might add two more remarks, relating to Bernd and Hilla Becher, from an engrossing essay by the art historian Blake Stimson in the *Tate Papers* series. He quotes the art critic Donald Kuspit, who wrote: "The Bechers are interested in the character implicit in a façade, just the way Sander was in the character implicit in a face." But Kuspit also insists that the Bechers' photographs, and the deliberately repetitive structures in them, are "macabre monuments to human self-distortion in the name of social reason".

Stimson disagrees: "Working objectivity against subjectivity, one comportment against the other and then back again, the Bechers have found the motor for their epic in an elastic liminal bearing that continually bounds between sides, between a cool, quasi-disembodied objectivity and a hot subjective comportment that speaks of its own history and desire in its bearing toward the world." The architecture of 4 Pancras Square produces the same oscillation between the coolly objective and a hot, subjective comportment – quite an achievement for a building that is absolutely not a Becheresque fantasy-object.

One Eagle Place, Piccadilly

One Eagle Place is also a standing wonder, but in a different way. Its most obviously remarkable aspect – which has been described as a risk-taking confrontation with "comfortable taste" by one critic – is its Piccadilly façade, and two features in particular: the gleaming faience of the punched reveals of six double-storey windows, whose crimson and white speckled surfaces – designed by Eric Parry – suggest tired lipstick after a night out...

1895

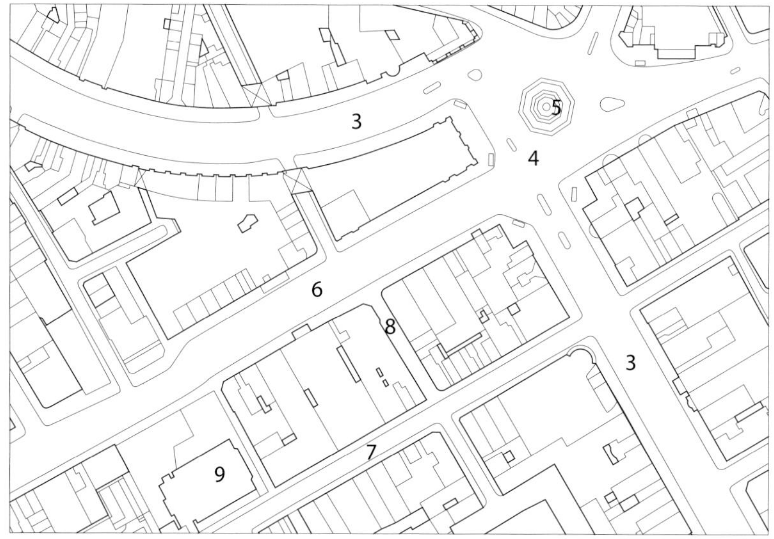

1953

One Eagle Place, Piccadilly, is an integral part of the practice's larger St James's Gateway scheme, whose design, for the Crown Estate, has delivered 57,000ft^2 of office floorplates, 28,000ft^2 of retail space and 18,000ft^2 of apartments in what amounts to three-quarters of the city block between Piccadilly and Jermyn Street at their eastern ends. The combination of newbuild, and major interventions behind retained fabric, has been commercially exemplary. But it is the evolutionary qualities of the design, and the echoes of civitas and creativity through time that make this such an interesting project.

The design of the scheme's public faces in Piccadilly, Jermyn Street and Eagle Place is absolutely embedded in the continuums of the history of Regent Street, Piccadilly and Piccadilly Circus as whole since the seventeenth century, which has seen extraordinary change. In his *History of England*, Lord Macaulay's description of London in 1685 includes this passage: "He who then rambled to what is now the gayest and most crowded part of Regent Street, found himself in a solitude, and was sometimes so fortunate as to have a shot at a woodcock. On the north the Oxford road ran between hedges. Three or four hundred yards to the south were the garden walls of a few great houses, which were considered as quite out of town."

Those great houses, which include Clarendon House and Burlington House, lay along the north side of Piccadilly. The south side was built up between Haymarket and St James's Street but, apart from Goring House, was less than impressive. John Strype's 1720 *Survey of London* mentions the White Horse Inn, Elephant Inn, and the King's Arms Inn east of Duke Street. Further along were Eagle Street and Fleece Yard, "which hath a Passage into Germin-street, very ordinary built and inhabited: And near unto this Yard is Sadler's Court, which is but small and mean".

By 1839, according to the *Survey of London*, the "south side of Piccadilly was composed largely of single-fronted houses, generally four storeys high and two windows wide above shop-fronts". In 1879, in *Dickens's Dictionary of London*, Piccadilly was "the nearest approach to the Parisian boulevard of which London can boast... one of the few streets left in London which are remarkable both from a commercial and a 'society' point of view".

Thirty years later, in Regent Street, the plastered neoclassicist terrace fronts and iron colonnades that characterised John Nash's "triumphal route" between Regent's Park and Carlton House were being torn down and replaced with Portland stone-faced buildings in a more fashionable and impressive Beaux-Arts manner, and that project was finally completed in 1927. Meanwhile, the replacement of the

1 One Eagle Place, Piccadilly
2 15 and 20 Jermyn Street and 27 Regent Street
3 Regent Street
4 Piccadilly Circus
5 Shaftesbury Memorial Fountain (Anteros sculpture)
6 Piccadilly
7 Jermyn Street
8 Eagle Place
9 St James's Church

N

2017

Chronological sequence of plans, showing the location of One Eagle Place, with its façades towards Piccadilly and Eagle Place, within the same urban block as 15 and 20 Jermyn Street and 27 Regent Street. In addition to the rapid transformation of late-nineteenth-century Piccadilly, much of the urban fabric was subjected to the heavy blows of the Blitz, from which London was still recovering during the 1950s, and that is still reflected in today's urbanity.

Quadrant, an adjoining stretch of the north side of Piccadilly as far as Piccadilly Place, and the remodelling of Piccadilly Circus, was proving to be a fraught process.

Norman Shaw produced a grand scheme for these pivotal components of London's West End, but his proposals for the Circus and Quadrant were shelved for various land-ownership and commercial reasons. Sir Reginald Blomfield took over, rebuilding the Quadrant between 1923 and 1928, and adapting Shaw's proposals for Piccadilly Circus. The only part of Shaw's overall scheme that survived was the 1908 Piccadilly Hotel, whose extraordinary architecture – including an heroic loggia terrace screened by two-storey columns – remains one of the most imposing Edwardian buildings in Central London. Shaw's design of the Quadrant would effectively have been an extension of the hotel's monumental architecture.

Blomfield disliked it, but admired Shaw's suavely effective manner. "How Shaw got away with it," he wrote in his 1940 biography of the architect, "how he persuaded his clients to expend very large sums on the screen, which serves no practical purpose whatever, remains a standing wonder, but Shaw was a magician in dealing with clients and committees. He seems to have had a way with him that no one could withstand, so clear, so pleasant, so convincing."

One Eagle Place is also a standing wonder, but in a different way. Its most obviously remarkable aspect – which has been described as a risk-taking confrontation with "comfortable taste" by one critic – is its Piccadilly façade, and two features in particular: the gleaming faience of the punched reveals of six double-storey windows whose crimson and white speckled surfaces suggest tired lipstick after a night out. The oriel windows that form the bottom half of the fenestrations recall those completed by the practice at 50 New Bond Street in 2009.

Even more vividly strange are the coloured asymmetric blocks of the 25m-wide cornice created by Richard Deacon. There is nothing remotely like this degree of architectural colour, modelling and abstraction in Piccadilly, or perhaps anywhere else in London. One Eagle Place offers the simultaneously different and oscillating realities of a background building and a foreground building – perhaps something like the "very erratic" realities described in Virginia's Woolf's novel, *A Room of One's Own*, which "overwhelms one walking home beneath the stars and makes the silent world more real than the world of speech – and then there it is again in an omnibus in the uproar of Piccadilly".

On 26 October 2017, the visual uproar was added to when the polychromatic vivacity of the building's artworked surfaces were

BARBOUR
INTERNATIONAL
MOTORCYCLE
CLOTHING
EVOLUTION
IN ACTION

above: View of the new façade from the Shaftesbury Memorial Fountain featuring a sculpture of Anteros popularly known as the 'Eros statue', here surrounded by the crowds and fast pace of Piccadilly Circus.

opposite: The façade of One Eagle Place looking over Piccadilly during the early hours of the morning.

amplified by the switching on of Piccadilly Lights, the new high-resolution advertising screen which swerves around the northern segment of the Circus. Its trillions of pixels instantly shimmered, an inferno of razor-sharp brand-names: Hyundai, Coca-Cola, Samsung, L'Oréal Paris, eBay, Hunter, Stella McCartney. Its biggest announcement read: "Bringing colour back to the city".

At dusk, looking up at the Piccadilly façade of One Eagle Place at its western end, the reflections of the pixelated advertising imagery tremble on the ceramic surfaces and on the vividly decal'd blocks of the deep, boldly projecting cornice. Deacon's combination of densely layered splotches and brindles of colour on the irregularly chopped blocks of the cornice were initially experimental. He composed forms using random clay off-cuts in his studio, and then refined them into 14 prismatic sections, butted together and individually rotated.

The faience elements of the façade were produced by Eric Parry's favoured ceramicists, Shaws of Darwen. In the case of the cornice, each facet of the sections – there are 39, in various permutations – is composed of a ceramic slip carrying an artwork decal, baked onto the faience with a triple-firing of the ceramic. It was the first time this particular decal-ceramic fusion had been used in a major public artwork in Britain, despite the fact that the technique was invented in Stoke-on-Trent in the eighteenth century.

The effect is sensationally and wildly neo-archaic, as if classical dentils and modillions had been compacted and splattered with paint. We have to look back at buildings such as Adler & Sullivan's 1891 Wainwright Building in St Louis to find cornices of such scale and artistic exuberance.

Thus, plasmas of fibrillating on-off photons from the Piccadilly Lights glance off the continuous analogue wavelengths of the colours on the façade's permanent, lime-mortared ceramic surfaces. What a far cry from the lone "Drink Perrier Water" sign erected, without permission, above the Café Monico in 1908, in more or less the same position as the Piccadilly Lights fascia.

However, the overriding point about the façade is that it is wholly in the tradition of Victorian and Edwardian architecture-as-stage-sets in Piccadilly. Shaw's hotel and Blomfield's Quadrant are opposite; Alfred Waterhouse's bank building is immediately to the west; Blomfield's 27 Lower Regent Street, which bookends the eastern end of Piccadilly and Jermyn Street where they meet the top of Haymarket, is just as dramatically grand.

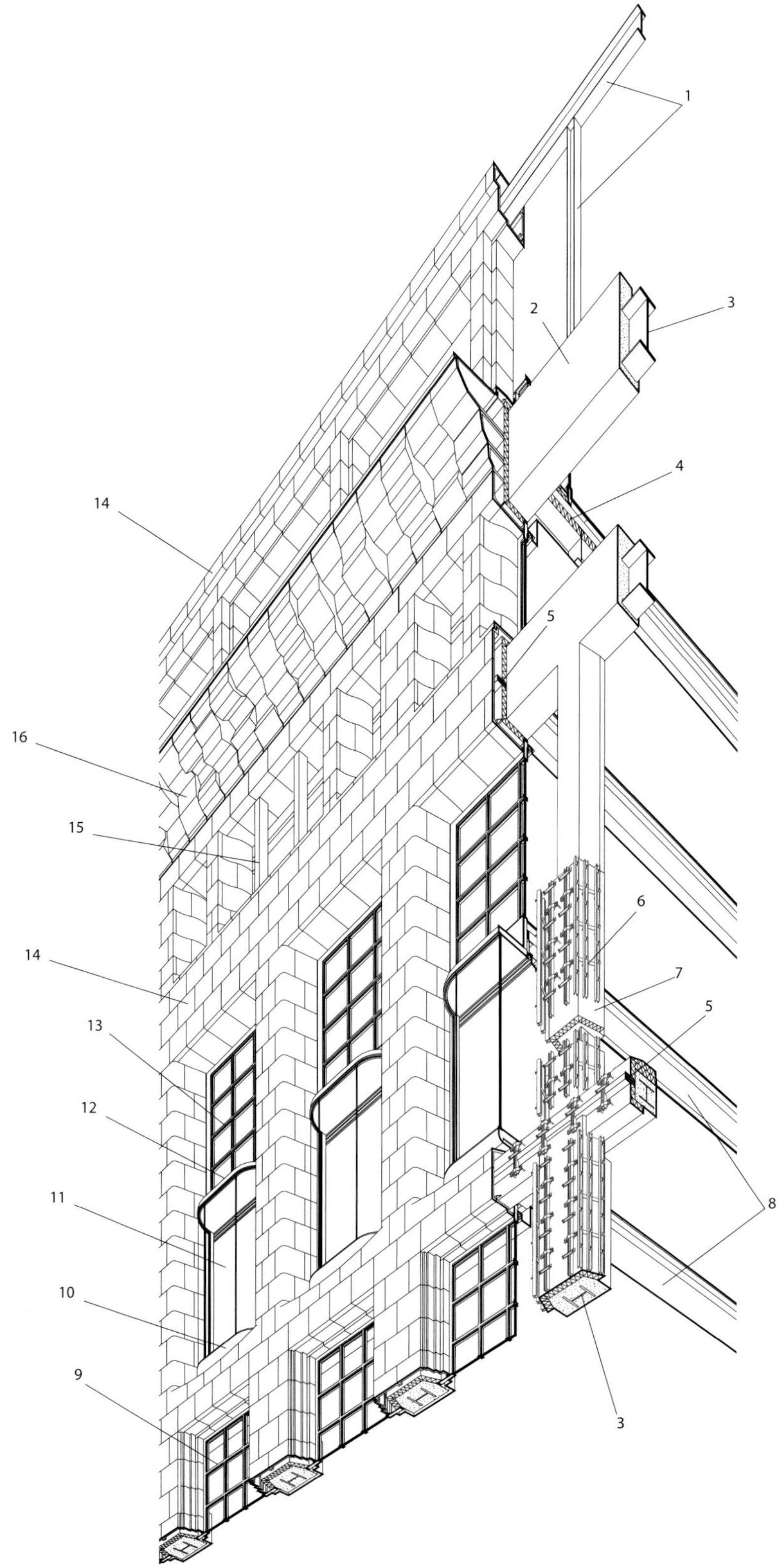

perspectival section

1 external steelwork galvanised for intumescent and corrosion protection
2 external weatherproof seal
3 concrete-encased steel beam
4 insulation beneath roof slab to improve U-value
5 continuous fire / smoke stop cavity barrier foil-faced block with intumescent strip fixed 25 mm from rear face of faience on proprietary clips 90mm
6 stainless steel support bracket bolted to cast-in channel
7 weatherproof seal
8 structural concrete slab
9 Oce fixed non-openable composite aluminium / timber frame to double-glazed window with semi-gloss powder-coated external nish, colour black; and timber with factory-applied paint internal nish, colour white (RAL 9010)
10 semi-gloss powder-coated aluminium corbel to bow window
11 double-glazing to bow window
12 semi-gloss powder-coated aluminium bow window top, colour black
13 Oce-fixed non-openable composite aluminium / timber frame to double-glazed window with semi-gloss powder-coated external nish, colour black; and timber with factory-applied paint internal nish, colour white (RAL 9010)
14 40mm faience (glazed terracotta) tile
15 anodised aluminium feature pillaret fixed to 4mm stainless steel spigots within 12mm lime mortar joint
16 polychromatic 40mm faience (glazed terracotta) cornice by sculptor Richard Deacon

left: Interior view of the façade looking over Piccadilly, framed by the glossy lipstick red of the external ceramic cladding.

right: Interior view of the main entrance lobby of One Eagle Place, with lift doors and frames also in red.

The face that One Eagle Place presents to Piccadilly defers to the Piccadilly elevations of 27 Lower Regent Street. From bottom to top: a plinth of shops, a band of mezzanine windows, double-height windows with an inserted one-storey-high glazed oriel, a line of attic windows, Deacon's oversized, powerfully modelled cornice, above which the top floor is set back to mediate between 27 Regent Street and the stretch of Piccadilly west of One Eagle Place.

The load-bearing masonry façade radiates the same weighty, highly crafted quality of its most important Edwardian neighbours, with one difference – the quite singular approach to the artworked elements of the façade is imperiously surreal. The effect is magnified by the otherwise precise ordering of the façade as a whole, which is as graphically defined as the clean, Modernist layering of Joseph Emberton's 1936 Simpsons building (now Waterstones), where raffish Bertie Wooster types could purchase what the shop advertised as "the smart ready-made two piece suit and Daks self-supporting trousers".

A comment in EPA's Design & Access Statement reveals the more fundamental, historically dutiful intent: "The [main] elevation will reflect the three buildings currently on the site, reinforced at ground floor level with the introduction of three shop units. This is particularly important, as the leitmotif for the inter-war vision of urban development was to create Piccadilly as a grand neoclassical avenue with a monumental gateway at Piccadilly Circus. This would give to this part of Piccadilly a similar urban prominence as Regent Street, which together with Shaftesbury Avenue, would form the rays of a star around the Circus, replacing the old frayed crossing."

However important the stage-set aspects of One Eagle Place are to Piccadilly, they are the servants of a much more challenging architectural and commercial performance: the redevelopment of the 2000m² Crown Estates site lying between Piccadilly and Jermyn Street – half a city block – to produce one big office building of seven storeys facing Piccadilly, and eight storeys facing lower Jermyn Street.

The second, physically separate, element in the Crown Estates' St James's Gateway brief was to reconfigure the interior of the southeastern corner of 27 Lower Regent Street to produce luxury apartments and improvements to the fenestration facing Lower Regent Street and Jermyn Street. The bulk of the development site lies within the St James's Conservation Area, with the 27 Regent Street element in the Regent Street Conservation Area.

View towards Piccadilly from Eagle Place, with the main building entrance through a new Portland stone façade in the foreground standing next to the reconstructed pre-existing corner building in the background.

Major interventions were required: the wholesale demolition and redevelopment of 212–215 Piccadilly, the internal demolition of 18–21 Jermyn Street, and the redevelopment of 210–211 Piccadilly, which turns the corner into the Eagle Place alley connecting Piccadilly with Jermyn Street. The latter posed what a Georgian might have called a "pretty problem".

The retained, turreted façade of the building on the corner of Piccadilly and Eagle Place – originally designed by John Gibson and later ruined by clumsy internal changes – had to be jacked up 1.5m and modified to align its cornices and floor levels with the key horizontals of the new building facing Piccadilly. The design of the new façade which forms two-thirds of the elevation along Eagle Place is as gripping, in its very different way, as the main Piccadilly frontage.

Commercially, this combination of newbuild and interventions within existing fabric has produced five large, L-shaped office floorplates overlooking Piccadilly and Eagle Place. There are also three new shopfronts facing Piccadilly and improved shopfronts in Eagle Place and Jermyn Street. Five apartments were created within 18–21 Jermyn Street, and eleven large apartments at 27 Lower Regent Street.

The interiors and fit-outs of the apartments were designed by EPA and reflect the gentrified-cum-dandyfied character of Jermyn Street. In describing the apartments within the 18–21 Jermyn Street segment, the practice resorts to suitably local argot: the apartments feel "made to measure" and "perfectly poised in cut, fit and style. The same principles as with a tailored suit or shirt apply". In the case of the bigger and even more luxurious apartments at 27 Lower Regent Street, Eric Parry takes evident pleasure in noting that it is possible to look out to the northeast to the bronze statue of Eros (although its sculptor Sir Alfred Gilbert actually designed it to represent Anteros, the god of requited love) poised above the fountain in Piccadilly Circus.

There is a notable finale to the design of the One Eagle Place scheme, an intervention that is purely creative, rather than referential to the cultural and architectural history of this fillet of London. At the top of the chamfered corner of the Eagle Place façade, where it turns at 45 degrees to meet Jermyn Street, there is an emblematic six-tonne sculpture made in 2013 by Stephen Cox, entitled *Elemental Head* – a face carved from Indian granite, simultaneously powerful and inscrutable, that seems to be emerging from a birth-caul.

A detail of Jermyn Street's new stone façade.

Parry describes the sculpture as "amazingly mysterious. The great thing with Stephen is that you never know what will come out when he carves into stone. We talked about an anthropomorphic piece, and how to mediate between sky and earth. Stephen carved it in India, and responded with this cosmic face. It's interrupted by a mask of gold, or a sun disc. The face is peering through: it catches the evening light, and glows and floats".

There is a subtly civic, if not metaphysical, sequel to Cox's dreaming-cum-birthing face, which is described in the essay about the practice's 7–8 St James's Square project (see page 68). The enigmatic sculpture certainly adds a surreal ripple to Jermyn Street's perspective, but it is also a coda to the vivid theatricality of the Piccadilly façade of One Eagle Place. The sculpture's face suggests a meditating magus who looks down on passers-by in a very different way to the data-gathering facial-recognition cameras embedded in the LED cosmos of the vast Piccadilly Lights screen 100m away.

left: Eagle Place and the corner with Jermyn Street seen from Babmaes Street. The urban corner is punctuated by sculptor Stephen Cox's *Elemental Head* (2013).

centre: Traced outline of the reverse, inscribed into the natural crust of the stone, seen from the offices.

right: A close-up of the sculpture seen from the street.

SHFT AVE
TRAF SQR

7–8 St James's Square

The 7–8 St James's Square project has two components: the replacement of a substantial office and apartment building running down from Apple Tree Yard to form the corner of the square opposite Chatham House, an eighteenth-century building. The stable mews in Apple Tree Yard was where Edwin Lutyens had his office between 1913 and 1924, when leading the design of the masterplan of New Delhi.

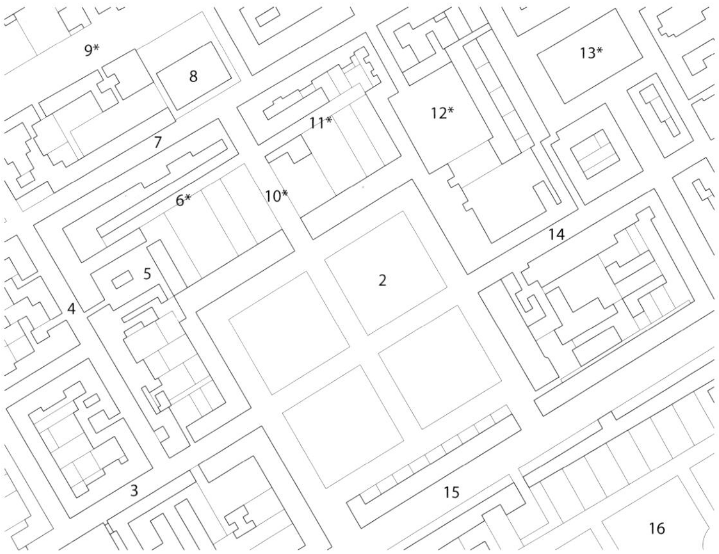

1685–1755

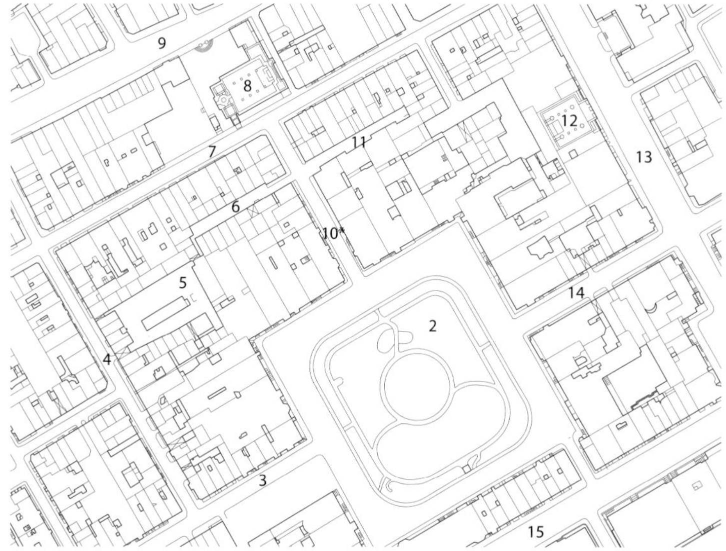

1893–1895

Chronological sequence of plans, showing the urban grid of St James's Square and its surroundings on the basis of the information provided by the historical plans of St James's by Richard Blome, 'The Parish of St Iames's Westminster' (1685); John Strype, 'The Parish of St Iames's Westminster' in John Stow, *Survey of the Cities of London and Westminster* (1720); Richard Blome, 'The Parish of St Iames's Westminster... with Corrections' (1755 reprint); followed by the London Ordnance Survey (1894–96 edition).

There is no square in London whose history is more profoundly aristocratic than St James's Square, and it remains talismanic in the twenty-first century as an integral part of clubland, and of the equally exclusive (and occasionally almost as historic) purveyors of clothing, accoutrements and comestibles in Jermyn Street and St James's.

To design an entirely new 65,000ft^2 office building that proceeds 60m down the east side of the sloping Duke of York Street and forms a cornerpiece of the historic square presented considerable challenges relating to scale, function and materiality. The scheme included work on an adjoining building originally designed by Edwin Lutyens. The long elevation of the new building is an exceptionally sophisticated addition to the street, suggesting the seventeenth century at one end, and the fifteenth or sixteenth century (and the Indian Raj) at the other.

The practice had produced an earlier design for the redevelopment of the site in 2006, which gained planning consent. But we see in the massing, materiality and core configurations of these proposals a relatively safe architecture whose long perspective conveys *firmitas* and *utilitas*, but not quite the expressive degree of *venustas* that has, in the last decade, become associated with EPA's work.

The final scheme, in 2010, was completed in 2017. It's quite different, and reflects the much bolder approach to architectural craft (and combinations of materials that might almost be described as luscious) which in London were first seen to striking effect in the practice's mottled green faience tiling on the façade of 50 New Bond Street in 2009. This was part of the major office and residential transformation of the 68,000ft^2 site which passes along the north side of Maddox Street between New Bond Street and St George's Street. The block-long north-south plan of the St James's Square scheme makes it broadly comparable in scale.

However blatantly money-sluiced the two Bond streets may be, they have nothing like the gravitas of St James's Square which, for architects who possess phenomenological tuning-forks, is one of the city's greatest civic and cultural stages, replete with layers of history. The square was created – perhaps decreed is a more suitable word – by Charles II's grant of the freehold of the site to Henry Jermyn, the Earl of St Albans, on 1 April 1665, and construction began in the 1670s. In its early days, the square's character was not entirely refined, as these remarks by the great historian Thomas Macaulay reveal:

"Saint James's Square was a receptacle for all the offal and cinders, for all the dead cats and dead dogs of Westminster. At one time a cudgel player kept the ring there. At another time an impudent

chronological sequence of plans

1 8 St James's Square by Eric Parry Architects
1* 7 St James's Square by Sir Edwin Lutyens
2 St James's Square
3 King Street
4 Duke Street
5 Masons Yard
6 Ormond Street
6* Blackamore Street
7 Jermyn Street
8 St James's Church
9 Piccadilly
9* Portugal Street / Piccadilly
10 Duke of York Street
10* York Street
11 Apple Tree Yard
11* Singer Street
12 St Philip's Chapel
12* Stable Yard
13 Regent Street
13* St James's Market
14 Charles Street
15 Pall Mall
16 The Kings Garden

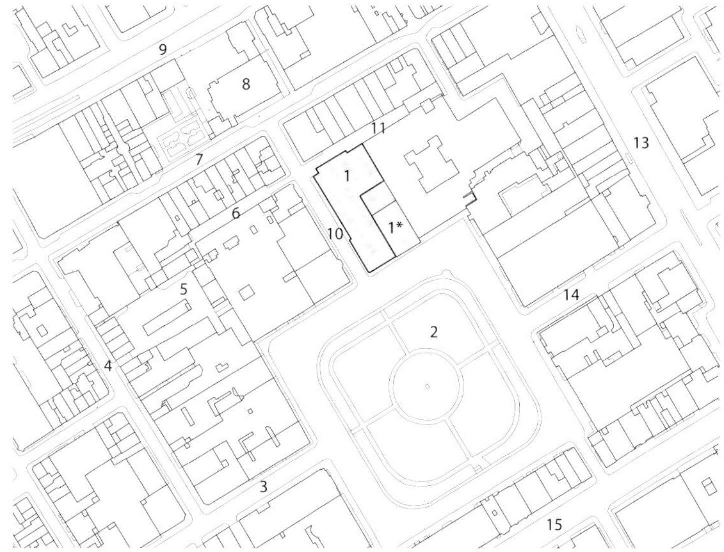

2015

N

0 10 25 50 100m

1:4000

7–8 St James's Square is located on the north side of the square, along Duke of York Street and Apple Tree Yard, in an urban fabric, which has changed little since the seventeenth century, despite the many modern building additions.

squatter settled himself there, and built a shed for rubbish under the windows of the gilded saloons in which the first magnates of the realm, Norfolk, Ormond, Kent, and Pembroke, gave banquets and balls. It was not till these nuisances had lasted through a whole generation, and till much had been written about them, that the inhabitants applied to Parliament for permission to put up rails, and to plant trees."

Very broadly speaking, the 1726 St James's Square Act set a precedent that encouraged subsequent groups of notable residents in other parts of London to establish private maintenance rates, and therefore degrees of exclusivity, for their locales. By 1727, St James's Square had been very neatly paved, by a certain Mr Mist, with "Square Cubick Stones, commonly called French Paving", and it possessed a circular, lamp-lit water basin 150ft in diameter, surrounded by octagonal railings and eight stone obelisks.

By 1721, along with six dukes living in the square, there were: a marchioness, seven earls, a countess, a baron and a baronet, among honourable others soon to be titled. At least ten of the houses were in diplomatic use, and between 1795 and 1823, John Soane worked here, surveying Nos. 8, 15 and 18, and altering the façade of No. 21. In the mid-nineteenth century, the square was still the most aristocratic in London, but its character was changing: it now contained a bank, an insurance society, the London Library and three clubs. Nevertheless, the intense aura of exclusivity remained: in his 1870 novel, *Lothair*, Benjamin Disraeli referred to the square as "our Faubourg St Germain".

The 7–8 St James's Square project has two components: the replacement of a substantial office and apartment building running down from Apple Tree Yard to form the corner of the square opposite Chatham House, an eighteenth-century building. The stable mews in Apple Tree Yard was where Edwin Lutyens had his office between 1913 and 1924, when leading the design of the masterplan of New Delhi.

Lutyens had been responsible for the rebuilding of No. 7 St James's Square in 1911, and EPA's brief included its interior refurbishments, improvements to the entrance, and the addition of a semi-glazed atrium at this Grade II* listed building (which had been altered, post-Lutyens). It is now a four-storey townhouse in the grand manner, undercut by a private subsurface swimming pool, spa and car park – the latter entered through a gate in Apple Tree Yard.

Nos. 7 and 8 had originally been built in 1676, and No. 8 became Josiah Wedgwood's ceramics showroom at the end of the eighteenth century. A century later, it was a private sports club; and then, in 1939,

1:750

South-facing elevations on the north side of St James's Square, including the façade of Eric Parry Architects' designed 7–8 St James's Square next to Duke of York Street, leading to Sir Christopher Wren's St James's Church.

despite the place-sensitive intentions of the 1932 Town and Country Planning Act, No. 8 and the three properties and chapel along Duke of York Street to the corner of Apple Tree Yard were demolished. They were replaced with a single, stylistically vague and crudely massed block whose seven-storey St James's Square elevation was two floors higher than most of its historic neighbours. Its frontage along Duke of York Street included a peculiar two-storey midriff, jettied over the lower two levels, with a severe setback above it to the upper floors.

This elevation, and the sharply rectilinear bulge in the perspective, presumably explains why the planners asked EPA to emphasise vertical clarity in its two earlier schemes for the site. And this has led, by happy contrast, to what is probably the practice's most interestingly orchestrated low-rise façade composition. We shall return to it in a moment, after considering the plan of No. 8, and its internal functional and material aspects.

The plan is L-shaped, with the long rectangular portion running from St James's Square up to Apple Tree Yard, where it turns east to bookend the rear of the Lutyens building. The 2006 scheme had two separated cores, with a single pillar interrupting the floorplates, but now the lifts and stairs are contained in an L-shaped core that fits compactly into the angle of the plan, producing clear floorplates with views over Duke of York Street, and north towards Jermyn Street and Wren's St James's Church.

There is a clever slot in the plan between the bank of four glazed lifts and the marble-surfaced party wall to No. 7. At the top of the slot, a narrow rectangular skylight allows daylight to fall eight storeys into the basement levels, and the party wall is treated as a canvas for the light-reflecting effects of Arabescato marble. In any case, a simple ride for ten or twenty seconds in one of these elevators is aesthetically pleasurable rather than hermetically banal.

We encounter the even more lavish Calacatta marble in the ground floor reception area that rises up, behind the roll-top reception desk – which, like the rest of the interiors, was designed by the practice. The walls are lined with book-matched American burr walnut-lined veneer, whose figurations have a faintly bloodied burnt umber cast, with beautifully made black walnut doors and furniture, including a big reading table that wouldn't look out of place at the London Library.

The atmosphere, beneath a plastered coffered ceiling, is club-like. The lift door casings are jet-black, and their interiors feature lacquered and walnut surfaces; even the building's lavatories radiate a crafted gloss, with walls coated with a rusty red polished lacquer. The obsessive

left: Eric Parry, 7–8 St James's Square, elevation study (May 2006).

middle: View of the construction site along Duke of York Street, towards Apple Tree Yard, with the recently rebuilt spire to Sir Christopher Wren's St James's Church in the background.

right: View of construction site with the back of No. 7 designed by Sir Edwin Lutyens, with the trees and garden of St James's Square in the distance.

care taken with the design and making of these elements (and the concealment of ventilation grilles and sprinklers) has become characteristic of the practice, but they don't overshadow the functional-cum-commercial clarity of the scheme.

The entrance interiors suit 'the house' portion of No. 8 at the corner of the square and Duke of York Street. The design produces an interesting stylisation of the Georgian manner – full-height windows on the first three floors, four bands of white-painted plaster which turn around the corner into Duke of York's Street, and charcoal-grey facing bricks. They were hand-made by Coleford Brick and Tile in the Forest of Dean, who produce no more than 1000 per day. Seen close-up, the charred finish of the Mixed Antique facings produces rich and dense variations of blacks, greys and subtle, rubicund blushing.

The most interesting aspect of the design is the way the long façade, and its turn into Apple Tree Yard, has been segmented into three sections with three frontage treatments. At the bottom of Duke of York Street, it is neo rather than pastiche Georgian; the central section steps back from a strongly defined, granite-faced plinth which rises to first floor level, where the fenestration is set back by approximately 1.8m. This produces a long, slim balcony-cum-loggia with glazed slots allowing natural light into the ground floor offices.

The plinth's deeply punched windows have thick, rounded granite cills, and the surface treatments of the Impala granite on this section of the façade is superbly effective: the trapezoidal windows get bigger as the base of the façade deepens along the slope, and the heavy blocks forming the horizontal cills are smoothly and lustrously polished; the façade to the base of the balcony has a picked finish.

The treatment of the façade above the plinth and setback is quite different. Here, the walls are rendered and the windows cased with limestone. The stone parapet of the fourth floor terrace has a metal balustrade, and the setback of the fourth and fifth storey layer has a very slightly canted glass cladding which has the effect of dematerlising the upper floors, and reflects light down into Duke of York Street. The sixth floor is set back even further, and its façade was designed to appear relatively lightweight. The earth-to-sky, weighty-to-delicate conceit is perfectly clear.

The third portion of the façade, at the north end, turns the corner into Apple Tree Yard. It erases any memory of the looming but utterly unremarkable five-storey backside of the earlier 1939 building, from which projected a two-storey shopfront, a dairy that had survived the war and later became Wheeler's Restaurant in 1952. Today, a projecting three-storey wraparound bay forms the northern corner

opposite: View of the completed building from Duke of York Street towards St James's Square. On the left of the image, the weight of the large granite and bronze camed hand-made glass oriel window is visually supported by large granite modillions projecting from the top of the granite street-level socle in line with the coffering of the interior ceiling. Descending along Duke of York Street, a limestone elevation is succeeded by a two-floor rendered façade over pilotis. The receding upper floors above lighten the visual weight of the massing and allow for a large veranda to the office spaces. The sequence is followed on the right of the image by a brick façade on arrival to St James's Square.

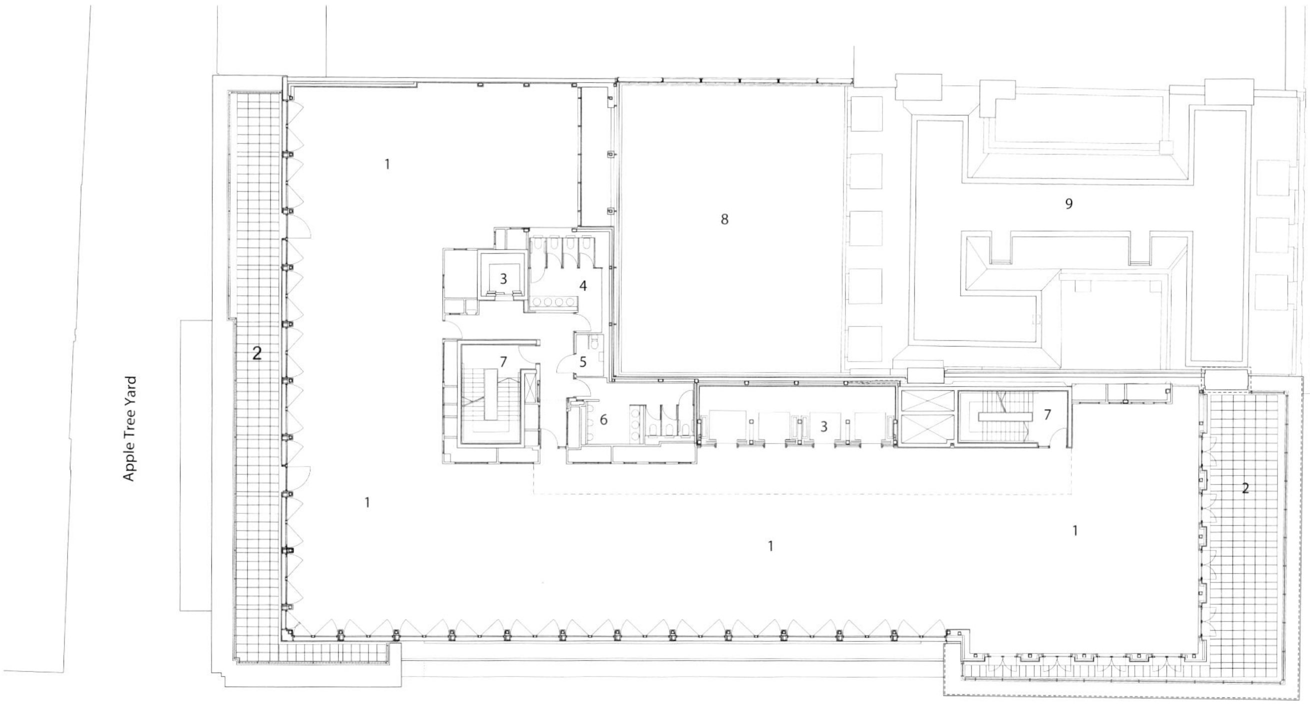

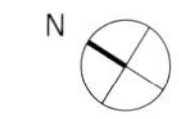

5th floor

1 office
2 terrace
3 passenger lift
4 female toilets
5 disabled toilets
6 male toilets
7 stairs
8 courtyard
9 existing building

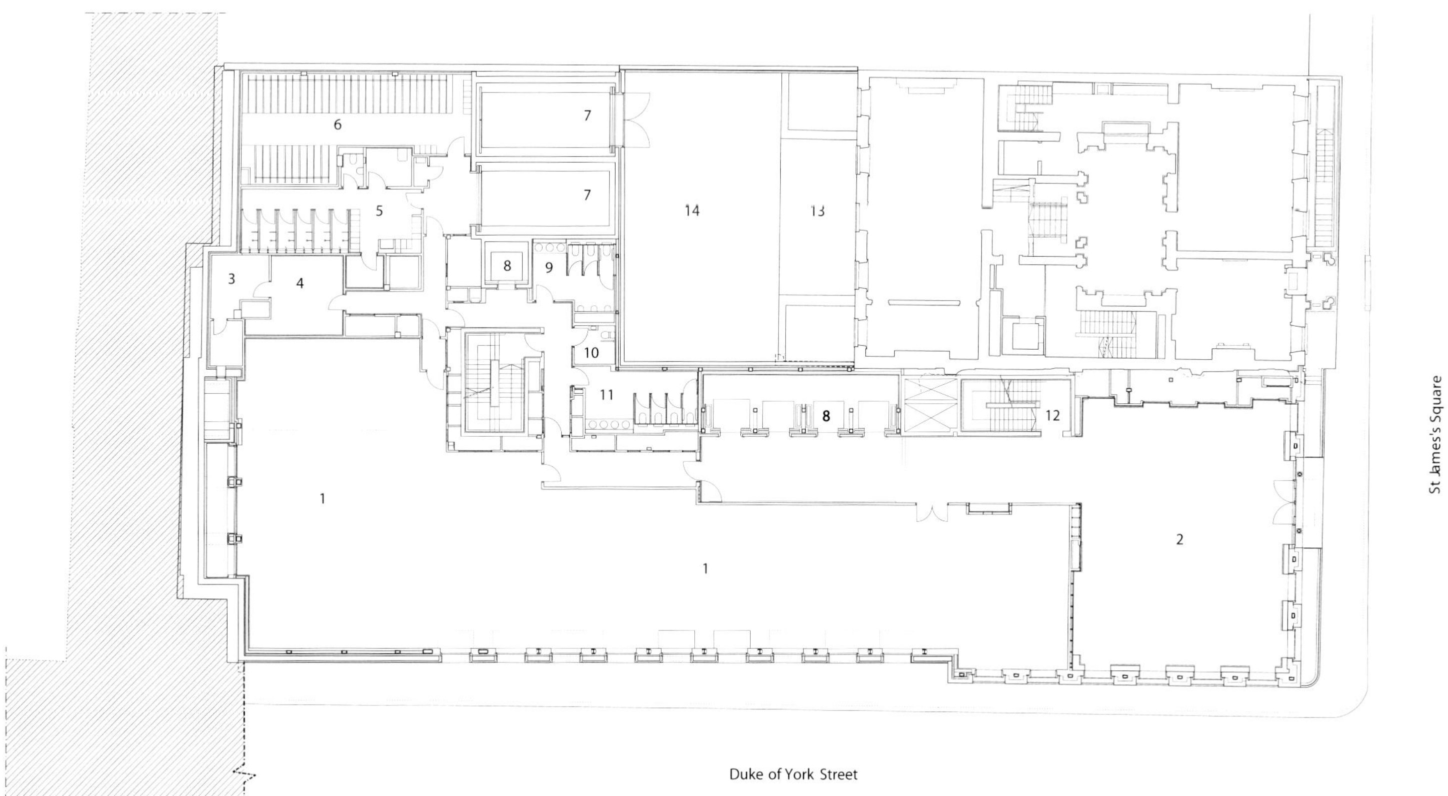

ground floor

1 office
2 reception
3 incoming services room
4 fire control room
5 showers / changing
6 bicycle parking
7 car lift
8 passenger lift
9 male toilets
10 disabled toilets
11 female toilets
12 stairs
13 existing building
14 courtyard

1:400

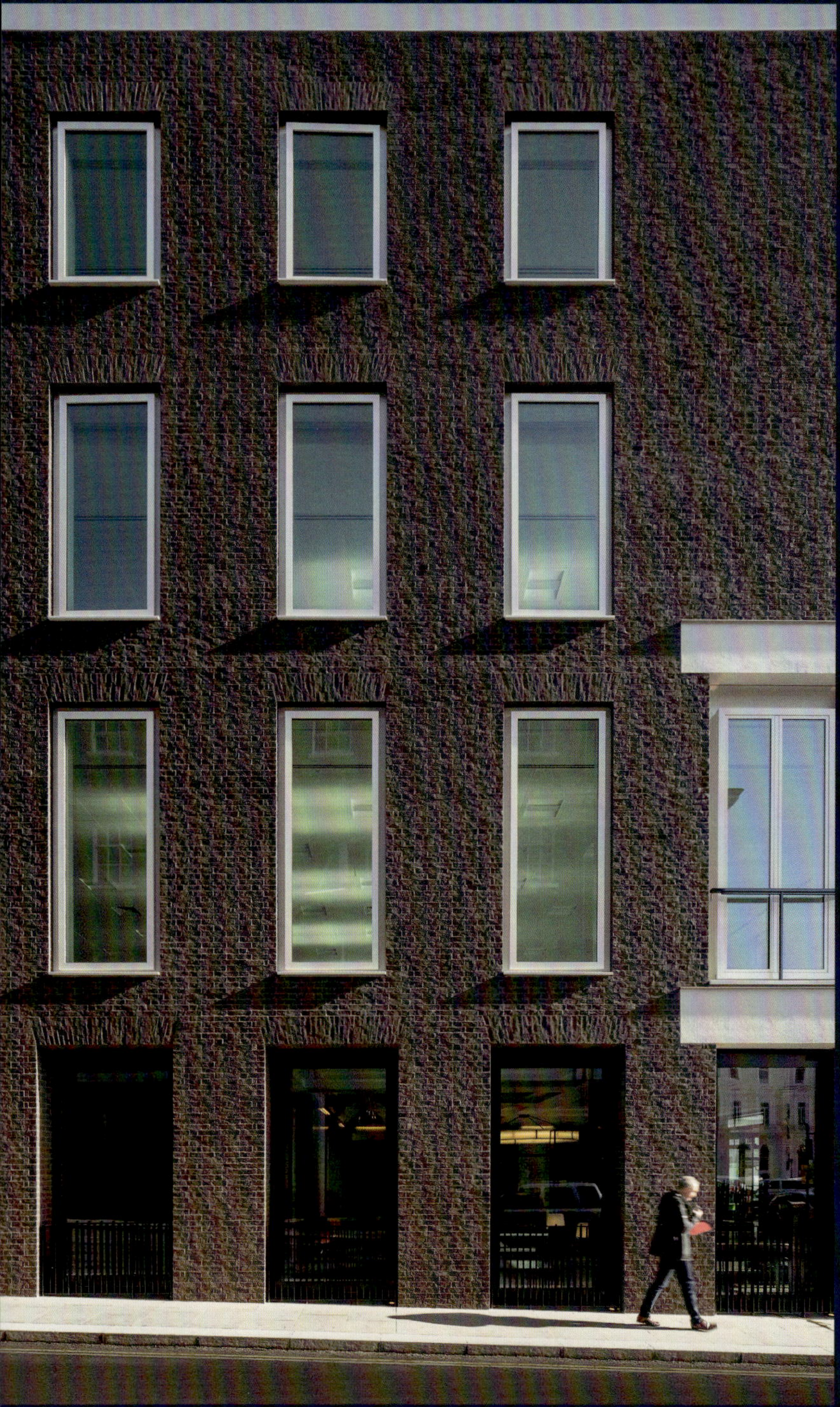

Partial view of the Duke of York Street façade and interior of the ground floor reception.

Apple Tree Yard façade

1 self-supporting picked granite lintel
2 specialist glass: hand-drawn glass within bronze cames
3 internal double glazing to window frame
4 3.6m-high granite pillar
5 picked granite slabs to false coffer
6 picked granite modillion
7 powder-coated aluminium window frame, colour dark grey
8 head to polished dark granite window casing

Apple Tree Yard and Duke of York Street corner façade

9 honed limestone pillar in anta
10 honed limestone mullion
11 double glazing to window frame
12 powder-coated aluminium mullion colour grey

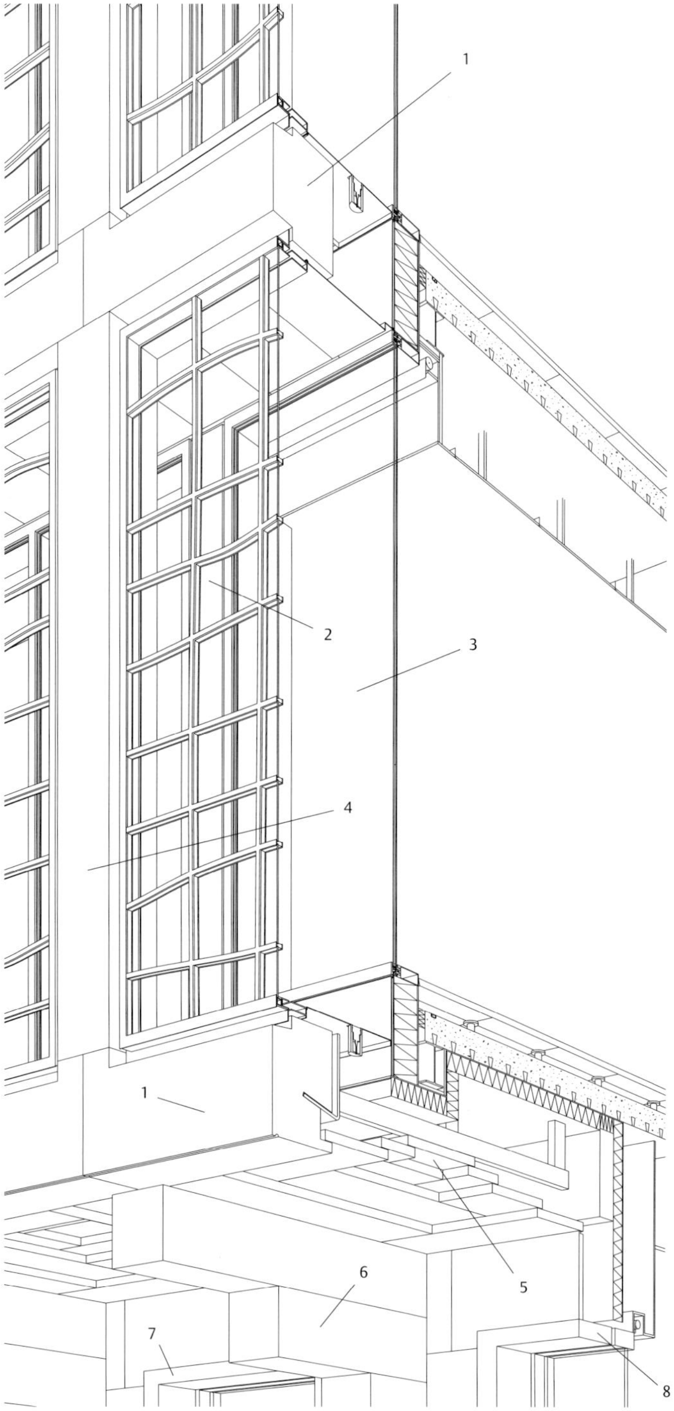

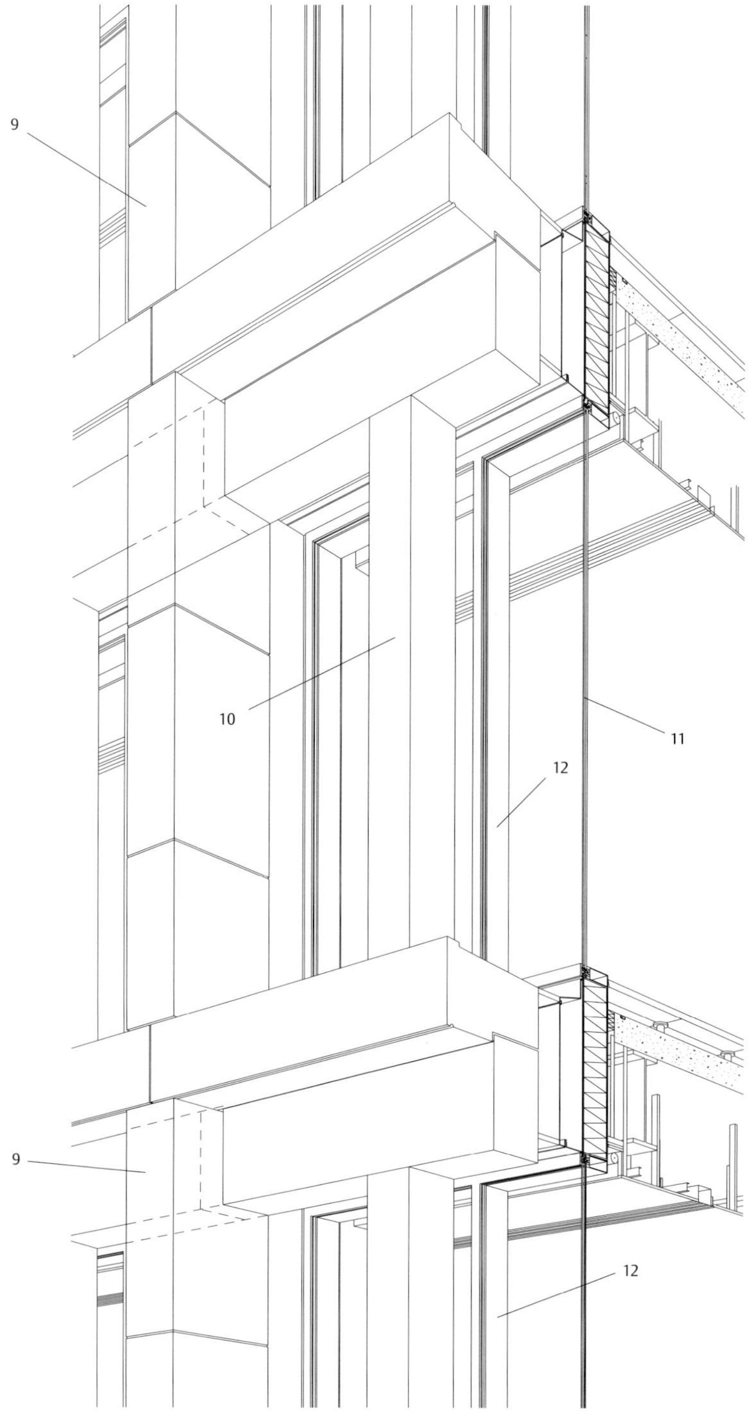

Duke of York Street façade

13 mineral-painted external lime render, colour white
14 head to honed limestone window casing
15 powder-coated aluminium window frame, colour white
16 double glazing to window frame
17 cill to honed limestone window casing
18 honed limestone architrave
19 painted steel pilotis, colour black
20 powder-coated aluminium soffit, colour grey

St James's Square façade

21 structural Flemish bond laid brick wall
22 plasterboard lining
23 powder-coated aluminium jamb reveal lining to window frame, colour white
24 double glazing to window frame
25 mineral-painted lime render cill shot-peened stainless steel drip on precast lintel
26 powder-coated aluminium to window frame, colour white

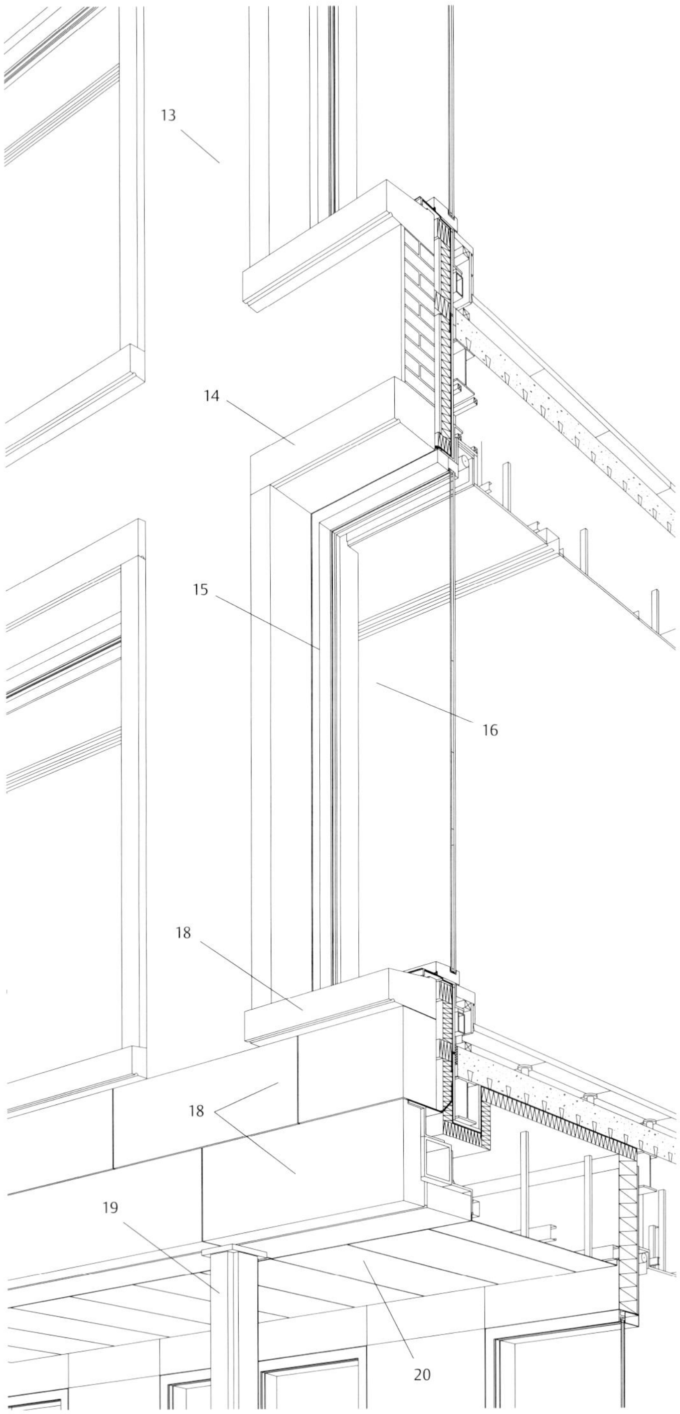

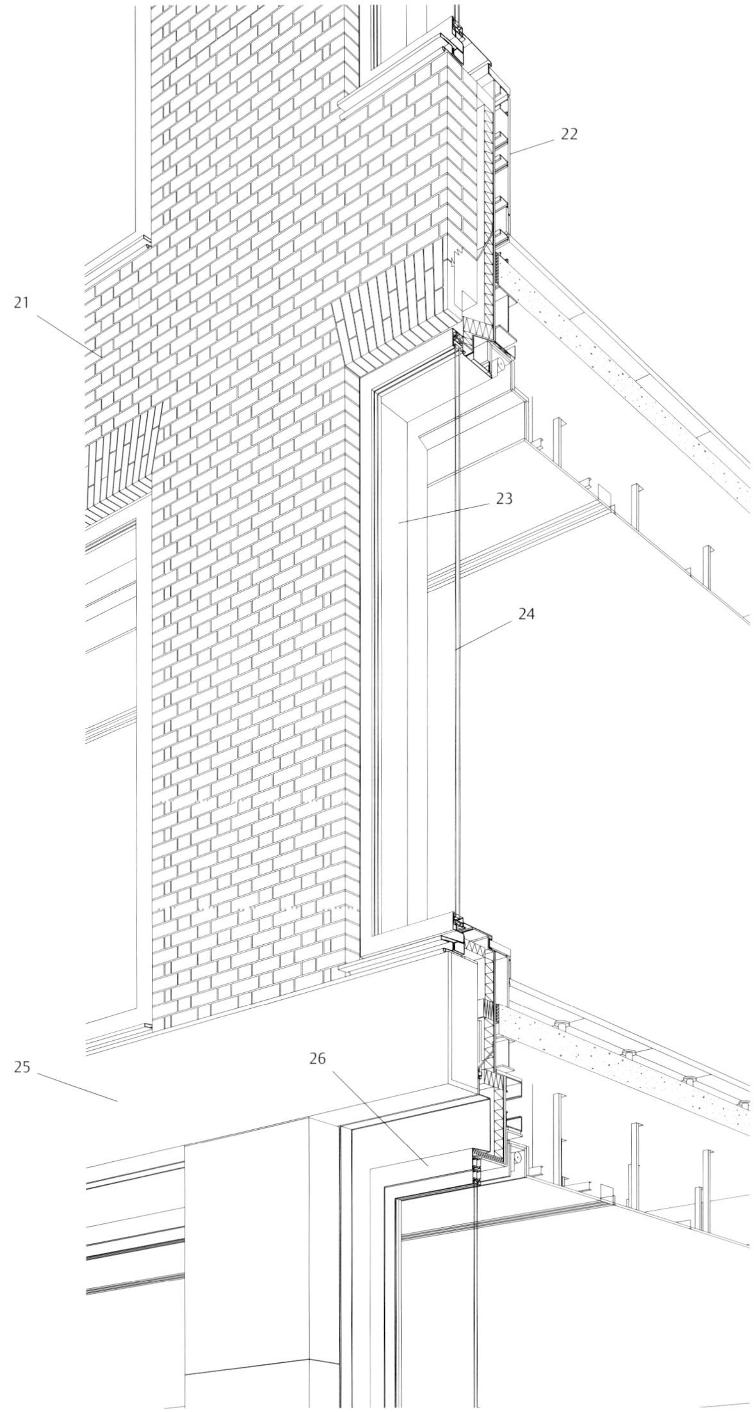

of No. 8, where the windows are set well back in double-stepped limestone casings. And from this, in Apple Tree Yard, juts an elevated two-storey segment rather like a partially extruded pavilion, framed with a structural grid of heavy limestone lintels, cills and pilasters which conceal the framing of the windows; the heavily rolled cills seem to echo the bespoke roll-top of the reception desk.

The whole projecting structure, coffered on the underside in an echo of the coffering in the reception volume, is poised up to first-storey height on six-stepped corbels; and it recalls, in a very general way, Eric Parry's raised rear extension at the Holburne Museum, Bath.

The architectural manner of the lifted pavilion might suggest Elizabethan jettying or an oriel-like Arabic *mashrabiya* from the Middle East, but it seems equally appropriate to think of the pavilion as an imagined, timeless addendum. The windows – hand-blown glass set into a bronze grid that appears to be melting – reference the glass in St James's Church, but the wavering metal in Shirazeh Houshiary's East Window at St Martin-in-the-Fields is a more aesthetically resonant precursor. Viewed from the top of Duke of York Street, the finesse of the elevation's modelling and perspective, its changes of materials and manner are experienced as visually balanced and continuous.

There is a charming coda to the scheme. In Apple Tree Yard, there is a memorial to Lutyens, designed by Eric Parry and Stephen Cox. The memorial features an 18-tonne figure, carved from granite from India's Deccan Plateau, set into the façade at ground level. It stands next to a four-panel granite fender which conceals an air- and light-well that drops down to ground and lower-ground floor levels. These massive, bevelled fenders carry a chiselled script which tells us that Sir Edwin Lutyens laid out his plans for New Delhi in Apple Tree Yard.

This is more than a merely decorous nod to Lutyens. If we recall the sculpture of the inscrutable face produced by Cox for the top of the southeast corner of EPA's One Eagle Place scheme, we realise that it is overlooking St James's Square. The sleeping face, in the same granite, is closer to the sky than the grounded figure beneath the corbelled pavilion in Apple Tree Yard. Is there something metaphysical about this subtle but not accidental connection – an occult addition to No. 8's contribution to time, place and city?

left: Sequence of images showing the gradual transformation of the reception space in its relation to the street and Square. Partial wooden screens and lacquered screens slide fully from within the walls.

opposite: By the corner of the façade, the finished work of Stephen Cox is shown next to his 'Inscribed Rail to Edwin Lutyens' – the latter in four granite blocks whose epigraph commemorates Sir Edwin Lutyens' project for New Delhi, largely conceived and designed in Apple Tree Yard. Above it, large granite modillions appear to hold the weight of the coffered soffit for the large oriel window, which is suspended over the street level – the urban surroundings are reflected against the blown glass panes held by bronze cames.

EDWIN LUTYENS ARCHITECT
DESIGNER OFNEWDELHI
IDOUTHIS PLANSHEREIN APPLETREEYARD

East Village

The practice has produced a set of buildings that are distinctly civic... the buildings radiate urban decorum within a development envelope which will ultimately gain buildings on six more plots, delivering 2000 more apartments.

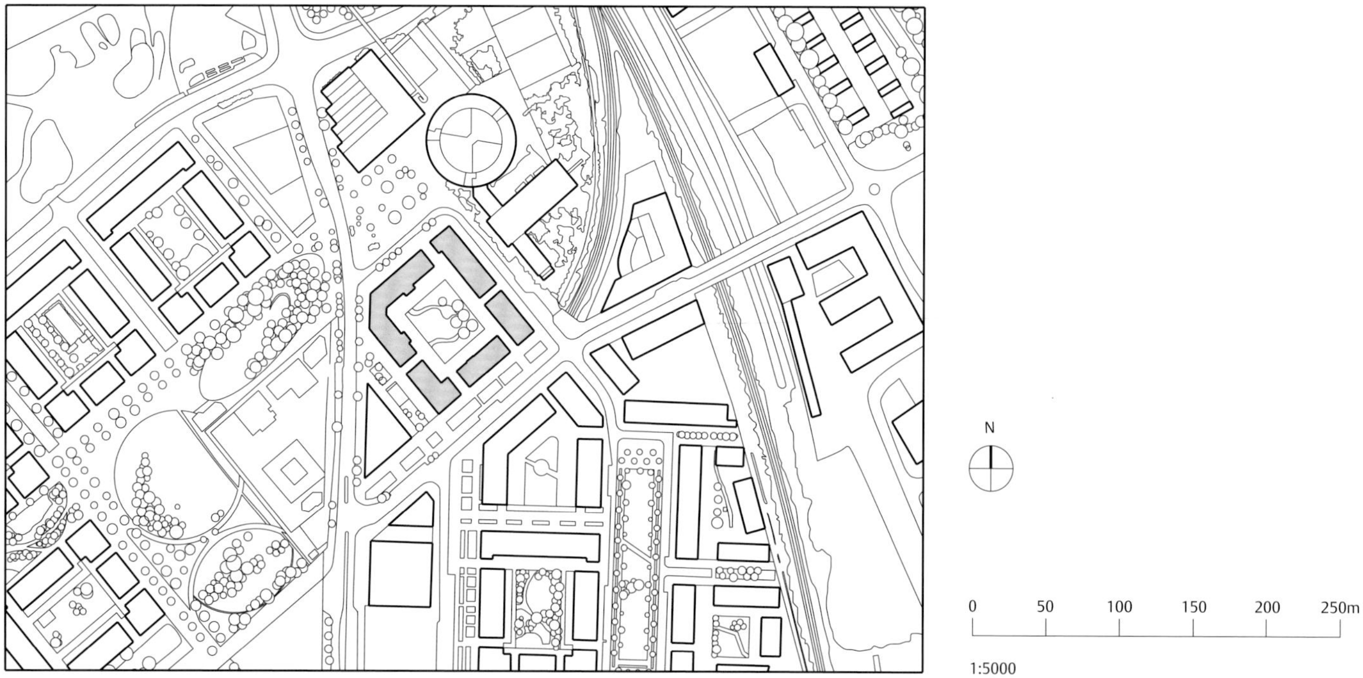

Millions of people pass through London's Stratford station every year. As their trains rumble past the platforms, how many travellers glance west towards East Village and the 63 apartment blocks that originally housed 17,000 athletes and officials at the 2012 London Olympics? How many of them know that this development, with more than 2800 apartments and townhouses inhabited by 6,000 people, is the biggest newbuild rentable and mixed-tenure estate in Britain?

The commuters can't take in the 67-acre setting or the architecture of the 63 individual buildings in any detail from their train seats. They can't, for example, see the façades of blocks partly composed of concrete bas-reliefs of the Elgin Marbles, which might have insulted some Greek athletes; they can't see the 25 acres of landscaped open space, or the secure bicycle compounds in the car parks below the raised gardens that form the central courtyards of the apartment block groupings; nor can they see the colourfully abstracted figurations on the balcony panels of EPA's five apartment buildings on Plot 10 at the northern edge of the Village.

There is not the slightest visual hint that EPA's scheme, or the apartment blocks designed by the 16 other practices distilled from an Architecture Foundation competition, are the products of a fraught financial and procurement backstory which led to a decidedly compressed masterplanning and planning approval process. EPA were one of only two practices who designed their portions of the Village solo, rather than in partnership with another practice.

As the masterplan was being finalised, the 2008 financial crash ruptured the project's original funding structure. Lendlease continued to lead the scheme, but could no longer fund its construction: ownership passed to the Qatari Diar–Delancey investment consortium in 2011, who bought the site, its long-term management rights and additional development land, for £557 million.

As a result, the architects had to work with predetermined plot and block plans, massings and a specific cast-concrete structural system – a fixed chassis, so to speak. As a whole, the layout and architecture of the Village drew sharp, but entirely reasonable criticism, encapsulated by *Building Design* magazine's barbs about the "gestural boulevards", the "forbidding wall of beige", and the salient fact that the "coarse resolution of the outline plan quickly became that of the detailed plan". The plot layouts were based on a default pattern: a north-facing slab with a wing on each side, and so-called pavilions on the south side. There were, of course, modulations to the standard plan as the project proceeded.

The completed internal courtyard.

The masterplan was developed by Fletcher Priest, Arup, West 8 and Vogt Landscape on behalf of the Olympic Delivery Authority and the site's original owner-developers, Lendlease. Fletcher Priest cited John Nash's nineteenth-century Regent's Park terraces as a general inspiration for the masterplan – a rather tenuous reference which, nevertheless, provides a telling historical link. As Nash began to set out his plan for the Prince Regent in 1811, hops were growing in the fields where the East Village now stands.

As the nineteenth century progressed, those fields and others to the south in the Lower Lea Valley became encrusted with dozens of factories and enterprises, which gradually degraded into an environmentally toxic industrial backwater. Living and working conditions in the area were deplored by Henry Morley in an 1857 broadside. He referred to its quite literal "shittiness", and to its inhabitants as "Londoners over the Border". By the late twentieth century the marshy swathe between Stratford and Canning Town had taken on a rust-belt aura, perfectly symbolised by Europe's biggest fridge-mountain on part of what became the Olympic site.

The masterplan's massing of the East Village buildings refers back to the architectural scale of schemes such as Boehmer and Gibbs' Edwardian mansion blocks in Maida Vale. There were also references to the 11,000-apartment Hammarby Sjöstad development in Sweden, built between 1995 and 2015, and the 1997 slab-blocks at Bercy-Gabriel, Paris. EPA's design reference is quite specific, recalling the large-panelled concrete structures of Berlin's Type WBS 70 *Plattenbau* buildings in the 1970s.

The masterplan set a compositional template, some of whose notable features were given slightly sarcastic quote-marks by the architecture critic, Oliver Wainwright: "a slab to the north, a wing either side, and a series of three 'pavilions' to the south, connected by glazed winter gardens. The lower three floors are devoted to 'townhouse' maisonettes, whose first floors open on to private back gardens"; and "apartments are stacked above", from fourth floor level.

The practice's responses to the formal, structural and tenure requirements of Plot 10 have been pragmatic where necessary, and artful in certain details. The design was intently focused on producing five ten-storey blocks that would have the appearance, character and *firmitas* of well-made masonry buildings – "a sense," as Eric Parry put it, "of traditional walls, and of things built upon each other". The construction cost restraints were absolutely binding: "A wonderful agony of differences. The architecture looks fairly simple, but everything was done to the cost per square inch."

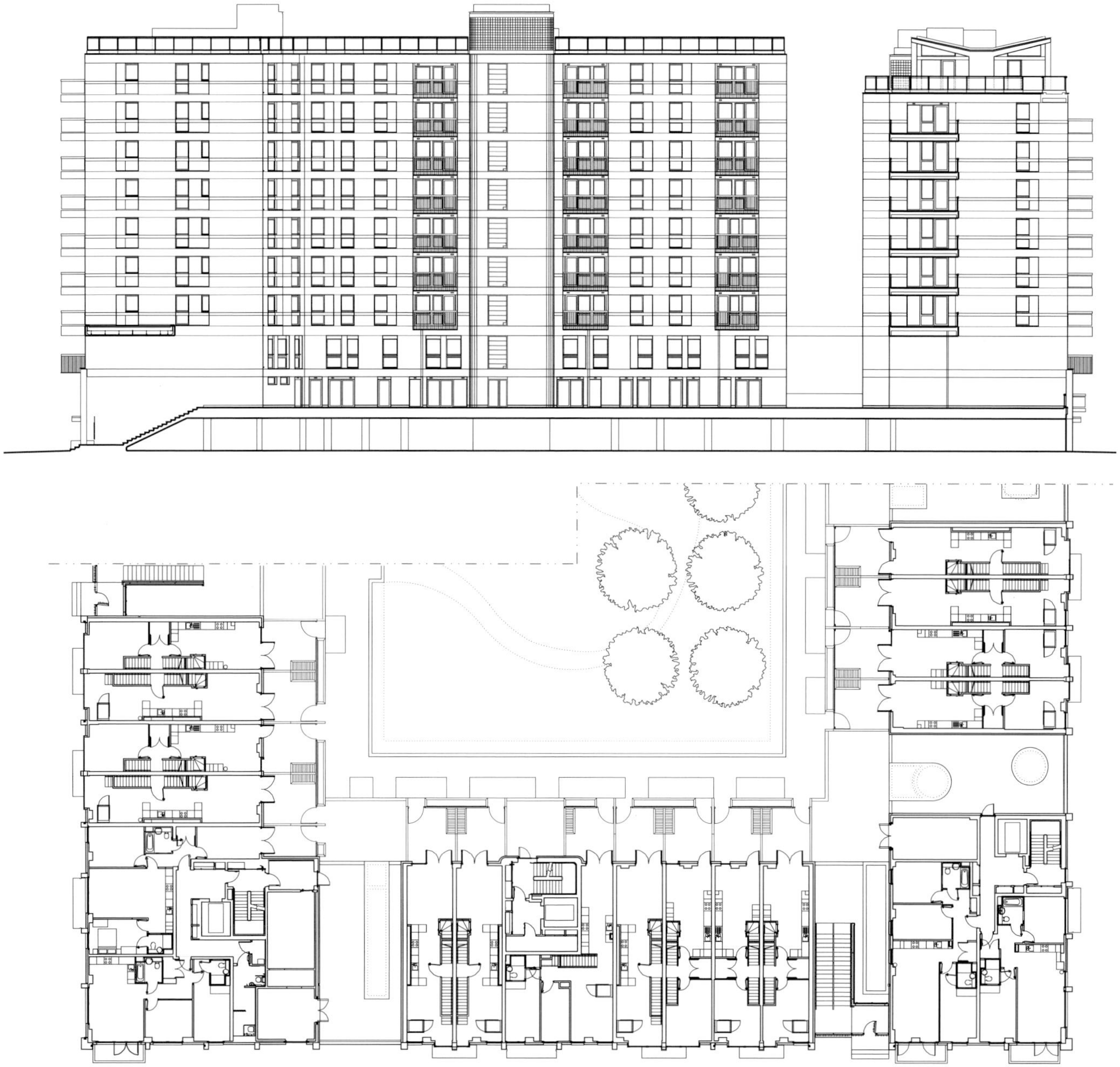

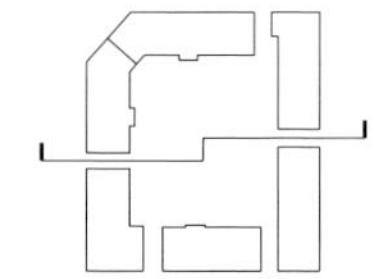

section diagram
1:5000

In the first instance, the block housed the athletes for the 2012 London Olympics and then was placed in the housing market, targeting a variety of social backgrounds – from market rental through intermediate rental for key workers to social housing typologies – which the plan on the page opposite represents.

Section through the internal courtyard and part of the first floor plan.

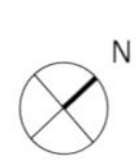

1:500

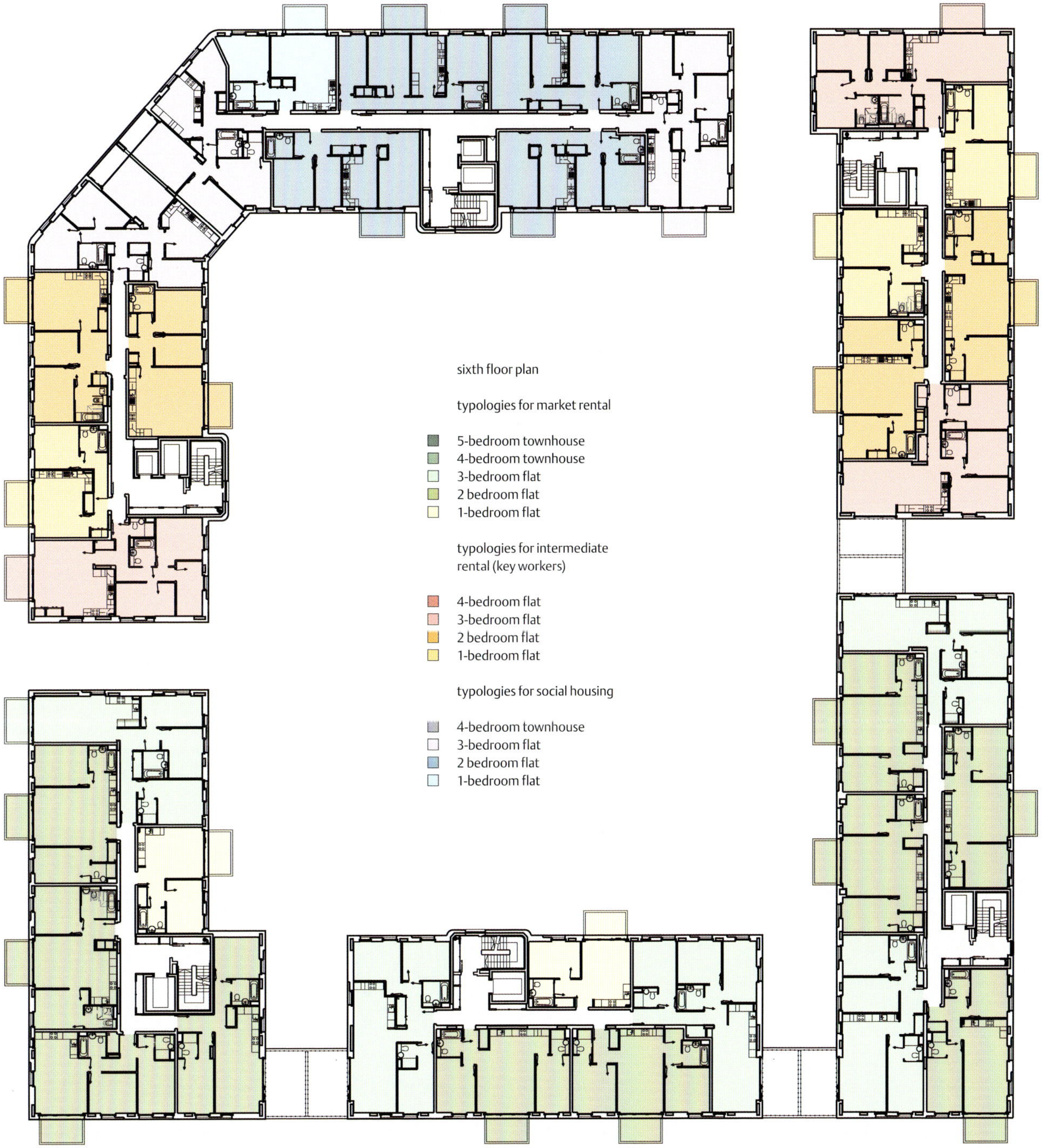
sixth floor plan
typologies for market rental
5-bedroom townhouse
4-bedroom townhouse
3-bedroom flat
2 bedroom flat
1-bedroom flat
typologies for intermediate rental (key workers)
4-bedroom flat
3-bedroom flat
2 bedroom flat
1-bedroom flat
typologies for social housing
4-bedroom townhouse
3-bedroom flat
2 bedroom flat
1-bedroom flat

left: The completed balconies with finished panels enamelled with paintings by Eric Parry.

above: Early detail study for the elevations, with enamelled panel to the parapet and vermiculated blocks to the concrete slab. The enamel would later be reduced to half of the parapet, reinforcing symmetry and transparency.

Early study for the elevations with particular emphasis on rhythm, depth and sciagraphy, already displaying vermiculation on one of the slabs.

The outward-facing sides of the five blocks on Plot 10 overlook different urban conditions: to the north across Cheering Lane, the open civic space next to Chobham Academy; to the southwest, the buildings face Prize Walk, Celebration Avenue – the Village's main north–south road – and Victory Park.

The footprint is rectangular, and measures 85.9m by 80.1m, with a chamfered corner on its west side so that the visual axis along Celebration Avenue remains clear, allowing the plan to angle into the southwest-facing elevation. The five buildings are arranged around a square central garden, beneath which lies a car park, plant rooms and refuse storage.

The blocks contain market apartments and three-storey townhouses, apart from the northern building's townhouses, which are social rent units. The buildings are arranged around a raised central garden. The larger, chamfered building to the west was designed to deliver a mix of social and intermediate units, with some market townhouses.

The remaining four buildings are all market units, except for the townhouses at the lower level of the northern block, which are social housing units. Winter gardens form glazed connections between four of the buildings on the upper levels. These buildings have outward-facing setbacks at the ninth floor, and the base of the blocks project 500mm, allowing their ledges to carry concealed drainage gutters.

The design of the elevations emphasises horizontals, to chime with the strong horizontal modelling of most of the Village's buildings, and notably the sharply angular, rather Expressionistic balconies of the single 13-storey block on Plot 9, immediately to the southwest.

EPA positioned three-storey townhouse segments centrally on each side of the development, with pairs of side-by-side front doors and front and rear gardens – "curiously English," says Parry. Double-height colonnades step out slightly out from the podium of each block and wrap around the base, which frames the first two floors of the townhouses, and creates distinct retail cornerpieces – part of the Village's 80,135ft^2 retail offer.

From the third storey up, the elevational treatments are consistent in materiality and key details, and therefore visually tenure-blind: if you walk past these buildings – or study them from the central courtyard – it's difficult to tell a premium rental apartment from a social-rent home. Internally, the only significant differences relate to room sizes and the fact that the non-market rent portions have fire escape stairs rather than sprinkler systems. The cantilevered precast balconies are extensions of the living rooms.

Some architectural features, such as window setbacks and recessed exterior wall panels, recall EPA's Foundress Court scheme at Pembroke College, Cambridge, completed in 1997 – "how to get 100 rooms in the elevation without creating a grid," as Parry recalls.

At Stratford, considerable thought was given to the expressions of horizontality and tectonic heft across the elevations. Above the townhouse level, bedroom windows are grouped within larger recessed concrete panels, with a cill-drain at the base. The cast concrete elevations are divided into layers by expressed bands at floor and balustrade levels, and this works because of the contrasts: the generally pale, acid-etched wall surface – white cement, fine aggregate and quartzite – with two different, slightly rougher etch-depths on the bands. Joint positions were arranged so that the concrete panels didn't read as a grid. For example, the floor-level spandrel-panels were jointed on a different line.

Grey, slightly roughly-surfaced horizontal concrete banding runs across the elevations facing the inner courtyard. They pass over the inset, two-part windows, which produces subtle effects of depth which add to the visual traction of the elevations and strongly emphasises the masonry quality. The gaps through the blocks created by the winter gardens, combined with projecting balconies (and the flat-fronted ones facing the busy traffic on Cheering Lane) reprise Parry's essential aim for the Foundress Court elevations – "sun, shadow, sciagraphy". Equally effective are the vermiculated bandings on the outward-facing elevations: they begin above the double-order base pilastrade, and appear on the elevations in line with the balconies, and wrap around their edges.

"Terragni is always there somewhere – Modernism plus materiality," Parry adds. The image of Terragni's and Pietro Lingeri's 1936 Casa Rustici in Milan hovers – particularly the elevation facing the Corso Sempione: flat-fronted corner-pieces which then step back to form narrow balconies running continuously across the structure's completely open midsection. The buildings on Plot 10 present asymmetric arrangements of those modulations.

Parry's remark about "things built upon each other" confirms a pleasure in conveying weight, but it has been done in a refined manner. The concrete panels and bandings in the elevations have very tight vertical joints. The surfaces are modelled by balconies and the projecting bays that run in a gentle bulge up the courtyard façades. Above them, V-shaped pavilions accentuate the rooftops like diacritics.

Some of the less obvious detailing is notable for adroit concealments: the barely noticeable heat exchanger vent-slits in the white powder-coated aluminium panelling on the undersides of the balconies; aluminium window framing – "pretty brutal," admits Parry – hidden behind precast concrete panels; drains above the third storey secreted in the vertical frame panels of balcony windows.

The practice has produced a set of buildings that are distinctly civic, but don't demand to be looked at. As individual objects, and in their relation with the townscape (the Village is not, of course, anything like a village) the buildings radiate urban decorum within a development envelope which will ultimately gain buildings on six more plots, delivering 2000 more apartments.

The formal and material decorum of the Plot 10 buildings is generally restrained, yet artfully accented. "I really felt that the Taste Police for the East Village were great, in general, except that there was an abandonment of colour," Parry recalls. His response was to personally produce a series of seven artworks which were, in both original and reversed versions, silk-screened onto panels fixed to two of the three balustrades on each balcony.

The imagery is colourful *con brio*. It has a vaguely Corbusian look, but the individual figurations are quite enigmatic; they have the spirit of cut-ups and their subject matter includes the 2010 Icelandic ash-cloud, the tanned hide of a skinned bear (perhaps prompted by EPA's Leathersellers' Hall project) and what Parry describes as "the fecundity of circles" – his wording infers a pagan rather than classically Olympian reference.

Equally pagan – at least in spirit – is the stone menhir that stands just outside one of the gated entrances to the courtyard garden on the west side of Plot 10. Why a menhir-cum-public artwork? "It's all to do with the raw, the crust," Parry explains. And that, in turn, seems an improvisation on the fundamentally weighty character of the architecture – "things built upon each other".

It's equally tempting to connect the stone, an entirely surreal object in the tightly and unremarkably ordered Village to the sketch of the Neolithic *menhir* at Locmariaquer, Brittany, on page 2 of Banister Fletcher's 1896 *A History of Architecture on the Comparative Method.* Fletcher was the first chairman of the Building Crafts College, established by the Worshipful Company of Carpenters in 1893. In 2001, the College moved from its premises in Great Titchfield Street to a new home in Stratford, about 15 minutes' walk from the Olympic Village. Is it the sense of weight and raw crust that defines the architecture of these buildings? Not quite. It is that these qualities have been civilised by the craft applied to their most salient features and details.

opposite: View of the southwest corner of the urban block.

DEO DANTE DEDI
SOLA VIRTUS INVICTA
LA VIRTU EST LA SEULE NOBLESSE
HONI SOIT QUI MAL Y

The Charterhouse

Everything about the design of this project has radiated from the careful reading of the physical and spatial details of this historically remarkable place, and its actual and potential thresholds. It is about the movement of people through time, in and around a building that embodies centuries.

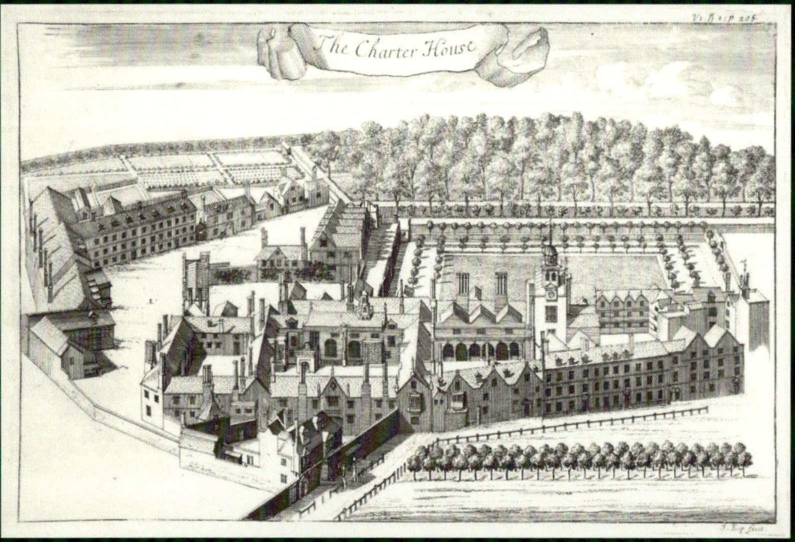

Copper plate etching of "The Charter House", dating from 1720, by Jan Kip (1652–1722)

On 27 January, 2017, the Grade I listed London Charterhouse opened its doors to the public for the first time in more than six centuries, following the completion of a Heritage Lottery-supported project entitled Revealing the Charterhouse. The scheme has reconfigured Charterhouse Square and created a new public entrance threshold at Chapel Court which leads visitors into a reception room, and spaces off it – a refurbished Learning Room, the new Wesley Exhibition Room, and access to other parts open to the public, such as the Chapel Cloister.

The history of the site is extraordinary, and the idea of revealing part of it to the public is enmeshed in something like the temporal riddle in TS Eliot's poem, "Burnt Norton": "Time present and time past/ Are both perhaps present in time future,/ And time future contained in time past."

Much of the Charterhouse's 13-acre site was used as a plague pit and burial ground for an estimated 50,000 bodies, in the year 1349 alone, during the Black Death, and 100,000 (including the bodies of the poor and destitute) by the time Sir Walter de Mauny established the Charterhouse. This was a cloistered retreat for Carthusian monks, and it existed from 1371 until the mid-sixteenth century, when the Dissolution of the Monasteries took brutal effect.

The buildings became tenements, and Sir Edward North began to demolish the monastery church and build a Tudor manor house with a Great Hall, Great Chamber, and a long brick-vaulted passage known as the Norfolk Cloister. In 1611, the philanthropist Thomas Sutton bought the site and transformed the buildings into almshouses and a school, together known as Sutton's Hospital.

The ages and restorations of the buildings' fabrics vary. The Chapter House, for example, is fifteenth century; the altar of St John the Baptist, next to it, is fourteenth century; part of the Master's Lodge is fourteenth century, as are most of the Library and Dining Room.

Today, the London Charterhouse houses more than 40 retired gentlemen, or secular 'brothers' of demonstrably limited means. In 1985, one of the brothers was the artist Adrian Daintrey. After visiting him on 28 March that year, the novelist Anthony Powell wrote this in his diary: "I went under an arch, entering a complex of utterly deserted quadrangles. It was like moving into the Fourth Dimension, several centuries back in Time, everything round about completely still, like a dream."

The Charterhouse left an even more illustrious nineteenth century visitor equally bemused. A report in an 1852 edition of the *Household Words* journal, published by Charles Dickens, presents the Charterhouse as a kind

location plan

1 Charterhouse Square
2 Entrance Court
3 Master's Court
4 Chapel Court
5 Wash House Court
6 Garden Yard
7 Preacher's Court
8 Brothers' Garden
9 Pensioners' Court
10 Master's Garden
11 Clerkenwell Road
12 St John's Street
13 Charterhouse Street
14 Florin Court
15 Carthusian Street
16 Metropolitan Railway
17 Farringdon East Crossrail

extent of proposed works

N

0 10 25 50m

1:2000

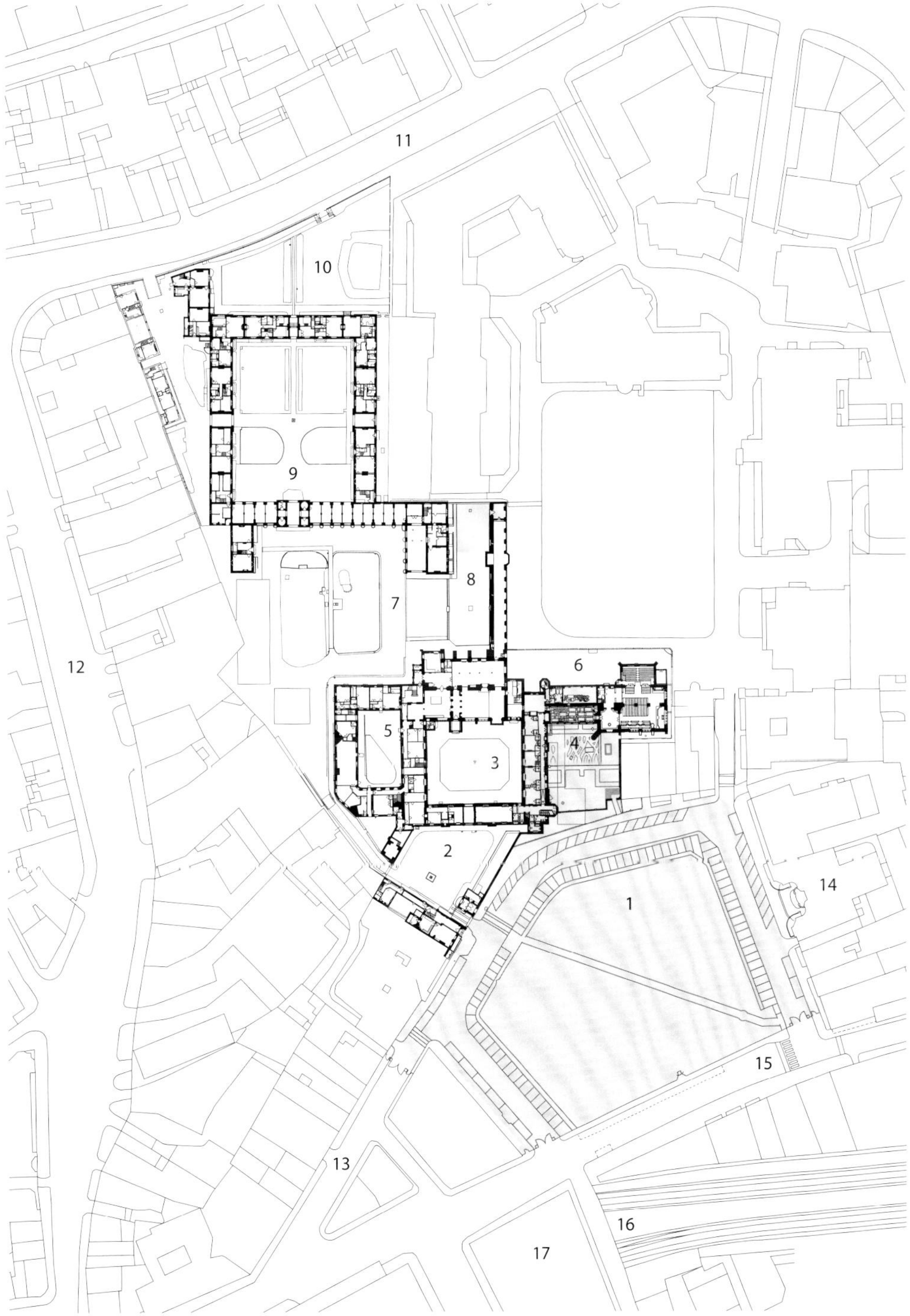

Study of the gates, portals and doorways from the pre-existing buildings of the Charterhouse.

of wanderer's riddle: "Out of the quiet of Charterhouse Square, we pass under an archway, by a porter's lodge, into the still greater quiet of the Charterhouse. Scattered buildings, many old monastic walls, a sort of lane leading to a silent square with a bit of green and a large pump; a chapel, a hall; an archway, other squares, cloisters, modern buildings like dull piles of law chambers constructed to match Pump Court in the Temple, a handsome modern house, an archway; a graveyard like a meadow, a boy's playground; monkish time-eaten cloisters, where monks spent an agony before death in the old grim days of persecution; then back, in some odd way, to the pump, or under an archway to the kitchen, or the chapel, or some other unexpected place – all this belongs to the confused image left upon the mind, by a first ramble over the acres covered by the Charterhouse, and shut out from the noise and tumult of the city."

The language used by Eric Parry and the project's landscape architect, Todd Longstaffe-Gowan, is in this tradition, emphasising this sense of obvious and less obvious historical and physical thresholds. Longstaffe-Gowan quotes Andrew Saint's 2008 *Survey of London*, which speaks of the "ancient impenetrability" of Charterhouse Square. In an essay about the project, Parry refers twice to the presence of the fugitive "shadow" of the fourteenth-century monastery. The shadow is time, and our sense of the movement of time is the crucial subtext of a project which recalls St Augustine's temporal puzzlement in his *Confessions*: "It appears to me that time is nothing other than extendedness; but extendedness of what I do not know. This is a marvel to me."

The Charterhouse's entry-point had been through a narrow arched medieval gateway and gatehouse facing the northwest side of Charterhouse Square, which is oversailed by part of No. 17 Charterhouse Square, known as the Physician's House when it was built in 1716. That entrance is a pinch-point, and leads into the roughly triangular Outer Court, which doesn't quite have the character of a courtyard, and so the first experience of the interior of the site is disappointing. Despite being surrounded by richly archaic brick and stone elevations, there is a faint sense of anticlimax, rather than arrival.

The design strategy for the new public entrance centred on the idea that Charterhouse Square and the actual point of entry had to coalesce into a narrative to form a *place* of approach and arrival which then culminated in a particular point of arrival. There is an important relationship between Chapel Court, the new entry threshold, and the wider setting of the square, which will become much busier with pedestrians when the Crossrail station opposite the southern corner of the square opens. It's forecast that the public-facing improvements to the Charterhouse have the potential

to attract between 80,000 and 100,000 visitors a year. Before the changes, the buildings were seen only by small weekly groups of visitors on guided tours.

In short, the design of changes inside the Charterhouse began with a study of what was outside it. Parry notes that, standing at the new southeastern gateway to the Square and looking towards the southern elevation of the Charterhouse, "the fabric of the buildings is broken by a dense foliage section with railings and a mysterious private garden beyond. This view is framed by the canopy of the mature plane trees and their massive trunks. It is an unusual place of deep repose in this densely occupied part of London... This verdant space marks a point of equilibrium between the east and west of the trapezoid square and forms an unseen ley-line that heralds the hidden world beyond, a length of more than three hundred metres to Clerkenwell Road".

His phrase "deep repose" is of significance to a project whose background is the Carthusian order, founded in 1084 by St Bruno of Cologne and which, in a recent description by Fr. Rosendo Roig, seeks "the ambience of solitude, the absence of any disturbing noise and of worldly desires and images, the quiet and calm attention of the mind to God... flow into that 'quies' or 'rest' of the soul in God".

How, then, do you make a place of "deep repose" more open to the public, without traducing the spirit of a place where the silts of time have produced particular physical and atmospheric imprints across seven centuries?

The Charterhouse buildings and the square retain a quite unique atmosphere, a long-gathered otherness that defies the fact that the they take up more than a third of the area of land bounded by the hurly-burly of Clerkenwell Road, St John Street, Goswell Road and Carthusian Street. The Barbican Underground station is 120m to the southeast, and yet, standing in the square or walking among the old buildings, the traffic and the footfall barely register.

The subtle orchestration of *without* into *within* begins with the new landscaping of the roughly pentangular garden which, with the road around three of its sides, is owned and maintained by the Charterhouse. In the 1960s, the central garden was reduced in size and given standard perimeter railings and low holly hedges to create more angled parking spaces along its north, west and east sides. The garden has reclaimed 760m^2 of its pre-war area, now covering just over 5000m^2 and ridding the square of 109 parking slots.

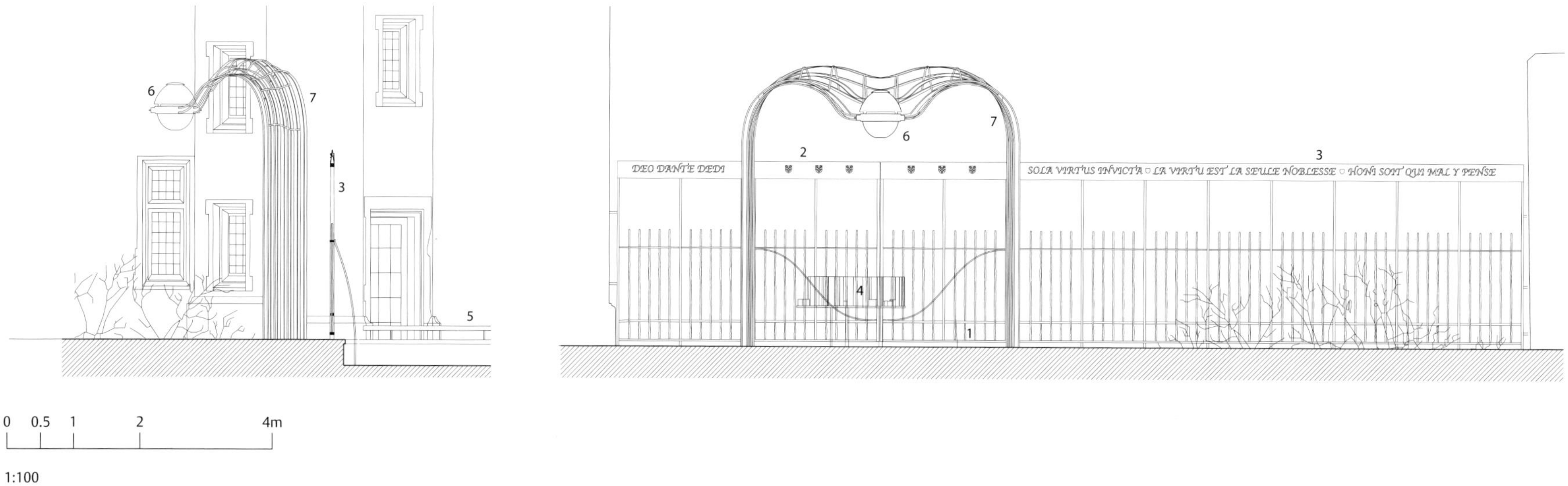

gate and fence
south elevation and cross-section

1 York stone paving
2 gates: bespoke mild-steel gates with decorative lettering to top rail
3 railings: bespoke mild-steel railings with decorative lettering to top rail and outriggers to garden side
4 bronze model of the Charterhouse precinct
5 metalwork edge rail with integral lighting
6 gas lantern: glass lamp with 16 mantles and vitreous enamelled hood
7 entrance arch: bespoke mild-steel arch, materials and nish to match gates

Most of the garden is greensward, but Longstaffe-Gowan has paid considerable attention to creating more diverse ecological conditions – particularly in attracting more bird species. The garden has small, meadow-like areas and traditional English hedging, including hawthorn, blackthorn, hazel, rowan and guelder rose; there are also sections of native woodland shrubs – holly, crab-apple, elder and so on.

There was previously only one path across the square, running in a straight line from its southeast corner to a point facing the gatehouse at the northwest corner – rather pragmatic compared to the diagonal saltire cross-path layout, lined with trees, shown in Stow's *Survey of London* in 1598, which lasted into the eighteenth century.

The new path layout has two main axes: a north–south path cutting directly across from the south side of the garden to gates facing the Charterhouse's public entrance threshold at Chapel Court; and there is a path from the garden's southeast corner – where a new octagonal pavilion stands – to a point opposite the original entrance arch. The pavilion has a floor composed of an octagonal perimeter band around four quartered segments of hand-set pebble-work illustrating the coats of arms of the four most significant owners of the Charterhouse.

There are two other paths, one leading from the centre of the garden to its western edge, and another which loops around the northeast portion. The loop, with seven long seats around its arc, gives walkers (or pausers) clear views of the southern elevations of the Charterhouse, and Chapel Court in particular.

The landscaping sets the scene for a more relaxed public engagement with the Charterhouse – it's a foreground designed to encourage deliberate (or simply inquisitive) movement toward the Chapel Court entrance, which contains vestiges of the foundations of the Charterhouse's first chapel, and a slab marking the grave of Sir Walter de Mauny. In 1941 a bomb destroyed an eighteenth-century building that stood on this part of the Charterhouse site, and in the 1950s a low wall and wrought-iron railings were put up on the Court's south edge; shielded by fig trees – it became the "mysterious private garden" described by Parry.

He recognised the historical and programmatic potential of Chapel Court, which has a cloister and chapel on its north side, the wall of Butchers' Hall on its east side, and a range which now contains the reception and Learning Room on the west. The threshold design has three components: a rebuilt and re-railed wall across Chapel Court where it meets the pavement; the removal of the two fig trees and

The arch and gates
to Entrance Court.

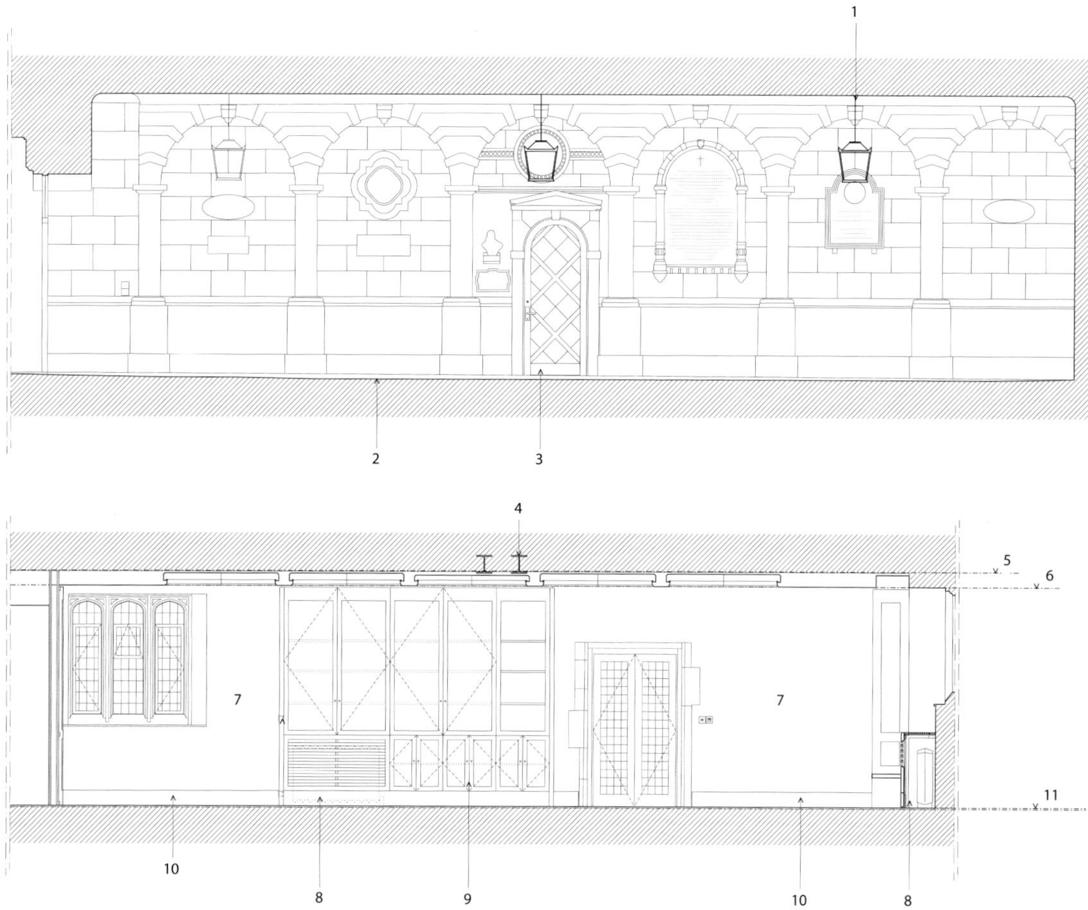

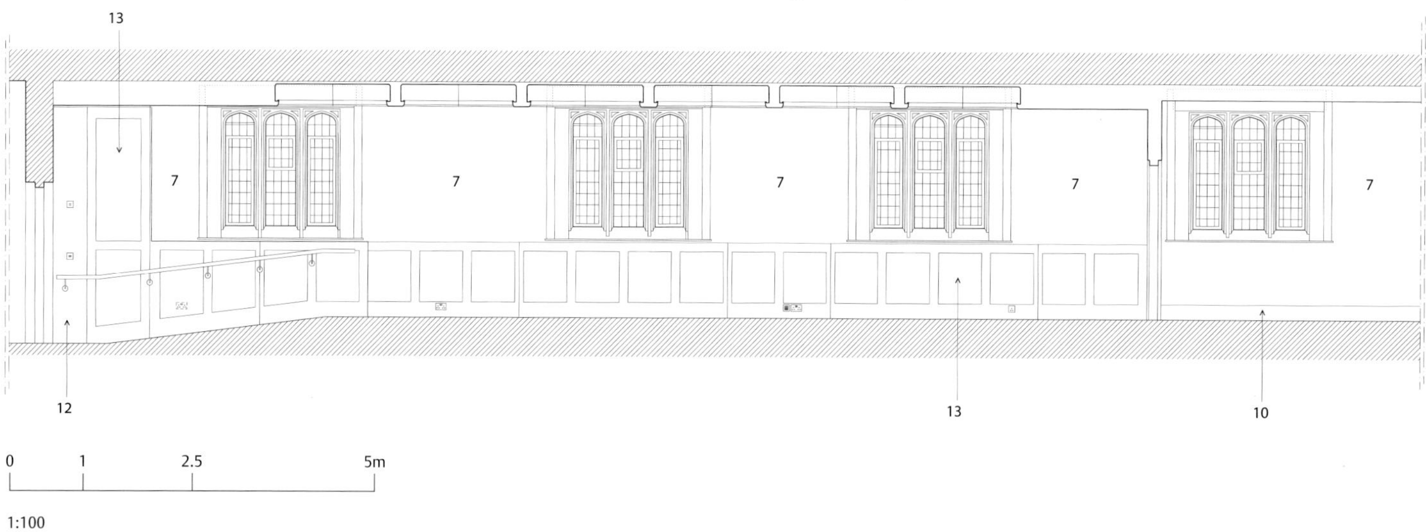

top to bottom: sections of the Chapel Cloister corridor, the Reception, and the Learning Room.

1 new lights to existing light fittings
2 conservation repairs to existing stone flooring
3 existing door retained and refurbished
4 I-profile steel beams
5 existing ceiling
6 dropped ceiling
7 painted finish to lime plaster
8 oak-panelled radiator housing integrated into display joinery
9 reception wall panelling
10 oak skirting
11 new cork floor surface
12 painted finish to dry wall
13 oak panelling

Interior of the reception.

a false acacia which had obscured the view into Chapel Court; the setting of a fourteenth-century plan of the monastery, in contrasting stones, into a single large stone slab with water-jetted lettering, positioned just outside the line of railings; and a three-dimensional bronze model of the current Charterhouse site, set on a canted bronze table, which stands a few steps into the courtyard.

But if we imagine somebody walking through the garden, it's obvious that those features alone would not signal the threshold effectively. Parry's first idea was to place a relatively substantial rectilinear baldacchino-cum-portico just outside the railings. But its relatively solid bulk would have interfered with a clear view into Chapel Court, and its architectural manner was not in tune with the elevations beyond it.

The revised portico is a botanical frame anchored into a stone base, and it was being made as this book went to press. It takes the form of a filigreed, gated bower composed of tapering and curved wrought-iron bars that recall the Tudor Rose and the sixteenth- and seventeenth-century rose decorations of the Charterhouse's Treasury and Great Chamber. The bower will eventually carry climbing roses and be overhung with a large gas luminaire which the practice associates, rather playfully, with London's grander Victorian and Edwardian pubs. Its soft light will fall over the bronze plan-slab beneath the bower.

Having dealt with the *without*, the *within* of the Charterhouse project was relatively straightforward, and affects three rooms in the Tudor mansion, whose north range had suffered bomb damage and, along with its east range, was rebuilt by the architects Seely and Paget in the 1950s. The western side of Chapel Court previously contained five brothers' rooms, and these have been transformed into a long Learning Room. The top half of the north range, alongside the Chapel Cloister, is now the Wesley Exhibition Room; and at the junction of these two new rooms is the rectangular reception area, which is twice the size of the original one, with a cloakroom and WCs. It is entered directly from Chapel Court through a glazed, step-free door.

In spirit, the design of the various transformed spaces reprises the unfussy, pre-war timber-lined walls, with contemporary detailing and lighting. For example, the flooring is either cork tiling or linoleum, walls are timber panelled in a very simple way, and there are suspended plasterboard ceilings. The interventions have created pleasant, clean-lined, properly unremarkable interiors which barely disturb the historic fabric or the atmosphere it produces.

Everything about the design of this project has radiated from the careful reading of the physical and spatial details of this historically remarkable place, and its actual and potential thresholds. It is about the movement of people through time, in and around a building that embodies centuries of time.

Visitors crossing the park, with the remaining shards of 600-year-old bones and teeth in the soil a few feet beneath their shoes, pass along the ley-line imagined by Parry and under the arc and the luminaire. They are unwitting participants in a contemporary mystery play, a subtle secular drama within this once-cloistered place of religious life.

left: Interior of one of the corridors of the permanent exhibition of the Charterhouse.

right: Model of the Charterhouse complex installed by the entrance.

opposite: The restored corridor of the Norfolk Cloister, which links the Old Library to the Privy Garden Room and Brothers' Garden.

The Welding Institute

What is beyond question – and more fundamentally important – is that the architecture of this expansion of the Welding Institute's Braithwaite Building serves the wider landscape, and its history, as much as it serves the science of electron-beam welding, friction stir-welding of rivets for jumbo jets, or the Big Pharma vibe that permeates Granta Park.

1 Granta Park
2 Franklin Building
3 Flowers Building
4 Vernalis Building
5 River Granta
6 McClintock Building
7 Portway Building
8 PPD
9 Milstein Building
10 Aaron Klug Building
11 St Mary's Church
12 TWI: Bevan Braithwaite Building
13 TWI: Building 1
14 TWI: Building 2
15 TWI: Building 3
16 Riverside
17 Abington Hall
18 Plot C
19 Plot D
20 Plot E
21 Plot A
22 Plot B
23 Plot F

0 100 250m

1:10,000

N

Plan showing the extent of the site with: Granta Park (1) a masterplan of Eric Parry Architects to the west (see *Vol. 1*, p. 144); the location of the existing Braithwaite Building (12) in the centre of the plan; and to the south, the completed expansion of The Welding Institute (13–15) by Eric Parry Architects as well as the forthcoming masterplan for Phase 2 (18–25).

The design of the expansion of the Welding Institute's Braithwaite Building at Granta Science Park, near Great Abington in Cambridgeshire, resists the architectural norms of science parks, a phenomenon which began in California with Stanford University's research park at Palo Alto in 1951. The first in Britain was Cambridge Science Park, established by Trinity College in 1970; and that was one year after the opening of the tech-based Fondation Sophia Antipolis, north of Antibes, which JG Ballard satirized as Eden-Olympia in his novel, *Super-Cannes*. The idea, as Ballard put it, is to create buildings and settings where "work is the ultimate play, and play the ultimate work".

If we exclude relatively rare High Tech buildings, such as Hopkins' 1985 Schlumberger Cambridge Research Centre, and the deliberately 'iconic' recent research buildings in California's Silicon Valley, epitomised by Apple's circular 2,800,000ft² headquarters and 71ha campus at Cupertino, this architectural genre tends to default to predictably banal forms: sleek metal skins and/or large areas of glazing, which impart a *Vorsprung durch Technik* simulacrum of innovation.

The buildings at Granta Science Park follow suit, and are arranged in a landscaped 120 acre rural setting which has been subject to three EPA masterplans. The first, in 1997, involved the eminent German landscape architects Latz + Partner, and established the layout of what is now the western half of the park. Latz's landscape scheme, regarded as "formidably good" by Parry, included water rills, hundreds of trees shading the so-called parking groves, and a blackwater reed-filtering system.

The second masterplan, developed between 2011 and 2015, covers the site around the Braithwaite Building and its expansion; and the third masterplan, Granta Park Phase 2, developed with input from Land Use Consultants and Todd Longstaffe-Gowan, deals with land to the south of the Institute. Here, the practice will design buildings on five plots, delivering 368,000ft² of new research space in large, flat-roofed pavilions with pale ceramic elevations set around the landscaped meandering edges of two lakes in a site that totals 1,221,000ft². This will introduce a very different kind of scientific stage-set and is an attempt, as Parry says, to civilise the architectural anarchy in Granta Park. The masterplan area currently contains one million square feet of laboratory and office space, with a working population of 2,500 people.

The 22,333m² expansion of the Braithwaite Building stands about 100m west of the Grade II* listed Abington Hall, a rather plain, decrepit brick building which dates from the early eighteenth century, and sits on the palimpsest of a landscape designed by Humphry Repton in about 1800.

View from the southwest, with Buildings 1 and 2 in the foreground. In addition to the main reception and library, Building 1 (left) also houses the Granta Conference Centre, as well as the Training Centre; Building 2 (right from centre) houses teaching laboratories and the administrative staff for the National Structural Integrity Research Centre; Building 3 (almost outside the frame), which houses the Engineering Hall, also includes testing facilities and laboratories, welder-training workshops and office space.

The non-profit Institute's presence on the site dates back to 1946 when the British Welding Research Association bought Abington Hall and outbuildings for £3,850 (the equivalent of about £85,000 in 2018) and set up a welding shop in the stables; metal fatigue researchers worked in an ex-Army hut. By 1965 there were also units for welding technology and applied non-destructive testing. The organisation was renamed the Welding Institute in 1968 and was government- funded until 1985.

In the twenty-first century the Institute's staff of around 800 staff at 13 facilities worldwide generates a range of world-leading research and commercial testing programmes on behalf of about 1,800 industrial member companies in more than 70 countries. Their work at Granta Park relates to structures, materials and welding techniques whose applications range from offshore oil-well structures, ceramics and plastics, to laparoscopy joints, friction-stir connections for aerospace parts, and bra-bonds.

The client's original brief for the Welding Institute's expansion was not inspirational – Eric Parry recalls the phrase "grey and watertight" being used more than once. However, one of the Institute's advisers, Ian Laing, an ex-director of Stanhope and a successful biotech entrepreneur, convinced the client to support a higher-quality design that would very distinctly convey technological and commercial progress.

EPA's design combines rational, cost-effective plans and sections with a number of formal, topographical and elevational treatments that are quite original in the context of Granta Park. An overriding design challenge was to ensure that the massive expansion would not insult the landscape around it: Latz's 1997 masterplan was based on retaining a sense of farmland, farm buildings and farmyards.

The Braithwaite expansion is the first at Granta Park whose formal, material and topographical innovations have given a potentially overwhelming architectural object a distinct relationship with the landscape around it; and, as Parry says, "to somehow create a calibration of the body against the landscape".

The extension has an E-shaped plan, with two pavilions and a massive barn-like structure projecting south from a 135m-long circulation street on an east–west axis, which is attached to the back of the 2003 Bevan Braithwaite building. The east end, known as Building 3, takes the form of three high-gabled volumes. One of these volumes contains a small section of offices and training rooms, the other two volumes form the Engineering Hall.

The amenity and conference spaces, in Building 1 at the west end, are partially embedded into a slope that falls to the boundary of the

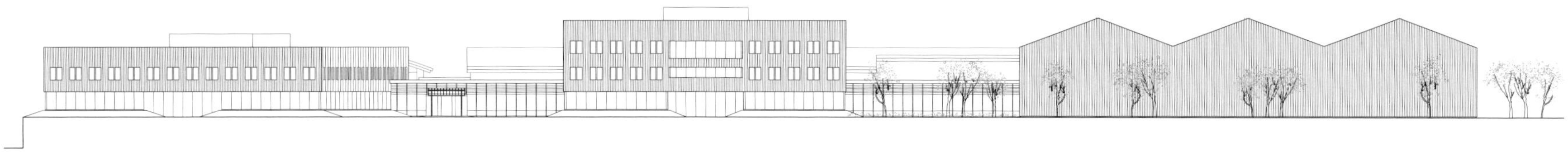

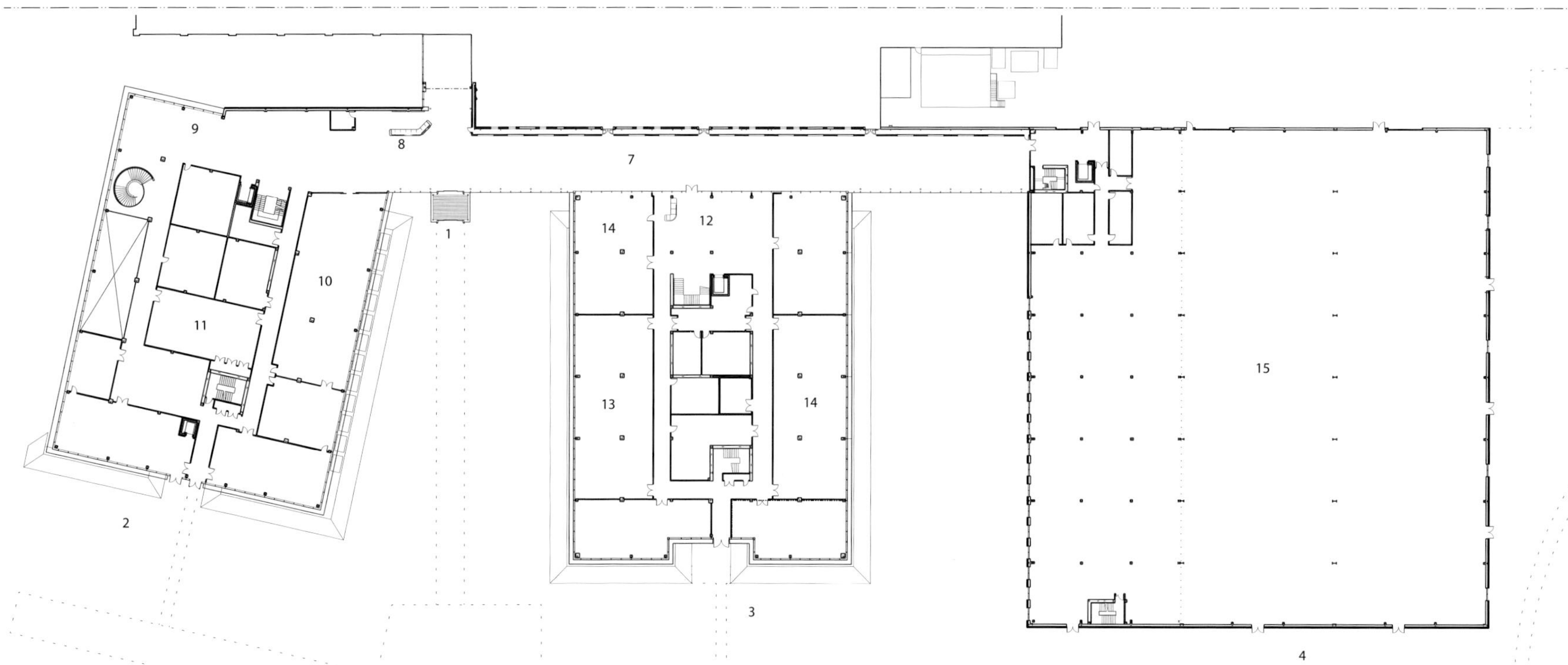

N

0 10 25 50m

1:1000

south elevation

1 entrance
2 Building 1
3 Building 2
4 Building 3
5 Beven Braithwaite building (existing)
6 service yard
7 The Street
8 reception
9 café
10 library
11 conference & meeting
12 reception & stair
13 teaching spaces
14 labs
15 Engineering Hall
16 offices (open-plan)

Detail of one of the corners of Building 1 that houses the reception and library, as well as a restaurant and café, among other amenities.

cricket pitch, which is the central, village-suggesting point in the 1997 masterplan. The north and west elevations of the double-height ground and first floors are glazed, producing pleasant light-filled circulation spaces. Viewed from outside, however, this is the only part of the scheme where the practice was unable to fend off clearly visible design-and-build rationalisations: the contractor's treatment of the berm and concrete upstand where the wing meets the falling ground at the southwest corner is pragmatic, to say the least.

Building 2, the central finger of the E-plan, houses the labs and teaching spaces of Britain's first structural integrity research foundation, which at any one time is occupied by academics from 16 universities, most of them from Brunel and Manchester at the time this monograph went to press.

Because of cost-restraints, the design sought very simple solutions to structure and internal finishes. The 9m structural grid is highly efficient; the structure of the Engineering Hall features spans from 6m to 22.5m between portal frames. The ceiling of the long link street is acoustically wood-slatted; and the external wall sections have highly insulated sections of more than 500mm, with steel and jumbo stud structural formats.

Internally, there are only two deliberately striking features: the angled metal balusters of the balcony handrail in Building 1, the amenity wing, and its gracefully articulated helical staircase – a necessarily restrained descendant of the practice's virtuosic stainless-steel staircase in the Babcock & Brown offices at 5 Aldermanbury Square, London.

Two of the three wings have flat roofs, and they project southwards into the landscape. Building 3, the Engineering Hall, is the dominant segment of the Braithwaite expansion, and it resembles three conjoined barns, forming a group that is 68.7m wide and 72.7m long. The treatment of the envelopes of all the buildings produces effects of colour, texture and shadow that introduce an entirely new architectural manner to Granta Park.

"How to dress the buildings was interesting," says Parry. "We needed something that wouldn't lose colour – so ceramic baguettes; and it's very cost-effective. Their spacing and depth was important, to catch shadow; and in the elevations of the research and amenity wings, large areas of glazing without frames. I also wanted to create a landscaped, bermed base for these wings, so that the glass immediately above them is veil-like, rather than distinctly anchored," adds Parry, who also referenced the three-layer glazing at the Holburne Museum, Bath.

opposite: View of the main entrance between Buildings 1 and 2 connected by The Street.

above: internal view of The Street which connects the three buildings, here seen from the reception toward Buildings 2 and 3.

At Granta Park, the veil effect is achieved with triple-glazed bands, with the internal layer set back by a minimum of 600mm to create ventilation and maintenance voids between the inner curtain-wall and the outer toughened glass, which is hung from steel perimeter beams flush with the cladding. This means that the glazing doesn't need UV filtering coatings, and that the external sheer glazing reflects the ceramic cladding very clearly – adding yet another visual quality to the elevations. The deep setback of the internal glazing produces three other important outcomes: it creates a ventilated façade, reduces solar gain on the southern elevations, and conceals the ordering of the office or work spaces inside the buildings.

The solar mediation ties in with a fairly sophisticated energy conservation strategy based on passive design analysis. This dictated the use of supporting technology such as PV arrays, low- or zero-carbon systems, a combined heat and power unit, stack ventilation of the street segment, and degrees of air-tightness and U-values that substantially exceed Building Regulations requirements.

Visually and conceptually, the most remarkable aspect of the scheme is the elevations of the buildings, which feature bands of slim, rectangular ceramic baguettes, in combinations of five pale, unglazed tones of brown, blue, and grey. The layouts of these hollow-sectioned ceramics, from the standard range of the German supplier, NBK, followed Parry's experiments with colours and rhythms, which he trialled using paint and tape on boards.

The effects the layers of baguettes produce on the long walls varies: the pale colorations and the small gaps between the individual vertical pieces can create anything from a subtly haptic surface shimmer to quite graphic articulations of light and shadow. Parry relates this treatment of gaps and joints to the design of the main façade of Finsbury Square.

The practice's profound concern with architectural materiality is concentrated in the ceramic screens, which convey two kinds of craft – the craft of formed and coloured clay, and the craft of its application. The two bolts on each of more than 100,000 baguettes were accurately hand-fixed to the backing rails on the insulated under-cladding. The visual treatment of the big, south-facing gable-ends of the testing facility is quite different. Here, the baguettes are set out in subtle patterns to produce a visual effect which Parry describes as "earthy, rising into woodlands".

Parry also speaks of the ceramic cladding as a kind of camouflage, and it might be, except that the detailing, by some perceptual alchemy, is so precisely minimal that the gaze locks onto it immediately.

opposite: View of the south façades of Buildings 2 and 3.

right: Interior of the ground floor and mezzanine of Building 1 linked with a spiral stair.

For example, the lines of baguettes run right up to the base of the cills of the recessed upper level-glazing; gutter downpipes are concealed behind the layers of baguettes; and the sharply folded zinc parapet profile, and the meticulously controlled shadow-gap between the top edges of the baguettes, seem impossibly straight: not so much design-and-build at £2,038.96/m^2 but built-as-designed. Full-scale mock-ups of these, and other parts of the project, benchmarked the effective outcomes of detail and architectural effects.

This intense attention to the refinement and visual qualities, even in architecture whose general forms are unremarkable, is typical of the practice. Questions of artistry and phenomenological connections also arise. One might, just, link the modulated colouring of the bands of ceramic with the faintly hallucinatory bars of wavering colour in Sean Scully's paintings – for example, the watercolour and graphite of *Land Land* (2016). Or are the equally wavering colours of the baguettes not quite vague enough for this comparison, bearing in mind Scully's remark, published in *Vice* magazine in the same year: "Art is the enemy of purity"?

What is beyond question – and more fundamentally important – is that the architecture of this expansion of the Welding Institute's Braithwaite Building serves the wider landscape, and its history, as much as it serves the science of electron-beam welding, friction stir-welding of rivets for jumbo jets, or the Big Pharma vibe that permeates Granta Park.

A short walk away, Abington Hall's Doric-columnated porch, pedimented south front and ironwork veranda continue to moulder. The Grade II* listed house was never an architectural beauty but, as the *Gentleman's Magazine* noted in 1815, it was once "pleasantly situated... surrounded by beautiful and thrifty plantations, where, during the summer's evenings, the nightingale 'Sings darkling; and in shadiest covert Tunes her nocturnal note'". The form and surfaces of the new building are a dutiful and metaphorical return to Repton's vision of the enclosures and grove of trees at Abington Hall in the eighteenth century, which appeared in a lithographed vignette of the original landscape in the 1803 edition of *Peacock's Polite Repository.*

The new buildings are considerably more than an architecturally polite repository for research; in the existing context, they are – camouflaged or not – a boldly counterfactual demonstration that the pursuit of science does not always have to take place in buildings that ape unknowable futures in the most predictably banal ways.

left: Interior of the café on the northwest corner of Building 1, looking over the cricket field.

right: Detail of the top of the stair at the mezzanine level, with a view to the fields and the broader campus.

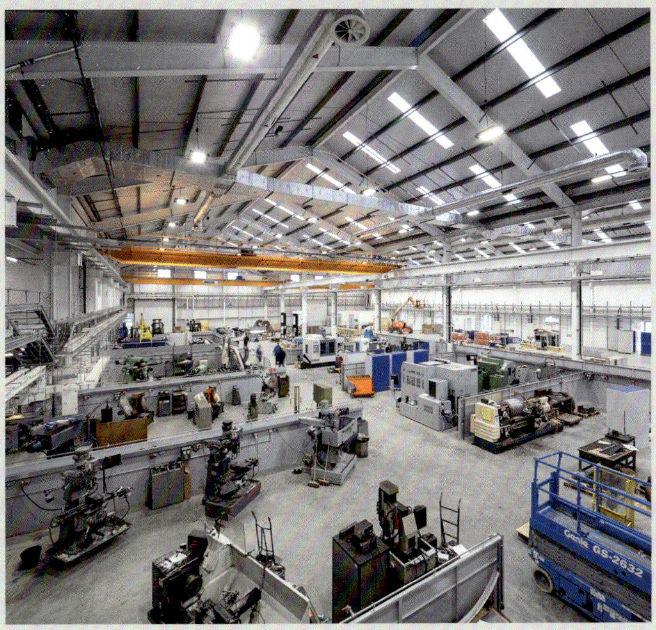

above: Interior of Building 3, which hosts the Engineering Hall and multiple facilities enabling teaching and testing, welder-training workshops and office space.

right: The large scale of Building 3 was mediated by the use of extruded terracotta units gauged to ascend in chroma and tone from earth to sky.

Wells Cathedral School

Ultimately, it was the positioning of Cedars Hall that convinced Stansfield Smith and the jury.... That contextual logic, and the formal and programmatic logic of the architecture, has produced an admirable building.

When I encountered the Cedars Hall performing arts building at Wells Cathedral School in Somerset, I immediately recalled a passage in Leo Tolstoy's *Recollections and Essays*. He describes how, as a boy, he and his brothers and sisters would push chairs close together, sit in them, and cover themselves with a blanket. This was their cabriolet – "and then having settled down in the carriage we changed from travellers to ant brothers. To them other people were joined up. It was very, very good, and I thank God we played it. We called it a game, but really everything in the world is a game, except that."

It's fair to say my reaction was unreasonable. Cedars Hall is not a *faux* cabriolet; its roof is not a metaphorical blanket; the music scholars who inhabit the building are not honorary ant brothers, though some may well think that everything in the world is a game except music. Nevertheless, there is something intriguing about the architecture of Cedars Hall which evades a purely architectural description. Why does this extremely distinct, handsome building also seem tantalizingly fugitive – to this observer, at least?

The temporary antidote to this reaction is a summary of the building's purpose and main characteristics. The school describes it as "the most substantial development" in its history. It must also be the most audacious example of contemporary architecture in Wells, a city which the 2011 Pevsner guide for *Somerset: North and Bristol*, updated by Andrew Foyle, said could be summarised by three "shockingly" accurate clichés – "jewel, venerable, unique".

Cedars Hall was designed to provide a substantial recital and performance hall; teaching, practice and community music workshop spaces; and recording facilities. The building is positioned so that it doesn't dominate the charming view northwards across Cedars Field from the Grade II* listed Cedars House, the school's Georgian main building. Cedars Hall sits less than 100m northwest of this building and is more or less screened by the densely glaucous branches of a mature blue Atlas cedar.

This means that the sylvan view from Cedars House northwards to Cedars Field, the cricket ground and the trees surrounding it (which include an ancient and stately *Wellingtonia*) is almost perfectly preserved. The two other buildings bundled into the Cedars Hall brief – a very simply designed zinc-roofed sports pavilion, and a maintenance building, both timber-built – stand out of sight, just west of Cedars Hall.

The structure of Cedars Hall is embedded in terrain that rises gently from the cricket ground to meet the level of the Recital Hall's gallery

left: Old etching of Wells Cathedral by John Buckler, "To the Right Reverend Richard Beadon. DD Lord Bishop/ of Bath and Wells; This North West View of the/ Cathedral Church of Wells is by Permission, most humbly/ Dedicated, by his Lordship's obliged and devoted Servant, John Buckler", engraved by FC Lewis (Bermondsey: J Buckler, 1806).

right: Early sketch by Eric Parry, showing the intended placement of the new Recital Hall by the cricket grounds of Wells Cathedral School, within sight of the College Road entrance (right of frame) and, importantly, within the visual and urban axis of Vicar's Close, leading to Wells Cathedral's Chapter House (bottom of frame).

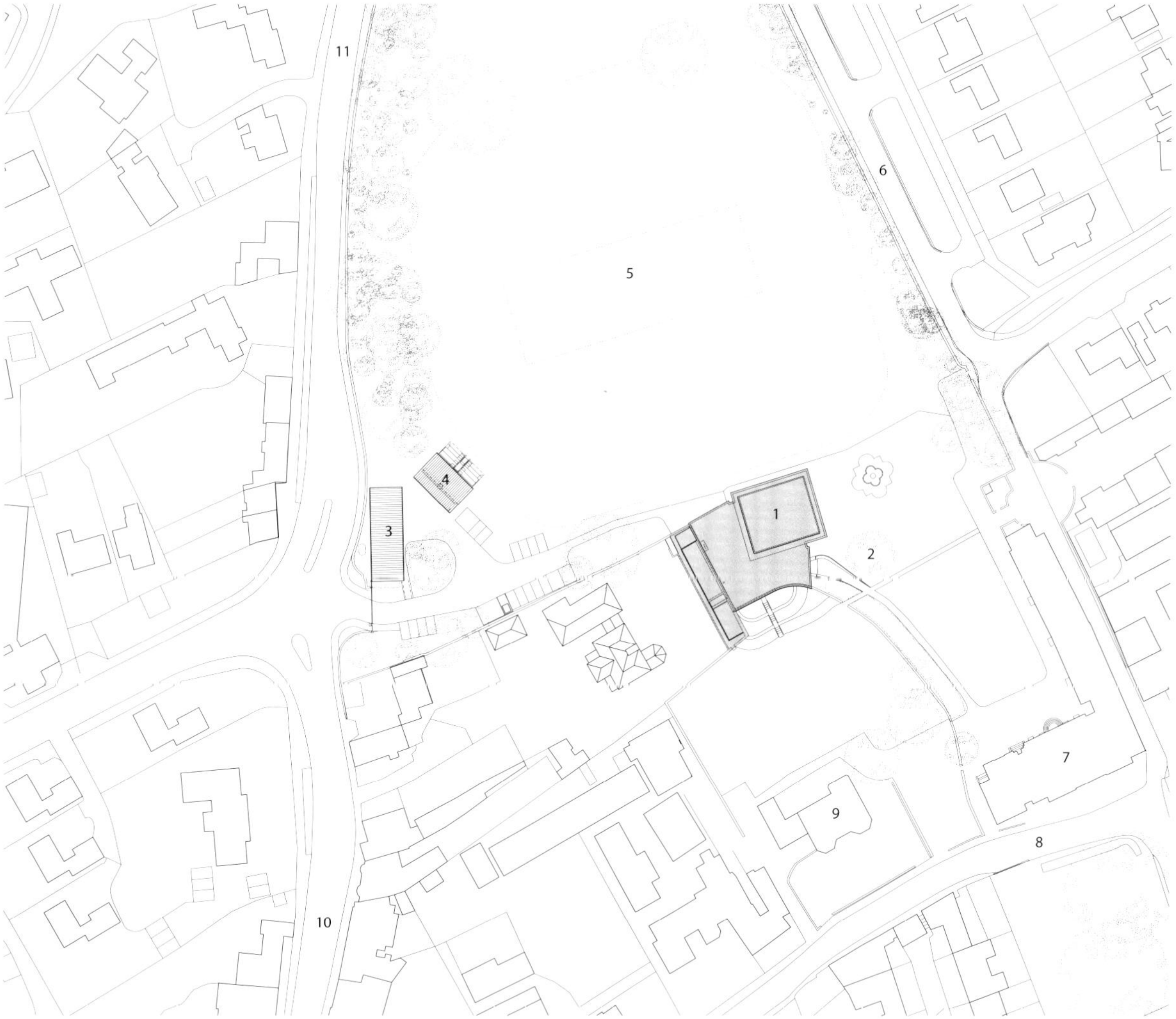

location plan

1 Recital Hall
2 Prince of Wales' Blue Spruce
3 maintenance building
4 Sports Pavilion
5 Cedars Field
6 College Road
7 Cedars House
8 The Liberty
9 Jocelyn House
10 New Street
11 A39

N

0 10 25 50m

1:2000

The Recital Hall within the broader grounds of Wells Cathedral School with the northwest tower of the Cathedral in the background and the old buildings of the School to the left of the frame; at night, the Recital Hall becomes a lantern in the landscape.

ground floor plan

1 Recital Hall
2 foyer
3 box office
4 bar
5 brass rehearsal
6 brass observation
7 backstage
8 front-of-house WCs
9 backstage WCs
10 store
11 dimmer racks
12 covered store
13 electrician's workshop
14 plant room

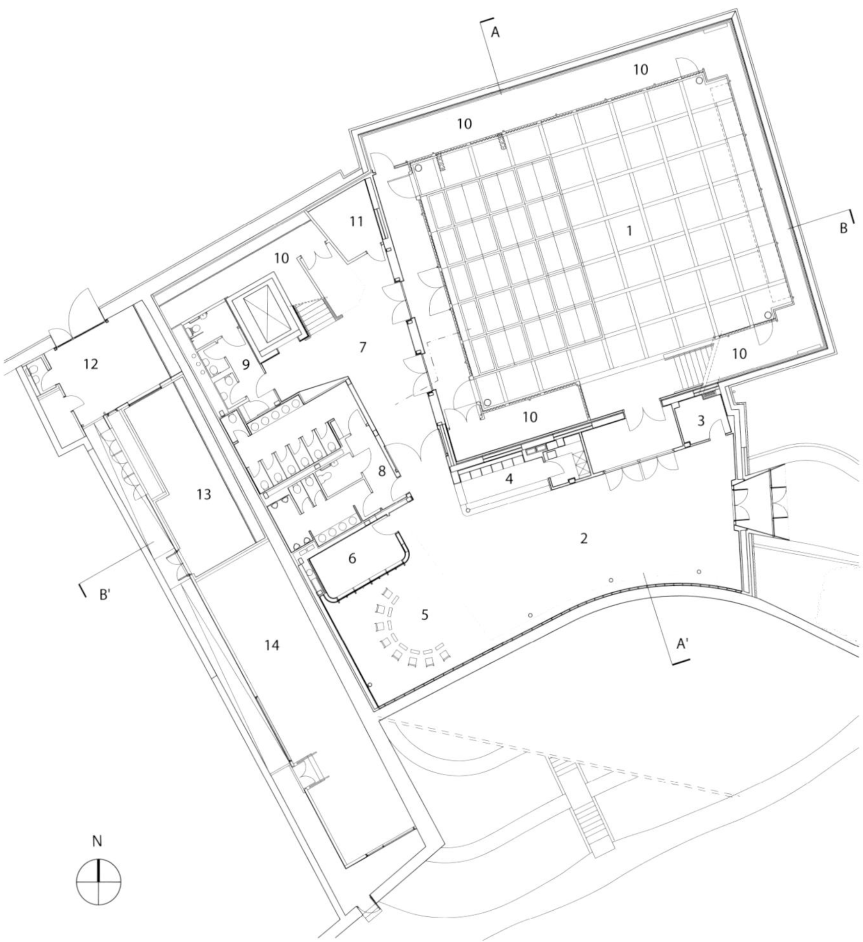

first floor plan

1 Recital Hall
2 upper entrance
3 circulation
4 office / green room
5 WC / shower
6 percussion rehearsal
7 percussion observation
8 woodwind rehearsal
9 woodwind observation
10 control room
11 amp room
12 amphitheatre
13 junior school garden
14 listed wall
15 yew hedge
16 backstage access

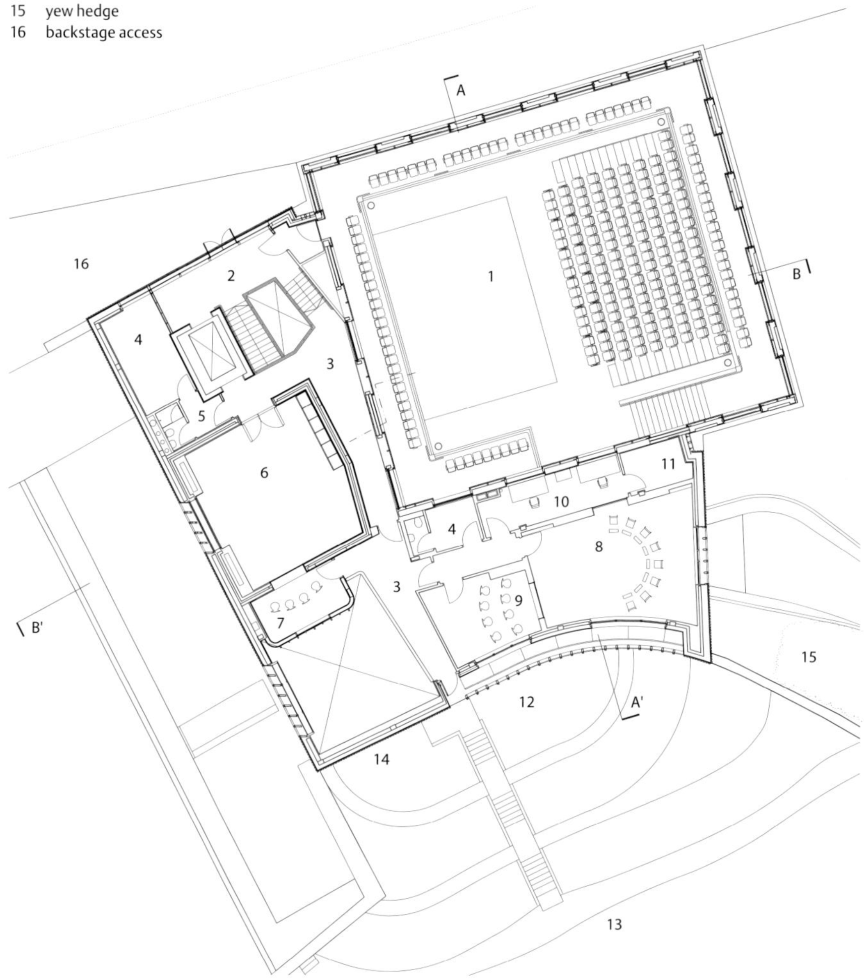

N

0 10m

1:400

View of the interior before a performance.

on the east- and north-facing façades. Inside, the auditorium steps take us from the gallery 2.3m down onto the stage, situated at the same level as the lobby and foyer, which are 3.44m deep in relation to the top of the old stone wall that retains the ground by the south façade. To the south, the grounds are landscaped into steps forming the slope that meets the south entrance, which looks over The Liberty, a road to the south of the school.

The practice suggests that Cedars Hall is encountered in the same way that one might notice a stable block or orangery found in a garden landscape. This might be true in the very broadest conceptual sense, but it doesn't begin to describe the building's remarkable object-quality and presence during daylight.

The elevations are composed of alternating vertical panels of seamless weathering steel and low-iron glazing, 5.5m high and 2m wide. The rich burnt sienna patina of the metal – which will darken further – might naturally suggest the trunks of the umbrous trees to the north of it; a logical, if not unavoidable metaphor, but one that doesn't explain the way such a relatively simple structure also seems poetic.

The first steps in the design process were practical and prosaic, and included visits to other recital halls where the school's various ensembles particularly enjoyed performing; and this established a volumetric and acoustically effective template for Cedars Hall, which delivers 10m^3 of volume per person at full seating capacity in the Eavis Hall, the central performance space, and 5m^3 in the spaces and practice rooms around it.

The Eavis Hall was designed to be adaptable to receive audiences of up to 359, but can be reconfigured in various ways; for example, the set-up for a typical symphony or concerto would allow a 60-strong orchestra and an audience of more than 200. An 8m-deep stage can also be deployed for theatrical performances.

The recital hall is about 10m high, 21m long and 18m wide, and can be acoustically tuned for full orchestras, amplified music, drama and lectures using the so-called folding shark's-fin, lacquered timber acoustic panels in the walls. Another more obvious, and aesthetically interesting, feature is the roof, which is inset from the main elevations and lifted 2.2m above them – a floating frieze-cum-clerestory which adds volume to the performance space and ensures the correct degree of sound reverberation. This attic is held up by four slim pilotis, with the clerestory mullions and window frames bearing onto the ring beam which caps the wall structures.

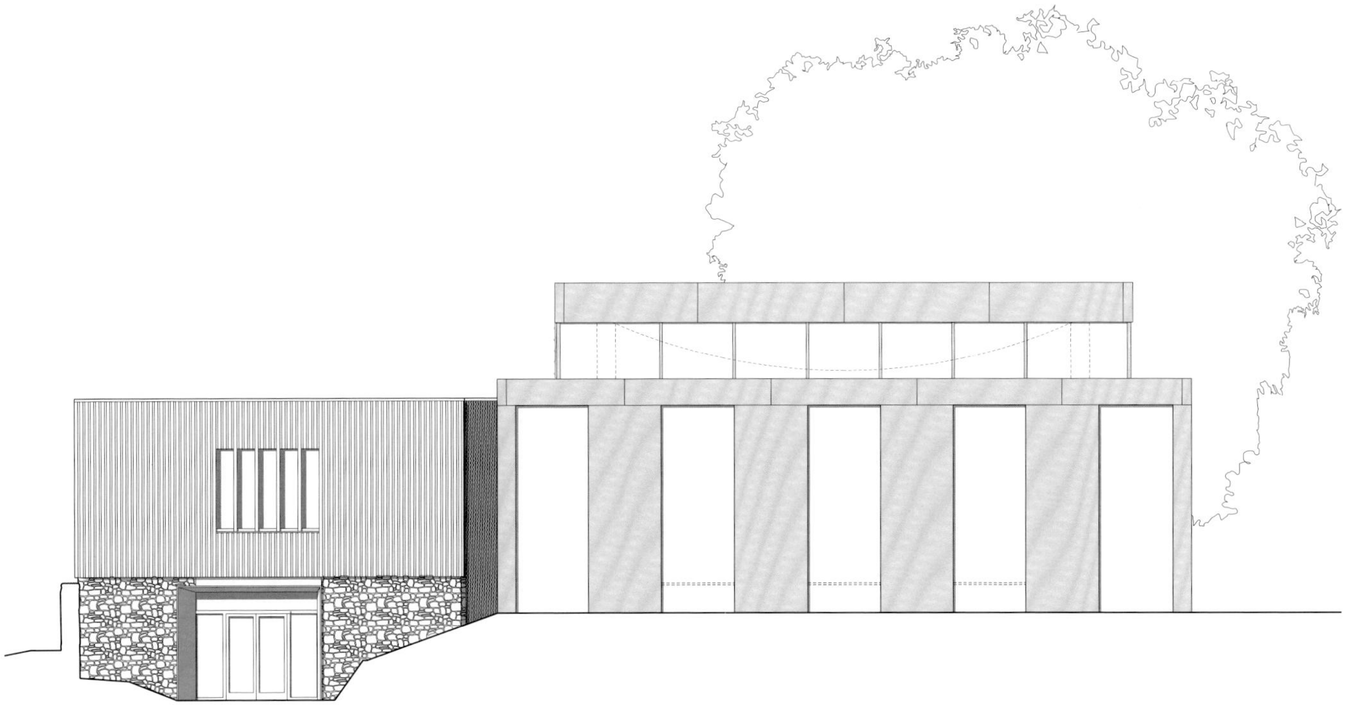

east elevation

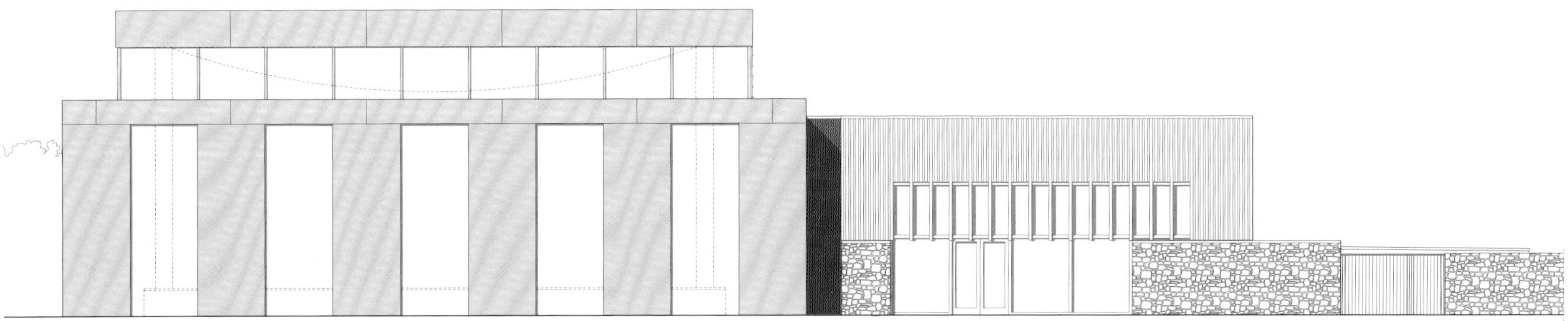

north elevation

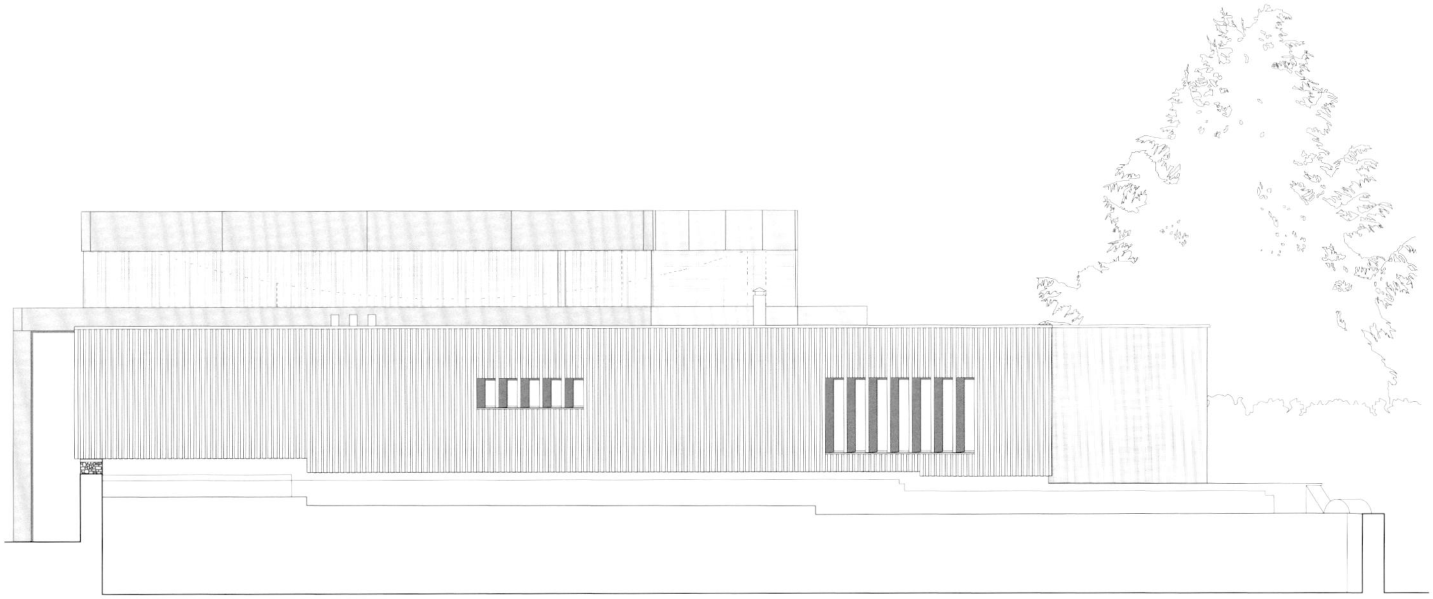

west elevation

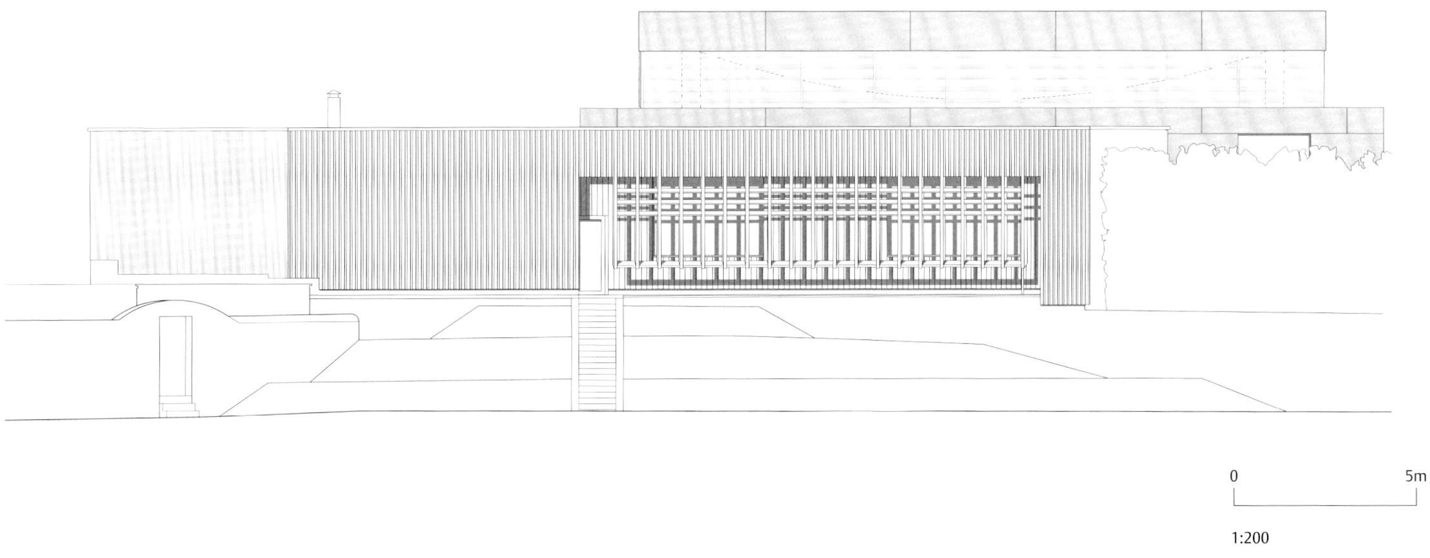

south elevation

left: The south façade incorporates a listed wall, forming the boundary of the building.

right: The spaces for brass rehearsal and observation (left of the frame) with the bar on the right.

The ceiling has a surprising, if not visually delightful, form: it's almost entirely composed of a timber grid which bulges downwards symmetrically like a lolling, soggy waffle, though it's more tempting to imagine the beautifully warped grid as a humbly functional, secular descendant of the fan-vaulting of the late thirteenth- to early fourteenth-century Chapter House of Wells Cathedral.

In plan, the Hall is clasped on its south and west sides by a roughly L-shaped, timber-clad segment whose curved south side follows the line of the Liberty Wall. This part of the building contains the foyer, practice rooms and spaces, and other administration and 'tech' rooms. There are spaces on the ground and first floor suitable for music practice, and their internal acoustics (and acoustic separations) were tested using full-scale mock-ups.

On the ground floor, brass section practices are held in the partially top-lit foyer. The acoustically buffered rooms on the south and west sides of the first floor are used by woodwind players and percussionists; and there is also enough space for impromptu performances.

On this upper level, observation rooms, an office, and the sound and lighting technician's booth overlook either the Eavis Hall or the rehearsal rooms. This arrangement is a very efficient use of space but, more importantly, creates a pervasive sense of loose-fit musical porosity, even in those parts of the building where there is complete acoustic insulation.

The architecture of Cedars Hall has an obvious precedent, from 2005 – the EPA-designed recital hall at Bedford School. It's smaller than Cedars Hall, but its structure and elevations are broadly similar, in that they're dominated by alternating vertical panels of glistening stainless steel and glass. There is no noticeable detailing of the steel elements, and the flat and rather thick cantilevered roof projecting over the west elevation completes the architecture's laconically modern-cum-classicist composure. The foyer and milling space at Cedars Hall has a much warmer atmosphere than the rather briskly functional equivalent space at Bedford.

The design of the Eavis Hall reprises the St Martin's conference room at the practice's celebrated transformation of St Martin-in-the-Fields church, London; that room sits at basement level beneath the pavement on the north side of Gibbs's church, and its upper portion is a fully-glazed, wraparound gallery, which allows visitors to gaze down into the space.

Eavis Hall sits below ground level and, internally, has a gallery whose 3m high fronts are lined with vertically slatted acoustic timber panels. Behind the gallery parapet – which forms a very distinct horizon-line – the

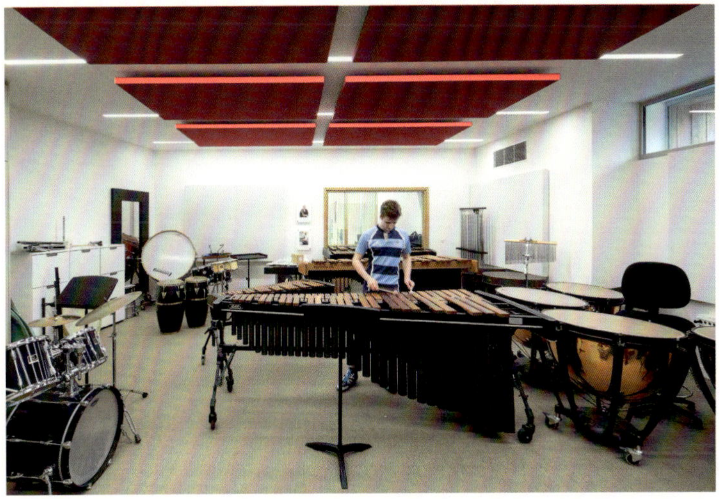

left: Interior of the foyer on the ground floor, with the red doors to Eavis Hall on the right, followed by the bar and a space for brass rehearsal and observation under the surveillance of the bust of Sir Yehudi Menuhin.

right: The percussion rehearsal room with an observation space in the background.

vertical glazing of the building's envelope, and the rustily-hued acoustic panels between them, form something akin to a giant-order gallery.

There is one other subtle but significant connection between Cedars Hall and St Martin's Hall. It was in the latter, in 2012, that Sir Colin Stansfield Smith, a brilliantly innovative and hugely influential local authority architect, took part in the conference programme on education then organised by EPA. He had been chairman of the Cedars Hall competition jury, and proved crucial to EPA's selection to design the building.

Ultimately, it was the positioning of Cedars Hall that convinced Stansfield Smith and the jury. Eric Parry's watercoloured sketch of the proposed site plan shows the decisive contextual idea: Cedars Hall at the northern end of an historically significant axis-line which passes between the fourteenth-century terraces of Vicar's Close and concludes at Wells Cathedral Chapter House.

That contextual logic, and the formal and programmatic logic of the architecture, has produced an admirable building. But that adjective cannot capture how remarkably *other* Cedars Hall seems when viewed from the east. At night, during performances, the elevation glows with rectangles of light; so do the reddish-brown acoustic wall panels inside Eavis Hall; the heads of those sitting at balcony level can be seen; the building is convivial. In this condition it's rather like a musical hearth set down firmly in the landscape.

In daylight, this hearth can seem to be something other than a modern pavilion in the classical manner. It might equally suggest a rusting iron henge; or John Summerson's remark about aedicule-shrines – "a sort of architectural canopy in the form of a rudimentary temple". In this way, Cedars Hall's qualities of presence seem simultaneously unearthly, yet also enduring and sheltering – not quite Tolstoy's huddle of chairs and blankets, but a shrine to something more than music, poised on that competition-winning ley-line sketched by Parry.

There is something about this architecture that is beyond type or manner or materiality or function. And there is, finally, something poetic about it, in relation to its setting in Cedars Field. One can almost imagine it appearing in an illustration by Alan Carr Linford or Sir Herbert Alker Tripp, popularised in inter-war British railway posters – such as "Wells in Smiling Somerset".

Almost, but not quite. "To verify images kills them, and it is always more enriching to *imagine* than to *experience*," wrote Gaston Bachelard in *The Poetics of Space*. Cedars Hall – whose architecture, given its setting, is unexpected and slightly surreal – is an interesting test of that remark.

section AA'

1 foyer
2 lobby
3 Recital Hall
4 store
5 control room
6 woodwind rehearsal room

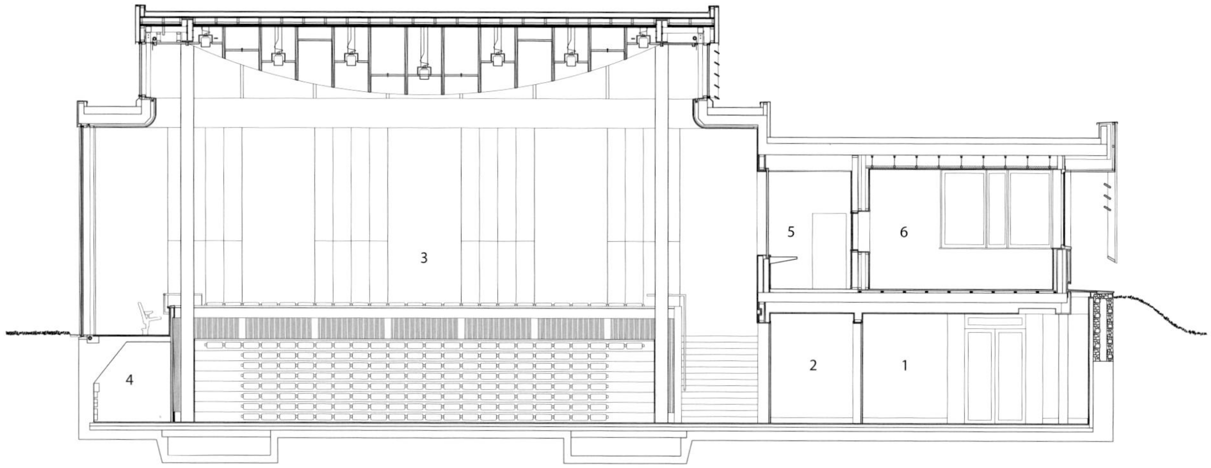

0 5m

1:200

section BB'

1 foyer
2 gallery level
3 back-of-house area
4 female WCs
5 first-floor circulation
6 percussion section rehearsal room

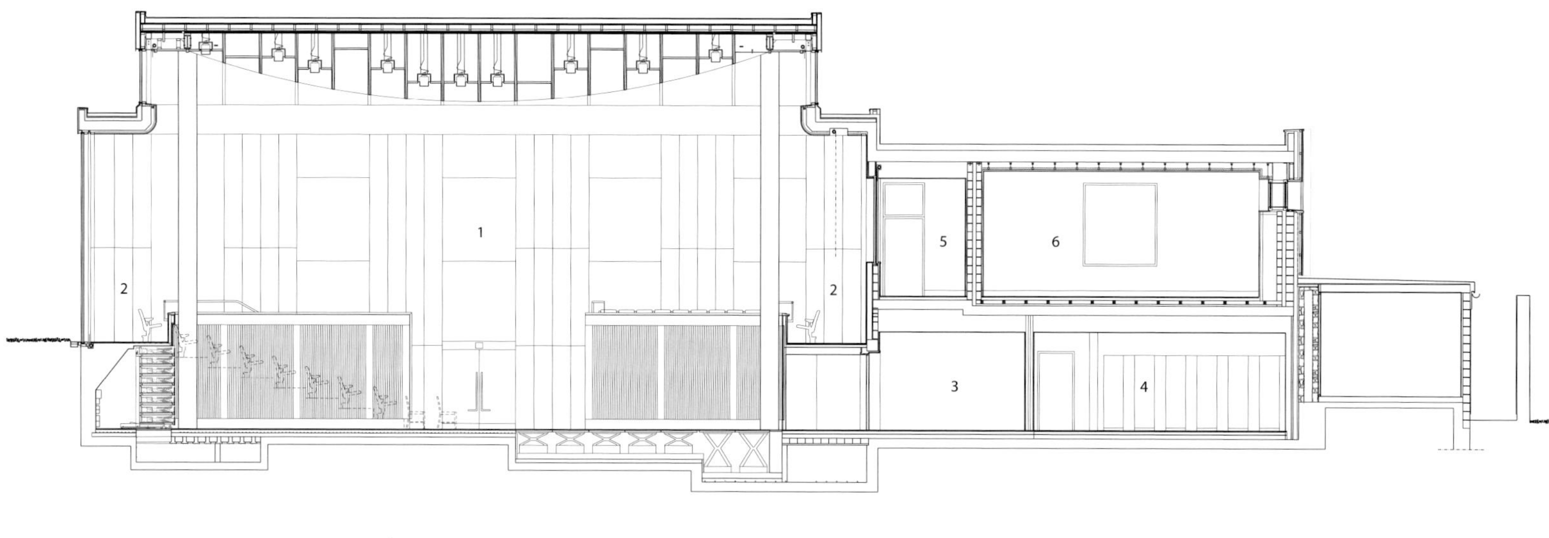

1 single-ply roofing membrane
2 140mm foil-faced rigid insulation
3 acoustic isolator pads
4 6mm weathering steel sheet coping
5 6mm weathering steel sheet cladding
6 recessed integral roller blind
7 EPDM membrane around windows
8 low-iron insulated double glazing to provide 50dB acoustic separation: 14.8mm acoustic laminated outer with selective solar control coating, 24mm cavity, 10.8mm acoustic laminated inner
9 75mm-thick beech laminated veneer lumber beams and soffit panels with cut-outs for lights and speakers
10 mild steel structural supporting frame
11 12mm cement particle board
12 3mm polyester powder-coated aluminium flashing
13 fibrous plaster
14 reinforced concrete slab
15 mineral wool acoustic insulation
16 lacquered timber reveal
17 guide rail to blackout blinds
18 45mm-thick lacquered timber acoustic panel as part of automated variable acoustic panelling
19 glazing frame flush with finished floor level
20 bark margin
21 300mm concrete retaining wall
22 external insulation
23 services zone
24 waterproofing
25 100mm rigid insulation
26 damp-proof membrane
27 beam and block floor with 50mm concrete topping
28 supply air plenum
29 80mm screed with underfloor heating pipes
30 engineered oak flooring in 2000x2000mm grid pattern
31 Schroeder quadratic-residue diffuser oak panelling

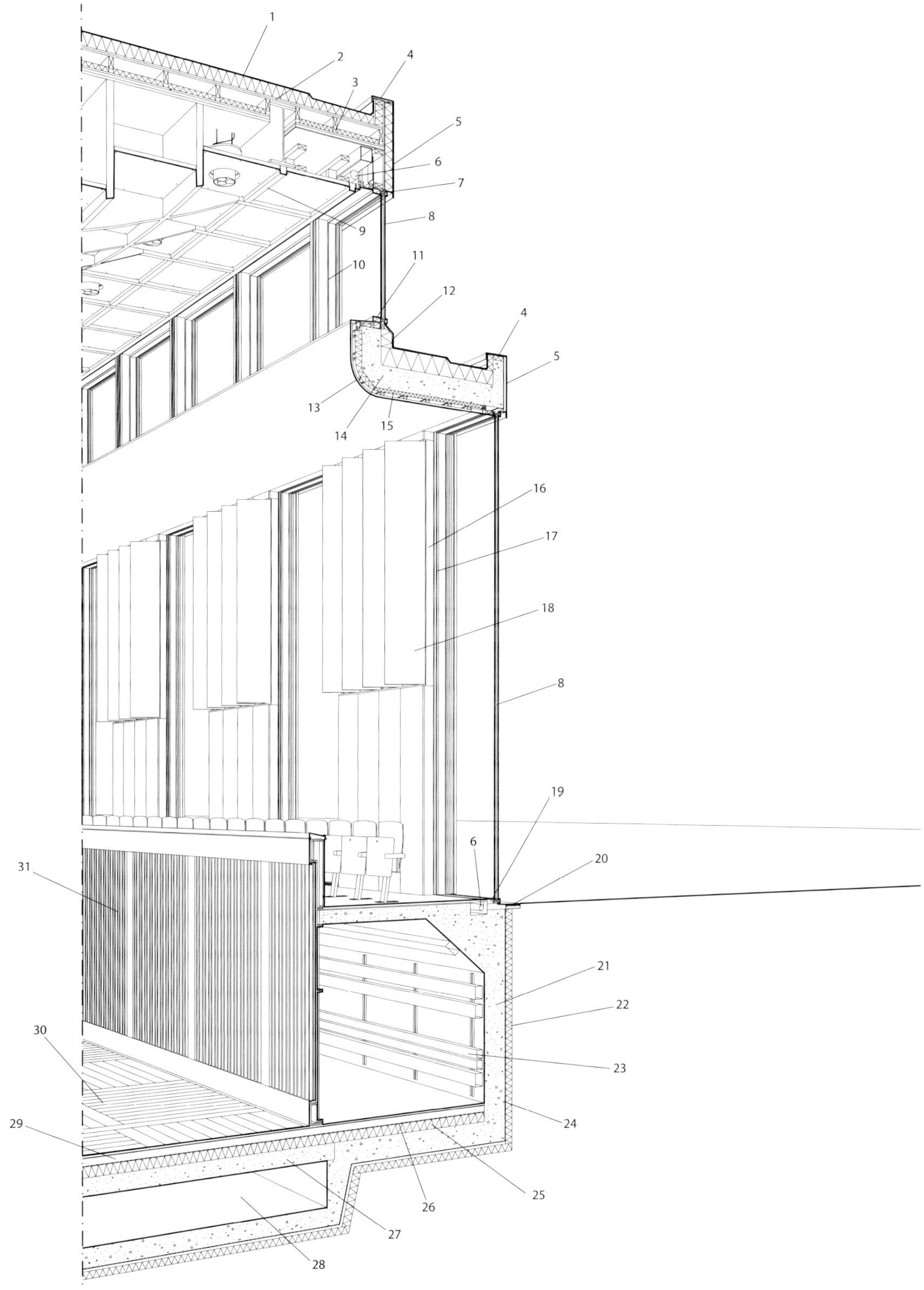

left: View of the Eavis Hall ceiling built of laminated lumber beams and soffit panels with cut-outs for lights and speakers.

opposite: Interior of the Eavis Hall during rehearsal against the background landscape.

Brighton College Music School

The coloured patterning of the Ceràmica Cumella roof tiles is intriguing. They're an obvious nod to Scott's and Jackson's decorative Victorian tiling, and Parry describes the pattern as fabric-like. But it's not so much fabric that comes to mind: the fragmented pattern is artfully contrived, almost Escheresque.

Drawing of Sir George Gilbert Scott's winning proposal for Brighton College, dating from the 1848 architectural competition.

The Music School at Brighton College is one of several recently completed architectural projects at a public school that has become extremely ambitious. The Music School is the first product of EPA's masterplan for the most spatially challenged portion of the College and includes an indicative design proposal for a Drama School, with a glazed foyer linking the two buildings. The Music School begins the process of unlocking the heart of the site and has done so with a mixture of formal adventure, effectively arranged functional spaces, and a crucial axial clarification.

The Music School, along with the other new buildings, signals the fact that in the last decade the College has risen into the educationally elite stratum of Britain's public schools, maintaining a position in the top ten in A level grades, with accelerating Oxbridge entrances. The College's success is the result of demanding student admission standards and a business and redevelopment strategy that has committed more than £100 million to new construction projects, directed by Steve Patten. The strategy was developed by the headmaster, Richard Cairns, following a lead set by the previous head, Sir Anthony Seldon.

Remarkably, this strategy gained full momentum after the 2008 economic crash, and has done so in a city that has experienced a significant and relatively recent demographic evolution. Mr Patten characterises Brighton as a kind of Islington-on-Sea, and it's certainly true that over the last 20 years, Brighton's past reputation as a rather *laissez-faire* place has evolved; its vibe is increasingly determined by a burgeoning population of aspirational residents for whom, among other things, outstanding (rather than merely reasonable) success at school and university is a secular grail.

The original tableau of Brighton College was designed by Sir George Gilbert Scott, who had previously only produced workhouses and churches. The conjoined chapel, school range and headmaster's house were designed in the Pugin-influenced Gothic manner between 1848 and 1859 and are listed as Grade II. A later dining hall, kitchen and octagonal latrine structure completed the original Victorian composition. The College's southern dormitory range, designed by Thomas Graham Jackson, faces Eastern Road and was completed in 1887; the central Cairns Tower, by Jackson, was completed by Richard Griffiths Architects in 2006. In plan, these early buildings and the Edwardian Burstow Gallery and Hall at the western end of the south range loosely resemble a courtyard or cloister.

By the latter part of the twentieth century, the area north of Scott's range had become rather clogged by buildings which proved increasingly challenging, in terms of circulation, for student numbers that have

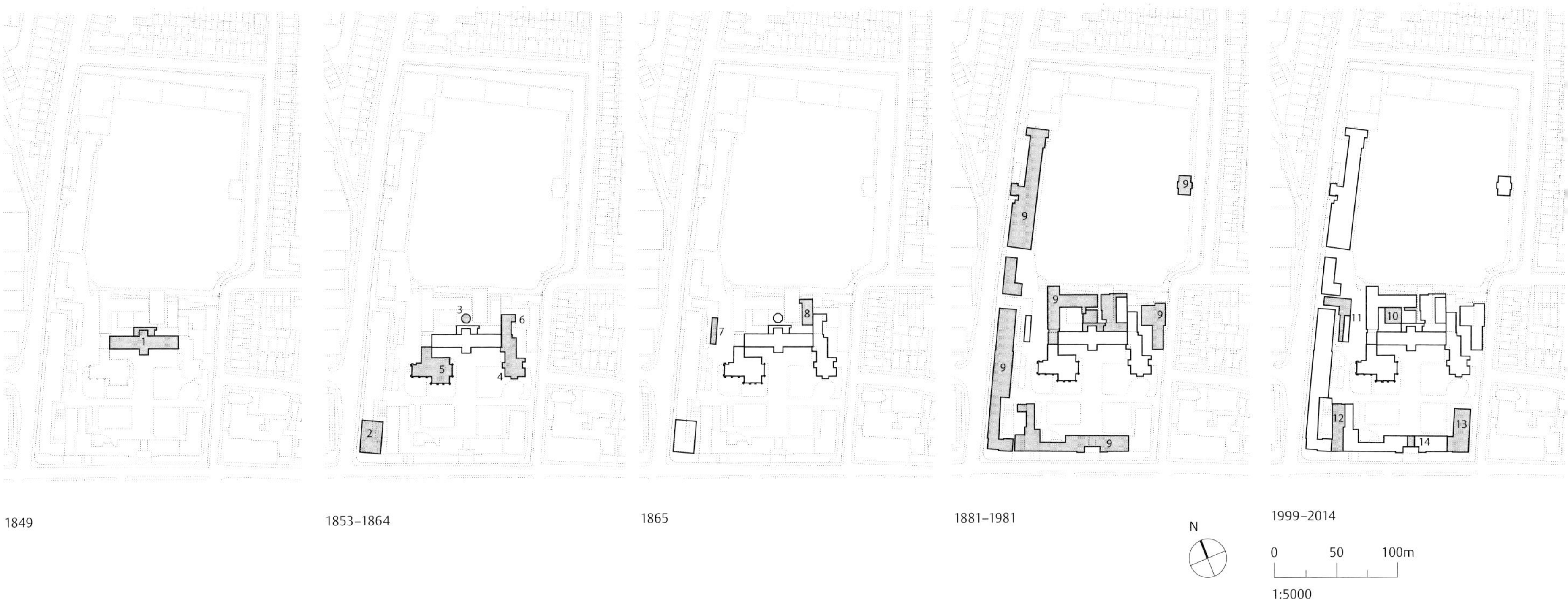

1 Brighton College (1849) by George Gilbert Scott
2 brewery buildings
3 latrine
4 principal's house (1853)
5 chapel (1859)
6 extension to principal's house (1864)
7 laboratory (1860s)
8 dining hall (1865)
9 developments along Sutherland Road and Eastern Road
10 Arts Centre (2000) by Tim Ronalds Architects
11 Skidelsky Building (2010) by Kirkland Fraser Moor
12 Simon Smith Building (2011) by Allies and Morrison
13 The Boarding House (2013) by Allies and Morrison
14 extension of Cairns Tower (2014) by Richard Griffiths Architects

since risen to more than 1000. One earlier attempt to clarify movement through this part of the site was the College's Arts Centre, an unfussy glass cube designed in the late 1990s by Tim Ronalds, which sits between the back of Scott's range and the stolid, concrete-framed 1958 science block.

Since 2010, development at the College has generated a building by Kirkland Fraser Moor, two buildings by Allies and Morrison, one by Hopkins Architects, and now EPA's Music School. A massive new sports and science building, designed by OMA in 2013, is currently on site on the west edge of the Home Ground sports field. The Victorian and modern buildings standing between the Home Ground and Eastern Road cover an area of less than 2ha.

The contextual responses of those built after 2000 are quite different, and highly individual. For example, the main elevation of OMA's asymmetrically layered offering is said to have been inspired by the terraced housing that faces it across the Home Ground. But if we take the Pevsner guide's comment on Scott's buildings as a guide, these architectural sports of nature continue a tradition of sorts. The Pevsner guide suggests that the College's Victorian buildings had "the kind of accidental-looking arrangement recommended in Scott's *Remarks on Secular and Domestic Architecture*".

Of the post-2012 buildings, the new Music School is unquestionably the most significant in placemaking terms. EPA's masterplan for the Music School and the forthcoming Drama School next to it will ultimately create a performing arts hub, and improve circulation and north–south views through this part of the College. The removal of the science block will make room for the forthcoming Drama School, which will be linked to both the Music School and the Arts Centre by a fully glazed foyer whose roof acts as a first-floor bridge between the two buildings.

There will also be a direct axial connection between the College's main entrance in Eastern Road, through the central Victorian courtyard and Scott's main range, and out to the Home Ground. Quite significantly, these changes will create a kind of courtyard, open to the north, where the Music and Drama Schools come together.

The rectangular site for the Music School originally contained a squash court, lavatory block, plant room and plate-wash facility. The eastern side of this ungainly stew of structures abutted the Grade II listed, collar-beamed Victorian dining hall. The 1982 Blackshaw dining room, a rather depressing volume which had been modernised in 2001, sat tightly between the dining hall and the obscured north side of Scott's range.

N

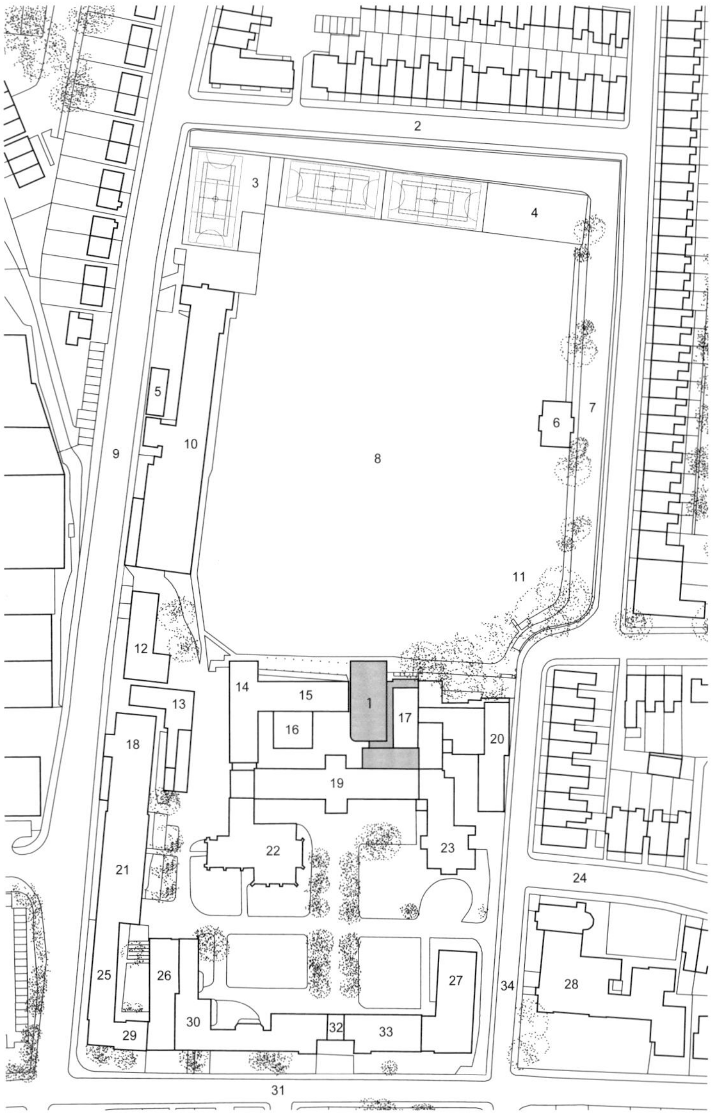

location plan for Phase 1

1 Brighton College Music School (2016) by Eric Parry Architects
2 College terrace
3 tennis courts
4 cricket nets
5 Chowen Building
6 pavilion
7 Walpole Terrace
8 Home Ground
9 Sutherland Road
10 sports hall
11 sports box
12 Aldrich House
13 Skidelsky Building
14 Lester Building
15 Science Department
16 PAC Building
17 dining hall and kitchen
18 swimming pool
19 Main School Building
20 Leach Building
21 Great Hall / Burstow Gallery
22 chapel
23 Fenwick House
24 Belle Vue Gardens
25 Woolton Building
26 Simon Smith Building
27 The Boarding House
28 Brighton College Preparatory School
29 lecture theatre – visual arts
30 Abraham House
31 Eastern Road
32 Cairns Tower
33 Dawson Building
34 Walpole Road

0 50 100m

1:2500

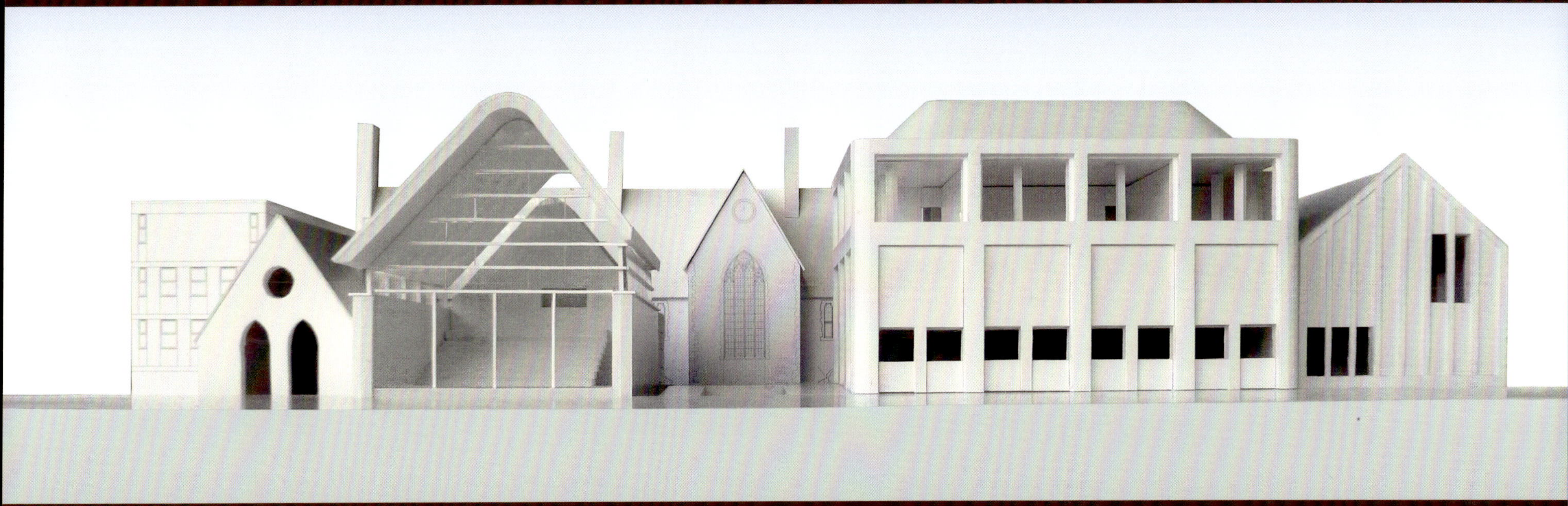

Working model of both Phase 1 (completed) and Phase 2 (forthcoming) as viewed from the Home Ground.

This arrangement has been clarified in a handful of moves that are simple in plan, axis and section. In the case of the new Recital Hall, the design has produced a boldly novel response to Scott's central gable, and his inclination to asymmetry. The ceiling and wall linings of the Blackshaw Room, now known as the Liu Room, were removed and replaced with a table-like structure which reveals the once-hidden flint walls of the Scott range. The original Porter's Lodge, connected to Scott's range next to the original Blackshaw Room, was demolished, and when the old Tuck Shop is eventually removed east–west movement across this part of the College site will be improved.

It was extremely important to open up the north–south axis through Scott's gable, and to achieve this the practice designed a glazed entrance in the Gothic manner on its north side. It sits beneath the first turn of the internal staircase, on a lowered floor, and between the plinths of octagonal columns which were extended to create space for two steps down to the new entrance level.

The four-level Music School sits on the eastern edge of the College's north–south axis, and its north end hunkers into the 3m rise in level where it meets the Home Ground. In its long section, it is effectively divided into two segments, with the triple-height Recital Hall sitting above a layer of practice rooms, offices and a kitchenette for visiting teachers; and, beneath them, there are lavatories, storerooms, and plant and services in the basement.

The back third of the building steps down one storey from the Recital Hall's roof ridge and is headed with a double-height percussion and rock music room with an interior in the shape of a truncated wedge. This isn't a big room, but something about its form, its large and elevated square window, its scale, and the orderly acoustic slatting give it an unusually satisfying atmosphere.

Effective acoustic separations were of critical importance and the practice worked with Gillieron Scott Acoustic Design to achieve targeted outcomes, such 90dB isolation between the Recital Hall and practice rooms, and 100dB between the Recital Hall and the percussion and rock music room.

Circulation was another challenging issue, and the design produced one particularly effective outcome: a top-lit, L-plan passage passes along the south edge of the Music School and then takes students along its east side and into the dining hall, and to stairs leading to the Home Ground (which Eric Parry refers to, playfully, as "the vomitorium"). In a nice touch, the windows of the ground-floor

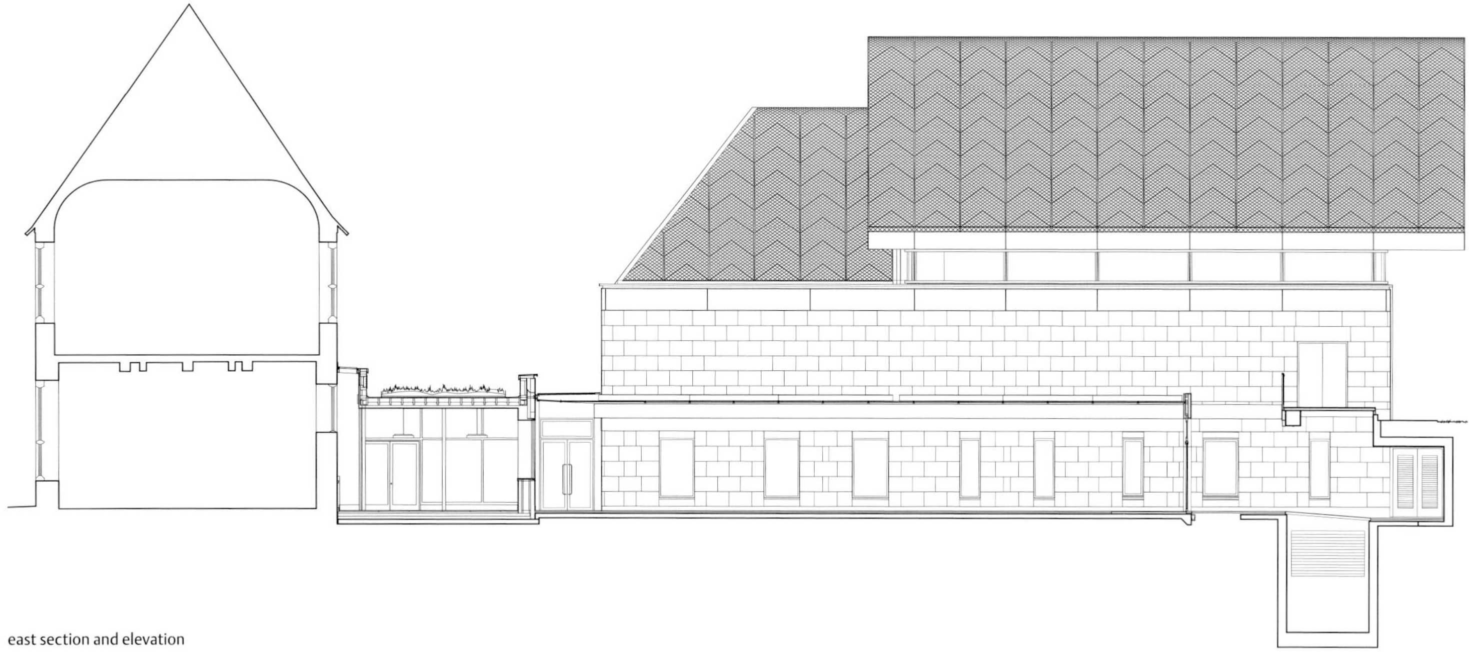

east section and elevation

0 5m

1:250

west section and elevation

longitudinal section

1 Recital Hall
2 percussion room
3 equipment room
4 store
5 Home Ground
6 GGS building
7 Liu dining hall
8 dining hall corridor
9 office
10 kitchenette
11 practice rooms
12 plant
13 female WC
14 lobby
15 WCs

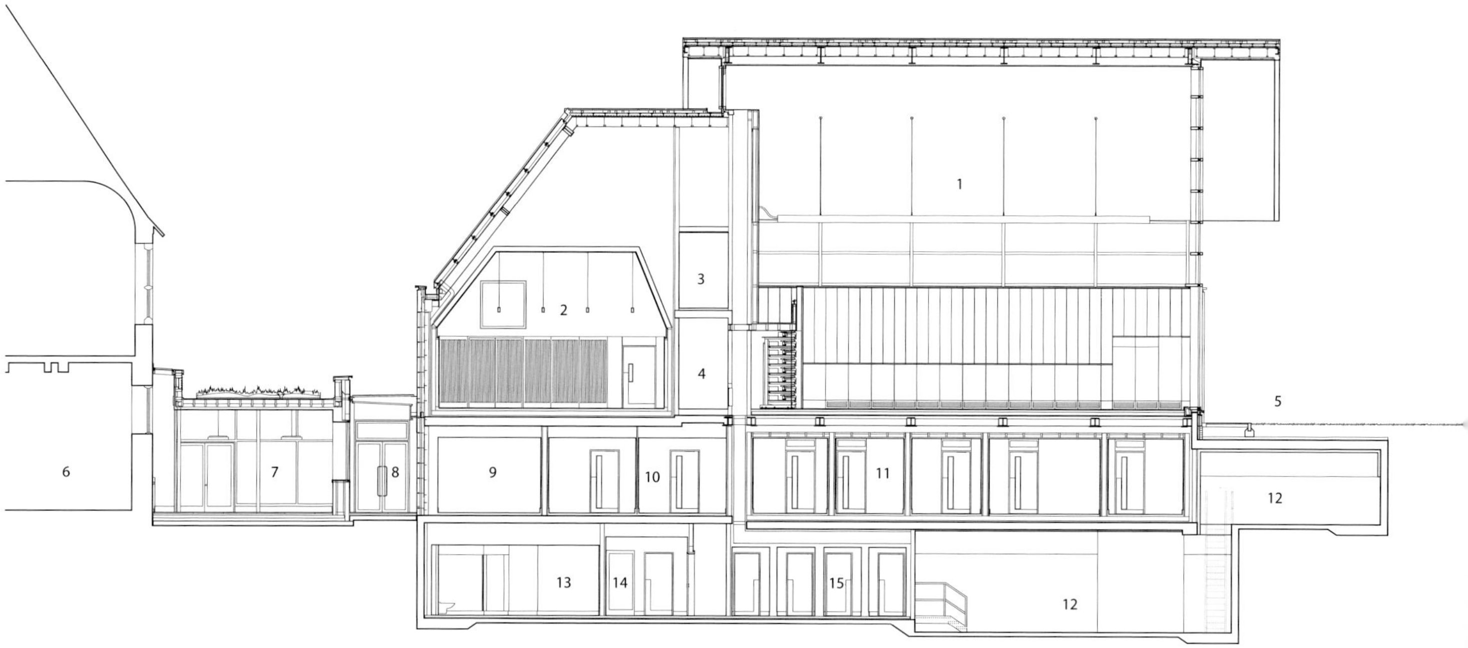

cross-section

1 pre-existing Recital Hall
2 Recital Hall
3 practice room
4 corridor
5 plant
6 pre-existing Science Building

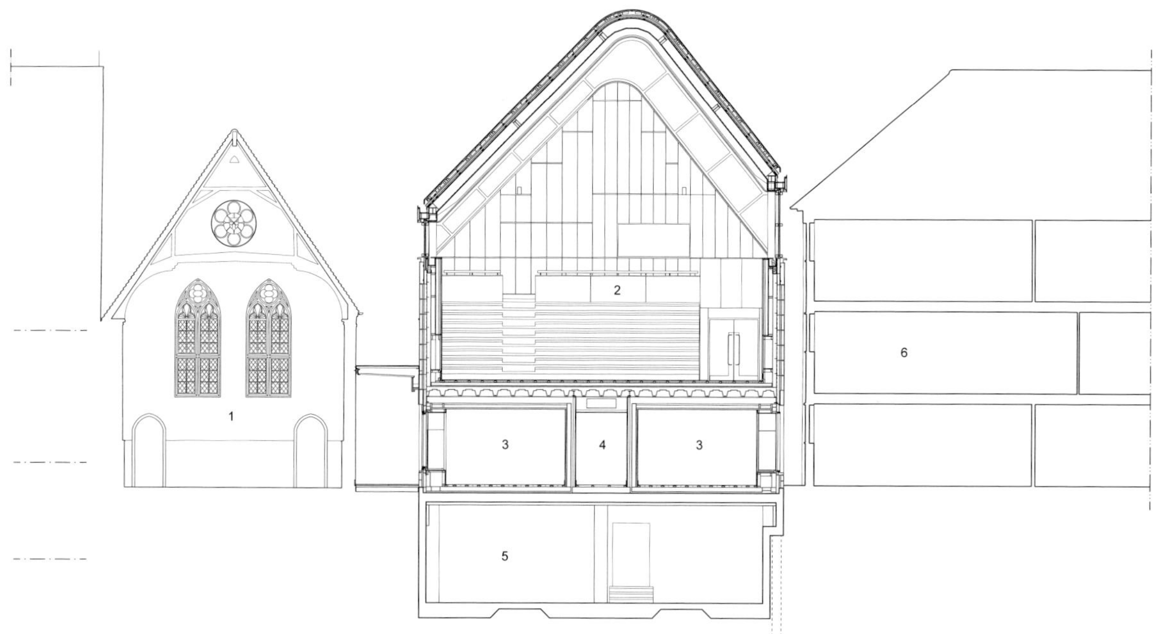

0 5m

1:250

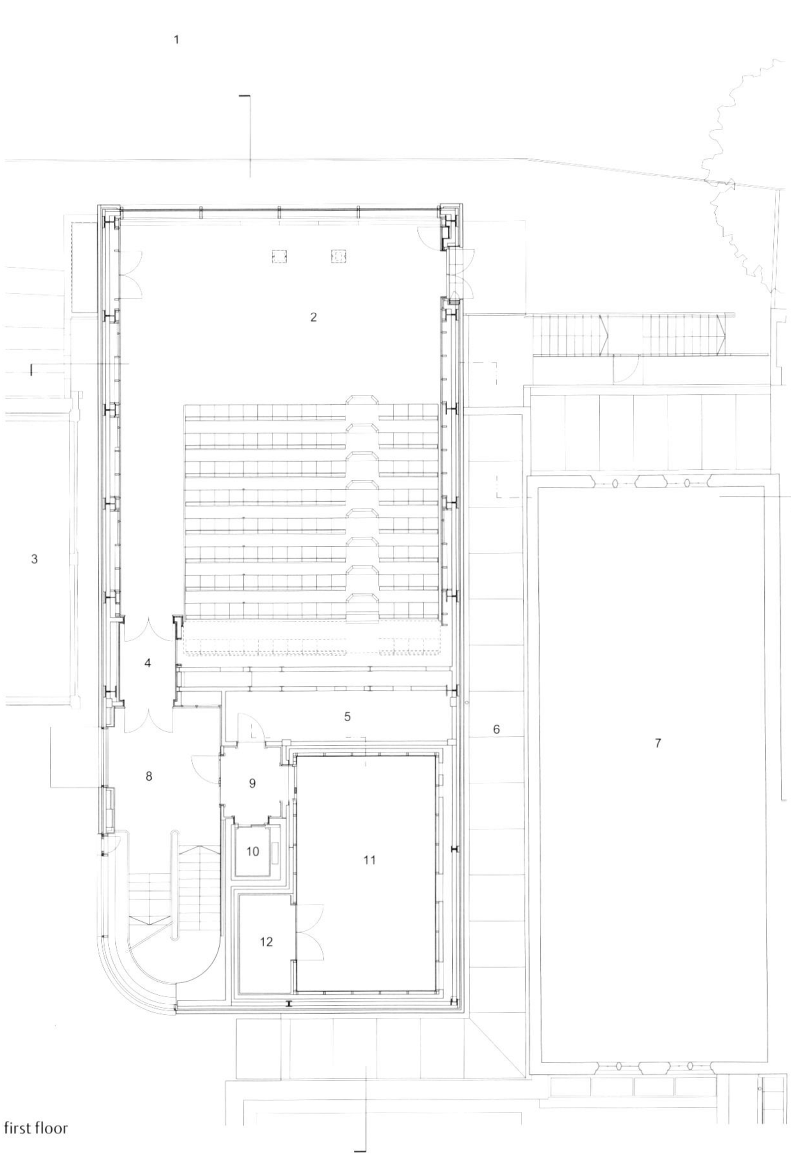

first floor

1 Home Ground
2 recital hall
3 existing Science Building
4 hall lobby
5 chair store
6 roof lights
7 existing dining hall
8 first stair
9 percussion lobby
10 lift
11 percussion room
12 percussion store

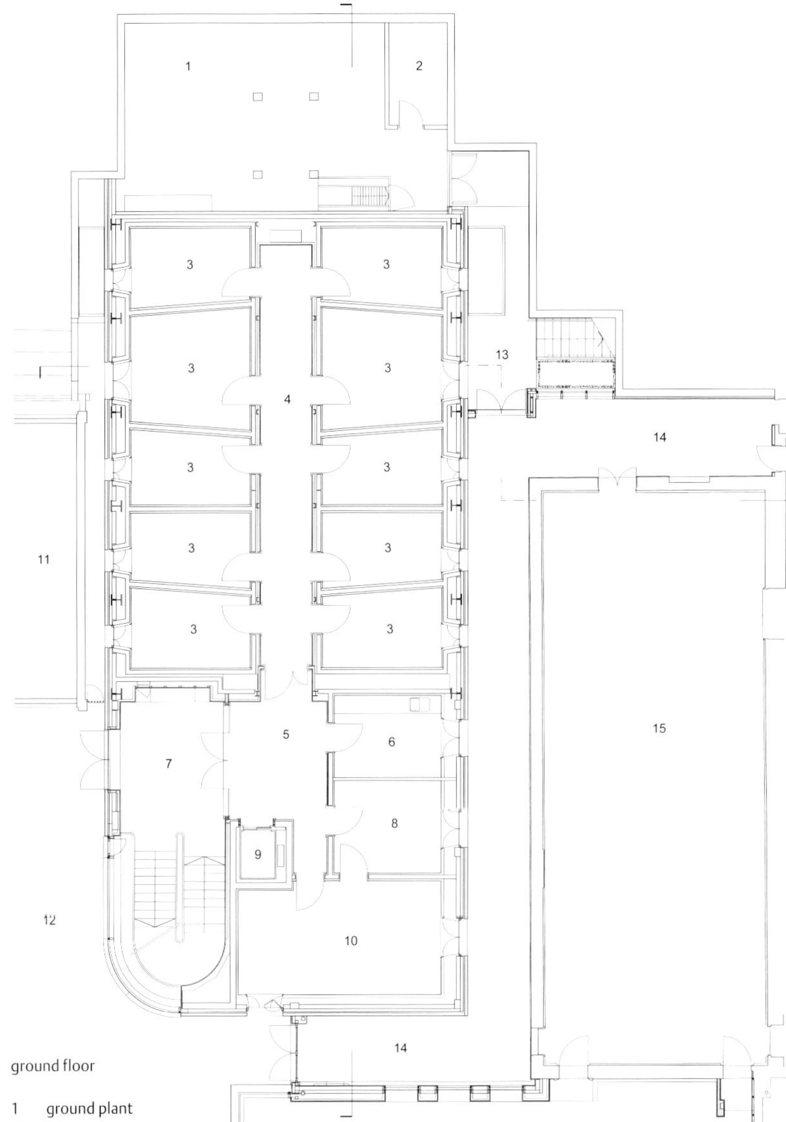

ground floor

1 ground plant
2 LV plant
3 practice rooms
4 corridor
5 lobby
6 tea kitchen
7 stair
8 admin office
9 lift
10 director's office
11 existing Science Building
12 new courtyard
13 corridor to Dining Hall
14 dining hall escape stair
15 existing Dining Hall

N

0 5m

1:250

above: Glazed terracotta tile setts mounted on glass-reinforced concrete are here laid on the proprietary aluminium standing seam roof under the surveillance of EPA architect and associate Damien Lee.

right: View of the construction site with the newly erected steel-frame structure of the Recital Hall.

perspectival section

1 aluminium carrier rails clamped to standing-seam roof
2 proprietary aluminium standing-seam roofing system
3 glazed terracotta tiles on glass-reinforced concrete (GRC)
4 mineral wool insulation
5 painted mild-steel portal frame (intumescent coating below level 1)
6 fibre-cement sheathing boards to underside of timber rafters
7 Recital Hall ceiling: two layers of high-density plasterboard combined with curved fibrous plaster elements; plastered and painted finish
8 bespoke steel stage lighting bar, suspended from portal frame
9 recessed blind box
10 spray lacquered timber wall panelling to recital hall, incorporating automated variable acoustic system
11 engineered oak floorboards over underfloor heating, laid onto a resilient acoustic separating layer
12 fresh air supply from AHU in plant room to the Recital Hall via plenum to the foot of the wall panelling
13 glazed roof to new dining hall corridor, with integral gutter
14 reinforced concrete hollow rib floor
15 practice rooms: constructed off acoustically isolated concrete rafts, with dense concrete block walls and heavily acoustically insulated ceilings
16 in-situ reinforced concrete basement contains plant room
17 ventilation shaft to plant room
18 aluminium framed windows to practice room, PPC finish; acoustic laminated insulated double glazing
19 cavity wall: Caen stone ashlar outer face, foil-faced phenolic foam insulation, high-density concrete block inner skin
20 precast concrete string course
21 bespoke aluminium window cill with PPC finish
22 spray-painted proprietary steel curtain-walling with bespoke stainless-steel cover caps; low-iron insulated glazing to provide 50dB acoustic separation: 14.8mm acoustic laminated outer with selective solar control coating, 24mm cavity, 10.8mm acoustic laminated inner
23 5mm aluminium plate fascia with a PPC finish
24 concealed gutters lined with single-ply roofing membrane

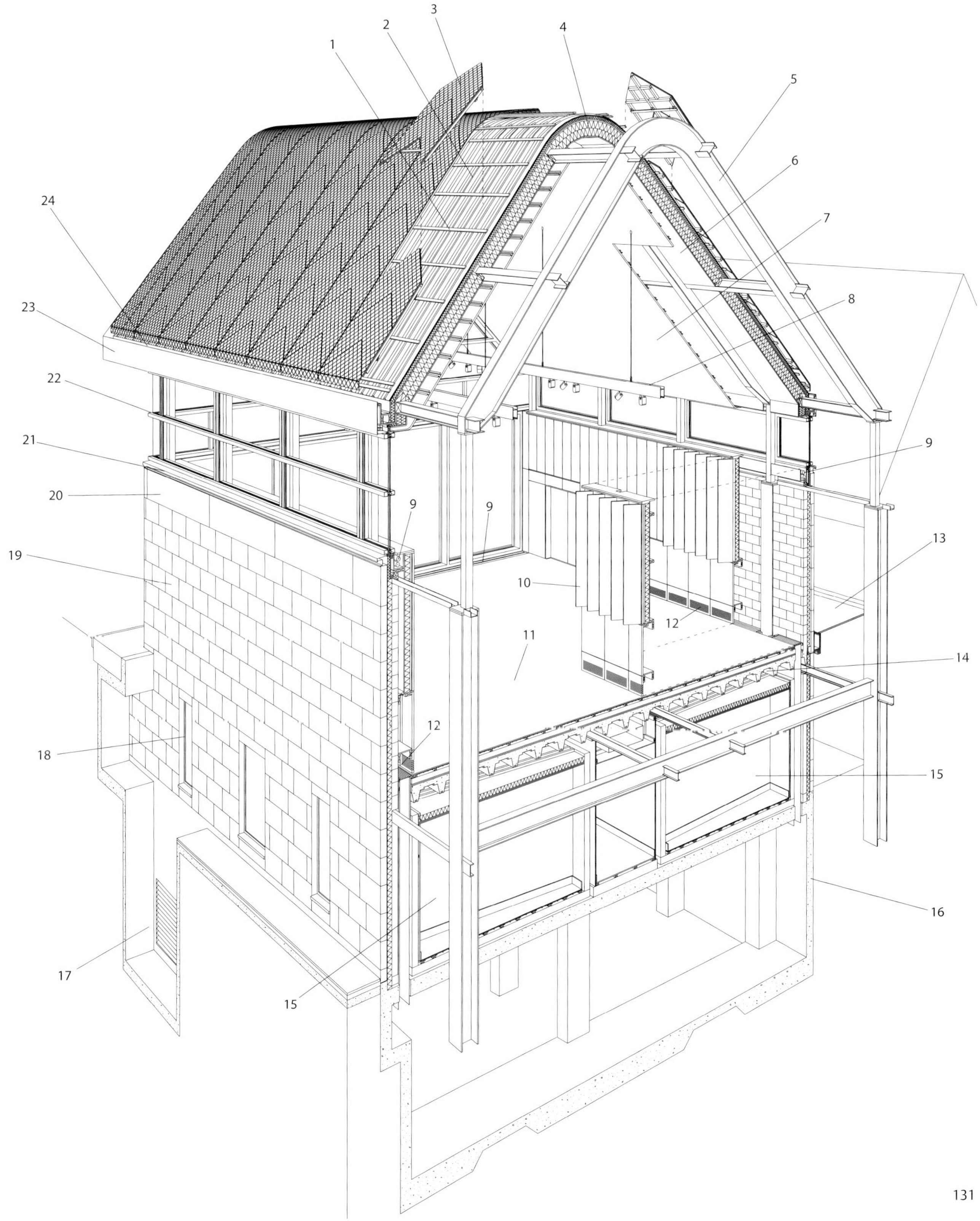

left: Recital Hall looking north to the playing fields.

right: Recital Hall looking south. The bleacher seating retracts to create a flat floor.

Interior of the percussion room on the first floor.

practice rooms on the east side face the lunch corridor, and musicians can either practise in the view of passing students or close the two-thirds height internal shutters.

Two aspects of the Music School's architecture are particularly striking. The staircase – white on the inside face of its continuous metal panelling, red on the outside – rises with a sinuous elegance through the radiused southwest corner of the building; above the staircase, the ceiling is curved in plan and section and, together, the stair core and its envelope are a fine essay in skilfully configured space and detailing. The wraparound glazing on the south and west corners gives the stairs an airy, well-lit ambience.

The Sarah Abraham Recital Hall, designed with input from Charcoalblue, is a boldly novel architectural response to Scott's central gable and the gable of the Dining Hall. The design of the 190-seat auditorium is finely resolved and so pure in both internal and external line and surface that, when viewed from the Home Ground, it has the quality of an insouciant yet precise sketch, if not a literally uplifting one.

The roof has a curved ridge and falls fairly steeply and asymmetrically, dropping towards the low roof edge of the Dining Hall on one side, but falling shorter on the other to ensure a clear, uncluttered view of Scott's gable and to let as much west light in as possible; south light also enters through a band of glazing that follows the roof profile at the back of the auditorium; the useful effect of the sun-path had always been a key concern during detailed design.

The coloured patterning of the Ceràmica Cumella roof tiles is intriguing. They're an obvious nod to Scott's and Jackson's decorative Victorian tiling, and Parry describes the pattern as fabric-like. But it's not so much fabric that comes to mind: the fragmented pattern is artfully contrived, almost Escheresque.

The roof cantilevers more than 2.7m out over the entirely glazed north elevation, and the clerestory glazing above the 800mm thick, stone-faced walls along the sides of the Recital Hall gives the roof a floating quality despite an acoustically isolating 910mm section with a soffit that steps up on the exterior to conceal this thickness at the gables.

The interior of the Recital Hall has a relaxed atmosphere. The ceiling, painted off-white, has a perfectly smooth, jointless soffit, producing a palpable, almost luscious sense of comfortable expectation which is amplified by the view of the Home Ground. The view is particularly uncluttered due to the minimal number of slim glazing mullions and transoms, and the carefully arranged sets of adjustable acoustic panels.

The metal stair connecting all the floors of the Recital Hall down to the multiple rehearsal rooms. In the background of the image, the walls of the pre-existing school buildings by Sir George Gilbert Scott.

Particular care was taken to ensure that the ventilation system of this big volume, designed in collaboration with Skelly + Couch, functioned as silently as possible. The concealed air-extract conduit behind the seating in the Recital Hall has a relatively large cross-sectional area of 2.8m^2 and the minimum number of turns as it runs down two levels to the plant room; which means that the air – drawn into the Recital Hall from a concealed plenum below the acoustic wall panelling – is moved at low velocity and imparts minimal vibration or mechanical sound.

The Music School has demonstrated the three Vitruvian ideals and added a fourth quality, visibility. Cricket matches and musical performances, sixes and sextets, batons and balls, have become simultaneous two-way visual spectacles, with the Pooterish houses of College Terrace rising 350m to the north on the ridge that remained after tens of thousands of tonne s of soil were shovelled away in the nineteenth century to create the level that became the Home Ground. The architecture of the Music School has brought together epicurean and quotidian pursuits in an admirably convivial, place-sensitive way.

The Leathersellers' Hall

Two things will immediately strike any visitor to the Hall. The remarkable quality and detail of the materials and finishes, and the practice's design of the fixtures and fittings.

The South-facing ceramic-clad façade which looks over St Helen's Church.

More than two hundred years ago, the German philosopher Friedrich Wilhelm Joseph von Schelling was the first to describe architecture as frozen music; Goethe was the second. It's a seductive phrase, but the idea of architecture as a petrified formal moment lacks resonance. If music is frozen, it's not music, let alone architecture. In St Helen's Place, a gated lacuna between Bishopsgate and St Mary Axe in the City of London, the only relevant music that can be discerned in the design of The Leathersellers' Hall is the music of the passage of time.

Here, with EPA's creation of the seventh Hall since 1444 (when Henry VI awarded a charter of incorporation to the Worshipful Company of Leathersellers) we encounter a spatially sophisticated, highly crafted arrangement of spaces, surfaces and atmospheres in a new building which lies between a retained Edwardian façade facing St Helen's Place, and the 800-year-old stones of the north wall of St Helen's Church. The building stands on the site of the second Leathersellers' Hall (1677–1799), whose banqueting hall had previously contained the nuns' dormitory of the Benedictine Priory of St Helen's.

These asymmetries – time and architecture, religious and secular – are matched by the asymmetry of the trapezoidal site; and this is within yet another kind of asymmetry – the overlay of the City's Eastern Cluster tower zone across the outline of the St Helen's Place Conservation Area. Within 200m of the Hall stand the so-called Gherkin and Cheesegrater towers; 22 Bishopsgate and the absurdly nicknamed Scalpel will join this gleaming, high-shouldered huddle in due course.

In fact, it was the churn of change in the Eastern Cluster which, in a sense, made this relocation of The Leathersellers' Hall possible. The Company made a commercial agreement with the developers of 100 Bishopsgate tower (Great Portland Estates and Brookfield Properties), which enabled it to develop the 5–7 St Helen's Place site and relocate The Leathersellers' Hall there.

In the simplest terms, the architecture of The Leathersellers' Hall could be seen essentially as an act of conservation: the building and many of its contents are literally rooted in history and, in this sense, it's a return to the past. But four other aspects of the scheme are equally significant: the architecture's unusually creative expressions of the heritage of The Leathersellers' Company; the relationship of the Court Room, Reception Room and Dining Room with the double-nave of St Helen's Church as a tableau of places of gathering; the absolutely outstanding quality of the designed fixtures and materials; and the way the building's ceramic-tiled south-facing elevation contributes to the cityscape.

1840

1945

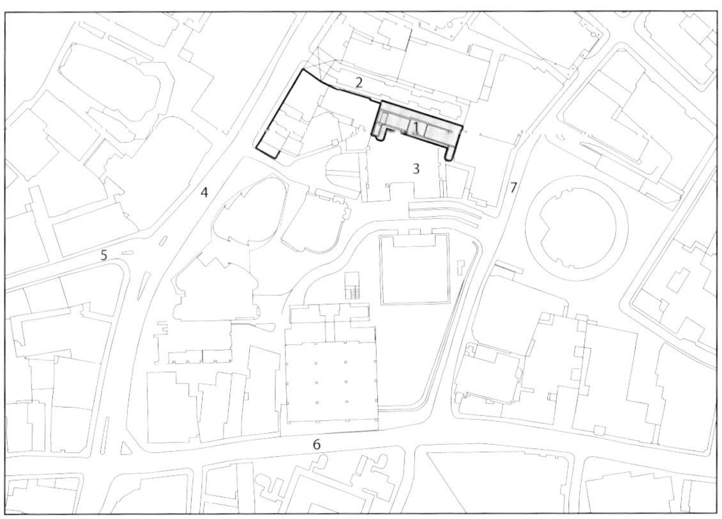

2018

Historical sequence of plans based on the information provided by James Wyld Jr., Wyld's *Plan of the City of London* (1842); Corporation of the City of London, *Report of the Improvements and Town Planning Committee... for post-war reconstruction in the City of London* (1945); followed by a current location plan (2018).

1 The Leathersellers' Hall
2 St Helen's Place
3 St Helen's Bishopsgate
4* Bishopsgate Street Within
4 Bishopsgate
5 Threadneedle Street
6 Leadenhall Street
7 St Mary Axe

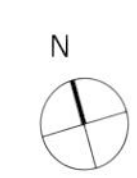

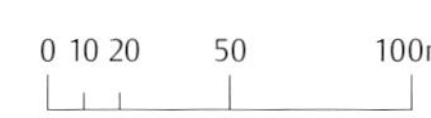

1:4000

opposite: The Reception Room, with a chandelier that was commissioned from sculptor Dale Chihuly, and a metal table and carpet designed by Eric Parry in the foreground. The lacquer-panelled walls incorporate shelved displays with unique exhibits belonging to The Leathersellers' private collection.

right: The walls and ceiling of the entrance lobby are intersected by scagliola pilasters. To the left of the frame, the external walls of St Helen's Church; to the right, the doors to the Reception Room.

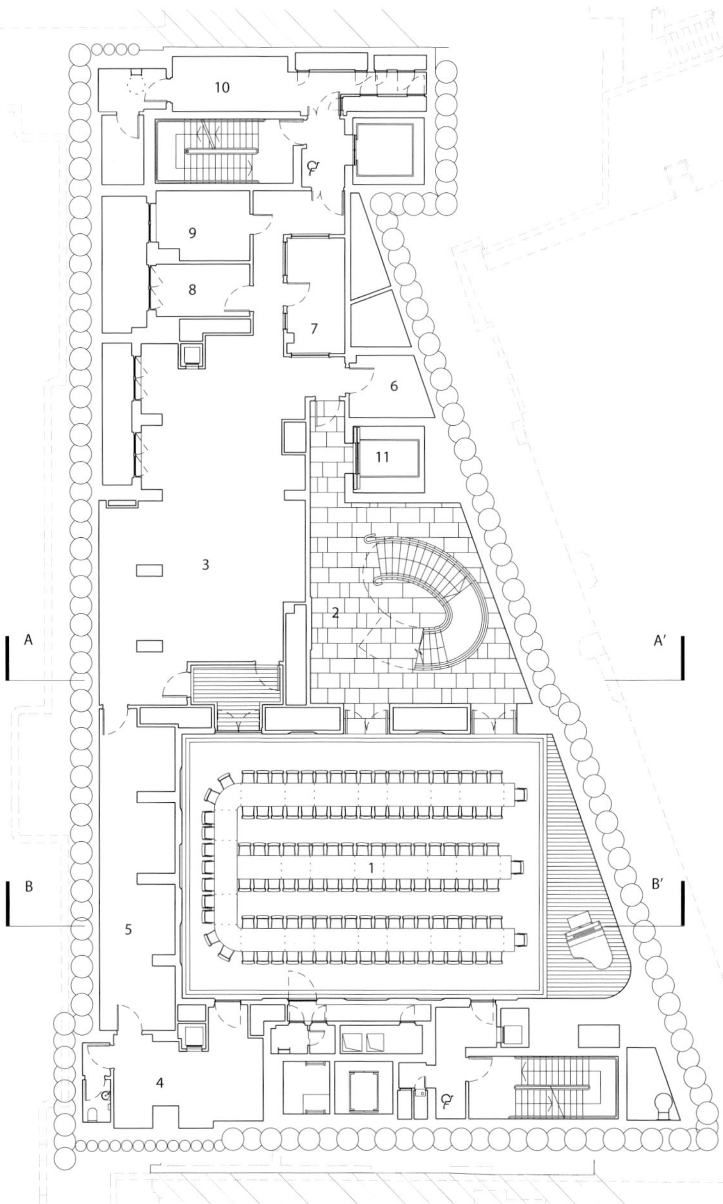

hall plan

1 Dining Hall
2 pre-dining
3 kitchen
4 butler's still
5 storage
6 chef's office
7 chilled prep
8 dry storage
9 cold store
10 bin store
11 lift

N

0 5 10m

1:300

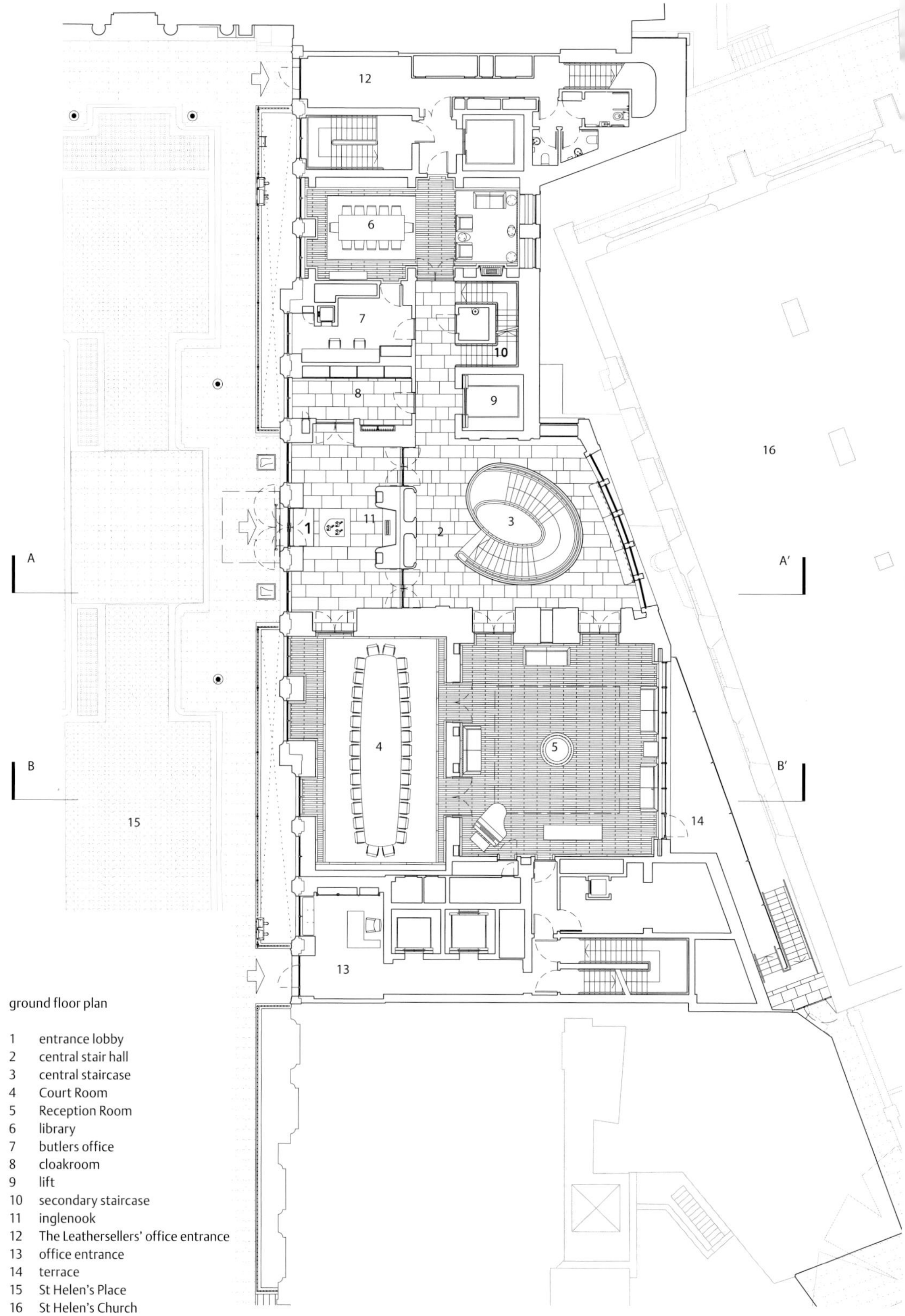

ground floor plan

1 entrance lobby
2 central stair hall
3 central staircase
4 Court Room
5 Reception Room
6 library
7 butlers office
8 cloakroom
9 lift
10 secondary staircase
11 inglenook
12 The Leathersellers' office entrance
13 office entrance
14 terrace
15 St Helen's Place
16 St Helen's Church

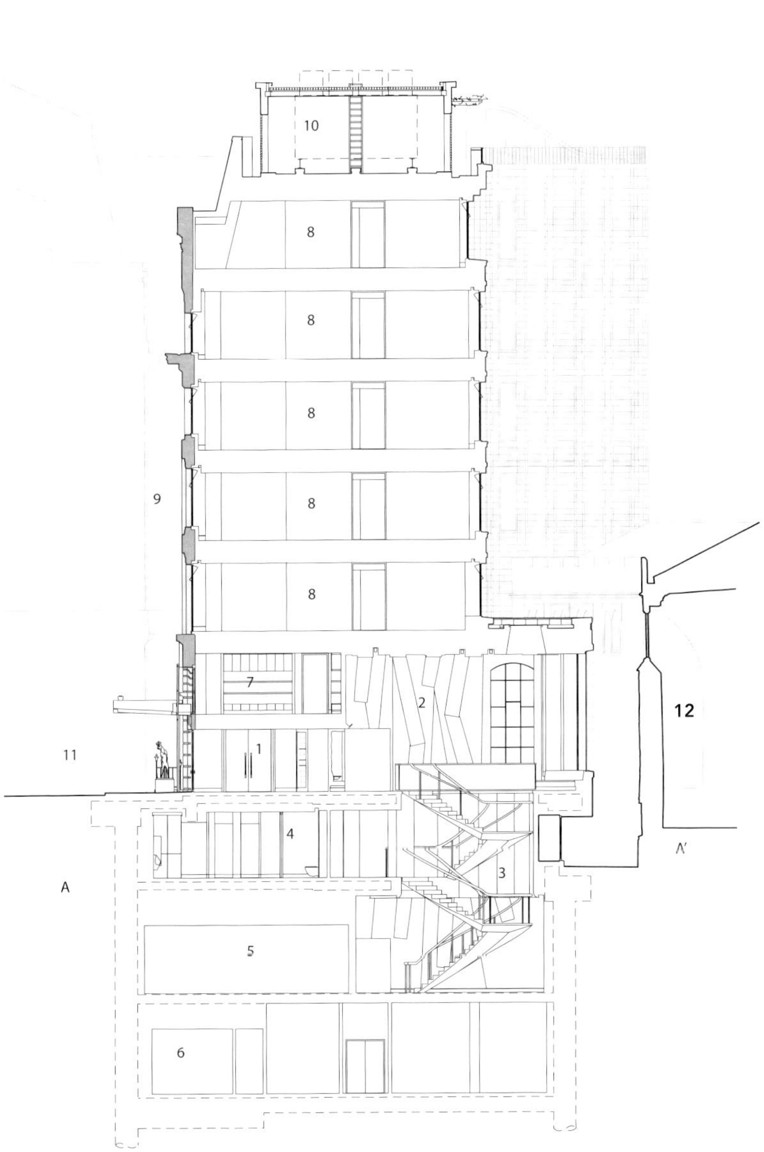

section AA'

1 entrance lobby
2 central stair hall
3 central staircase
4 changing rooms
5 kitchen
6 The Leathersellers' back-of-house areas
7 The Leathersellers' offices
8 offices
9 retained façade
10 plant
11 St Helen's Place
12 St Helen's Church

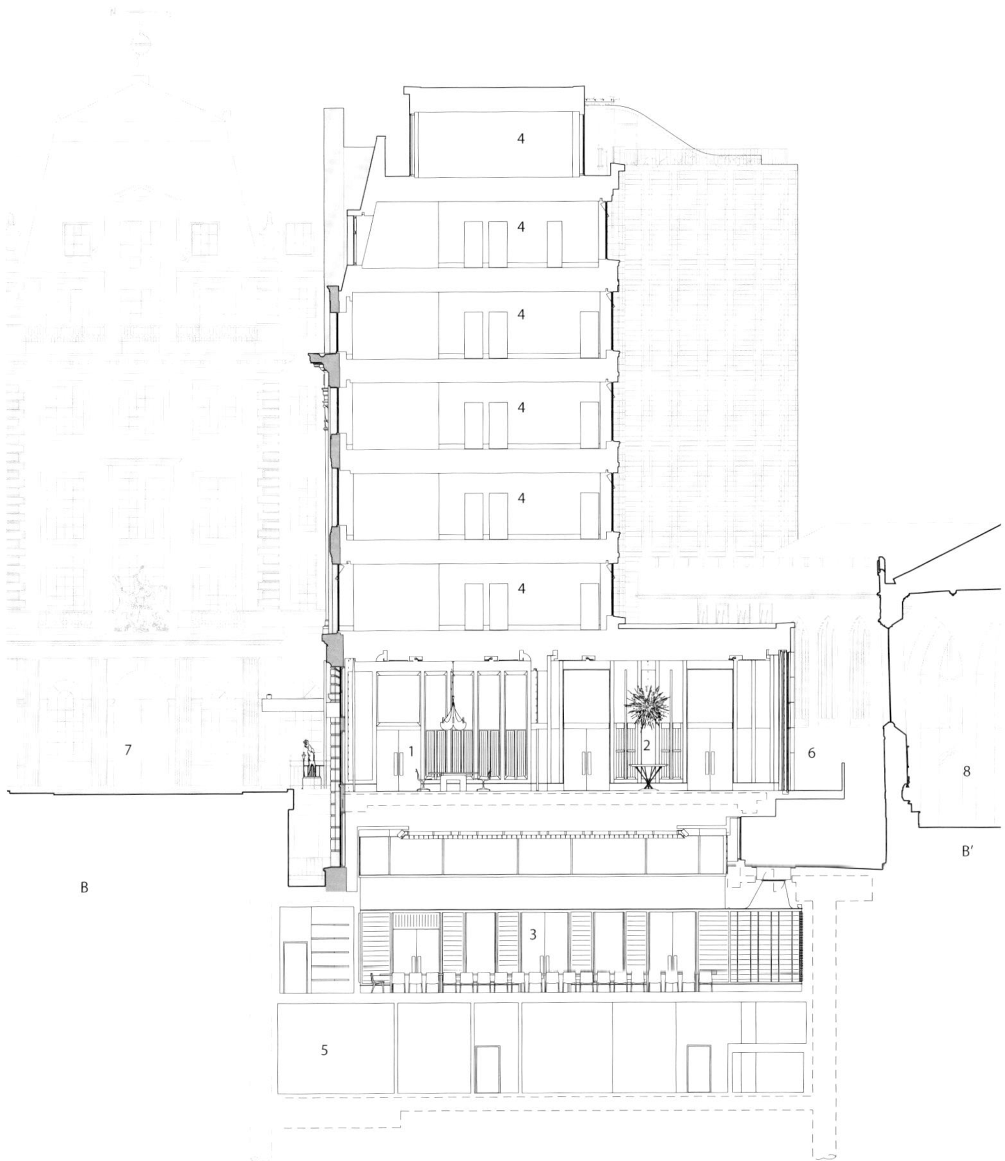

section BB'

1 Court Room
2 Reception Room
3 Dining Hall
4 office
5 The Leathersellers' back-of-house areas
6 terrace
7 St Helen's Place
8 St Helen's Church

0 5 10m

1:300

opposite: The Court Room, with walls in American black walnut, alternating between plain and vertical slotted panels. The walls hold the royal charters granted to the Leathersellers as well as a portrait of Henry VI, who instituted the royal livery company.

left: View from the main ground floor corridor with walls panelled in green leather panels, looking towards the main stair hall.

right: Partial view of the library, which bridges between from St Helen's Place to the new south ceramic-clad façade looking over the walls of St Helen's Church in the background.

The Company's original brief required the reconfiguring of the interiors of the sixth Leathersellers' Hall. But the company had second thoughts, related to maximising the development potential of 100 Bishopsgate, and asked EPA if it could design the required reception, offices and ceremonial spaces within the volume of a smaller building on the opposite side of St Helen's Place. This would also allow The Leathersellers' Company to own and manage the entire building. The only way this could be done was to meet the planning requirement to retain the limestone façade facing St Helen's Place and produce an entirely new building behind it, with a 9.5m deep dig-out that would create enough subterranean volume at the wider east end of the plan to contain a high-ceilinged dining hall capable of seating 122 guests, with room for a large, commercial hotel-standard kitchen and other functional spaces, including a wine cellar, staff facilities and still rooms. This left enough above-ground volume within the envelope of the original building to put the remaining ceremonial rooms on the ground floor, with five floors of offices and, above them, a small office and roof terrace. Another adjustment – lowering the ground floor to pavement level – produced step-free entry to the building, and allowed the Stair Hall, Reception Room and Court Room to be double-height, with enough room at the east end of the plan to insert a mezzanine-level office for The Leathersellers' Company staff.

The office levels fall across most of the width of the plan on the five upper floors, with lift cores at each end, one of which serves as the Hall's ceremonial entrance; the other two entrances at the east and west ends of the building are for the Hall's staff, and the commercial office floors, respectively.

Two things will immediately strike any visitor to the Hall. The remarkable quality and detail of the materials and finishes, and the practice's design of the fixtures and fittings. This is historically apt: one only has to glance at James Peller Malcolm's 1799 engraving of The Leathersellers' Hall, when it was on the same site as the current Hall, to see a decisive precedent for the Worshipful Company's expressive twenty-first-century interiors.

The design of the reception and ceremonial rooms has produced Reception, Court, Hall, and Stair volumes, and a staircase whose surfaces, fittings, and materials can safely be described as exquisite; furthermore, the atmosphere of these volumes – light-filled in the case of the Stair Hall and Reception Room – is individual rather than repetitive, and each is finished in a way that would enrage the writer, Paul Theroux. He complains in *Ghost Train to the Eastern Star*, that "luxury is the enemy of observation, a costly indulgence that induces such a good feeling that you notice nothing. Luxury spoils and infantilises you and prevents you from knowing the world. That is its purpose".

The interiors of The Leathersellers' Hall are certainly luxurious. But so fine are the materials, and the way they've been deployed, that they induce an acute observation of the results of supremely skilled hands and craft implements (and their own histories). They have translated the scheme's design into rooms that refer, in highly sensual ways, to the guild's history, the church a few feet away from the rear of the building, and the building's urban context.

In other words, these rooms are unabashedly creative set-pieces which, to reverse Theroux's remark, trigger such a good feeling that you notice everything – in the same way that the interiors of Adolf Loos's Villa Müller cause the gaze to lock onto every detail of the *cipollino* marble-clad walls, mahogany and granite dining table, Delft tiles and lemon wood cabinets. In both buildings, we are acutely and equally aware of design, and the superbly crafted *making* of the design.

The interiors at St Helen's Place transform the accumulated historical inertia of the guild's first six halls into something like a theatrical experience, which begins even before one enters the building. The fifth Hall had been the only building in St Helen's Place with a substantial stone portico, designed by Henry Saul in the 1920s, with elaborate nineteenth-century wrought-iron gates by John Starkie Gardner from the fourth Hall. These gates survived the fire-bombing of the Hall in 1941 and were reinstated in the sixth Hall. The gates have now been re-hung in front of the new Hall's bronze entrance door, with bronze sculptures of a ram and roebuck mounted on plinths to each side.

Above them is an unusual cantilevered bronze canopy resembling a thin and rather lax Ionic volute, carrying two flambeaux. It was inspired by the copper canopy over an entrance to Prague Castle, designed in the 1920s by the Slovenian architect Jože Plečnik. The soffit of The Leathersellers' Hall canopy has a white vitreous enamel surface, which is lit from below when the Worshipful Company holds evening events.

The tableau of canopy and sculptures carries an element of the Hall's nineteenth- and twentieth-century architecture into the future; and, as the project architect Christopher Burton put it, they punctuate the view from the Bishopsgate entrance of St Helen's Place, prompting curiosity about the Hall's distinctly singular, relatively theatrical threshold.

The Reception Room, entrance lobby and the cloakroom off it, has a contemporary cast-iron fireplace with a mirror above it, with vitrines either side displaying a selection of the Company's historic treasures. This relatively compressed space not only sets up the entry to the double-height ceremonial rooms, but leaves room for an office above the entrance lobby at mezzanine level.

left: The carpet designed by Eric Parry for the Reception Room of The Leathersellers' Hall.

right: Detail of lacquered doors and vertical slotted wall panelling. The doors feature bespoke leather-clad handles.

opposite: Leather niches and seating in the Stair Hall.

The creative and phenomenological ambition of the scheme becomes vividly obvious on entering the granite-floored Stair Hall. We see the wall of the nave of St Helen's Church, about 9ft away, through the full-height windows running across the slightly faceted south side of the room; set into the opposite wall are two inglenooked banquettes with flawless, perfectly stitched leather surfaces; in the middle of the room is the precise ellipse of the glazed balustrade at the top of the granite-edged staircase which spirals down to the changing rooms' level and the Dining Hall.

The Bill Amberg-designed leather lining the curving, vitrine-inset walls of the staircase have a veined rubicund finish not unlike the ceramic tiles visible on the window reveals and the building's rear façade; we get a glimpse of the stair carpeting – a royal purple that references mauveine, the colour of the world's first aniline dye, invented and patented by the 18-year-old chemist, William Perkin, in 1856. Perkin, later Sir William, became a Master of The Leathersellers' Company. The spiral stairs are the second in the history of the Halls: the first appeared in the fourth Hall, designed by William Fuller Pocock, which opened in 1822.

The ceiling of the Stair Hall is abstracted by a trapezoidal skylight and yellow-toned scagliola pilasters, which were removed from the sixth Hall, and have been scattered across the polished plaster ceiling, sometimes flat, sometimes turning down onto the walls. Eric Parry sees them as symbolising the vortex of the descent into the lower floors, a frozen moment of "collapsing weave" that he associates with the changing history of the seven Halls, and with the falling columns in the fresco at the Palazzo del Te, Mantua.

This richly symbolised space leads, via two sets of double-doors, to the Reception Room, whose ivory-painted walls and vertical, flush-mounted display cases are a cool backdrop for the extraordinary Dale Chihuly-designed explosion of drawn-glass icicles – indigo at the core, glitteringly clear at the tips – that hangs from the centre of the ceiling. Beneath it is a high circular table whose cast bronze edge carries a Latin phrase from the 1444 Charter, and a square rug, both designed by Parry.

The latter, in the paler colour tones of Chihuly's scintillae, takes its geometric patterning from medieval paving layouts; and this produces an effect that suggests both Art Deco and thirteenth- and sixteenth-century astrological drawings of constellations in the Burney and Egerton collections. In an otherwise convivial space, these three pieces symbolise an ascent through the medieval and Late Middle Ages, into a future starburst. The large window in the south wall looks onto St Helen's Church. A grand piano and four Jaan sofas upholstered with black-and-white cowhide – an arch-Modernist touch – complete the setting.

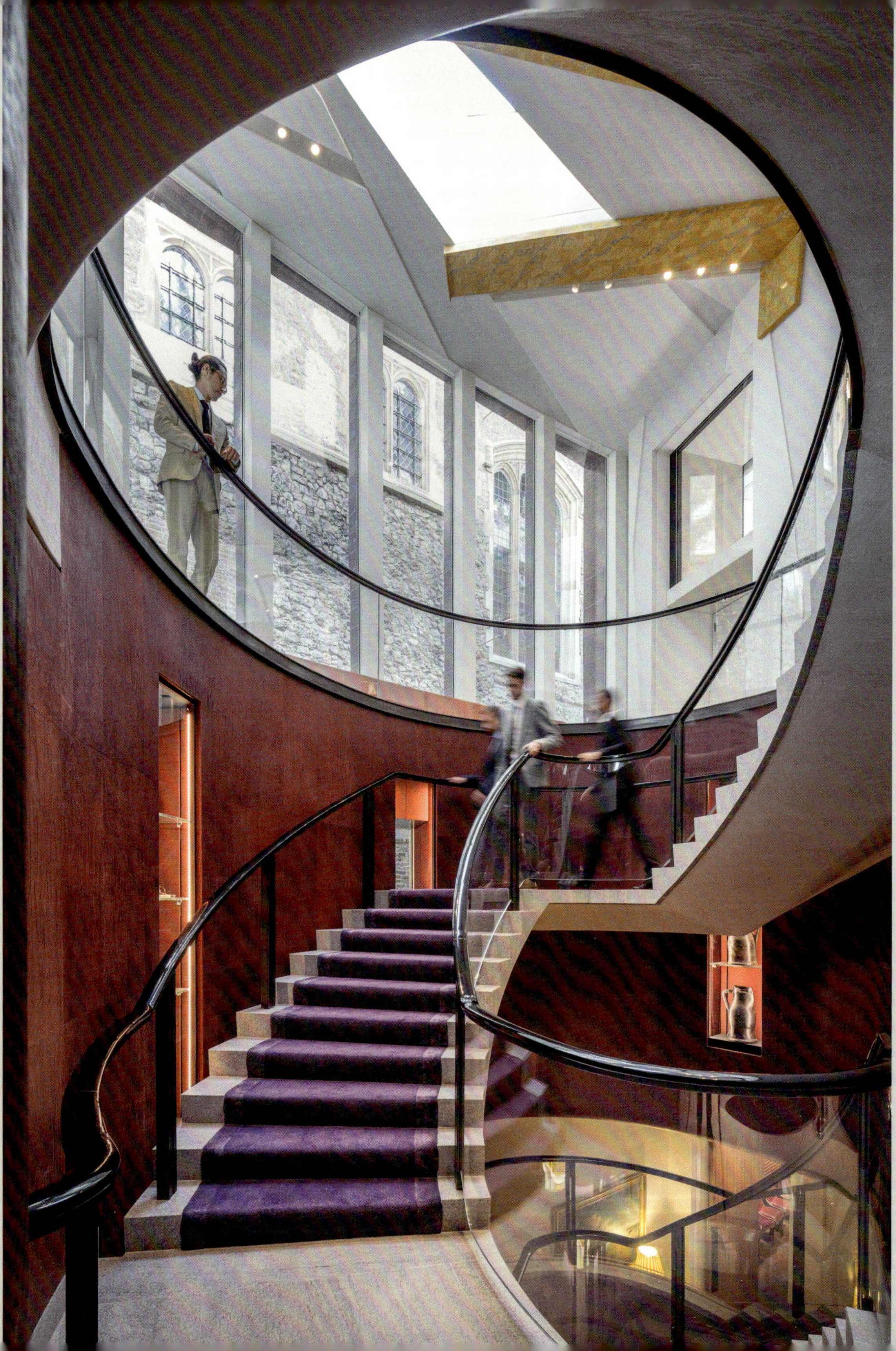

The stairwell descends from the main entrance lobby through the various levels of the interior.

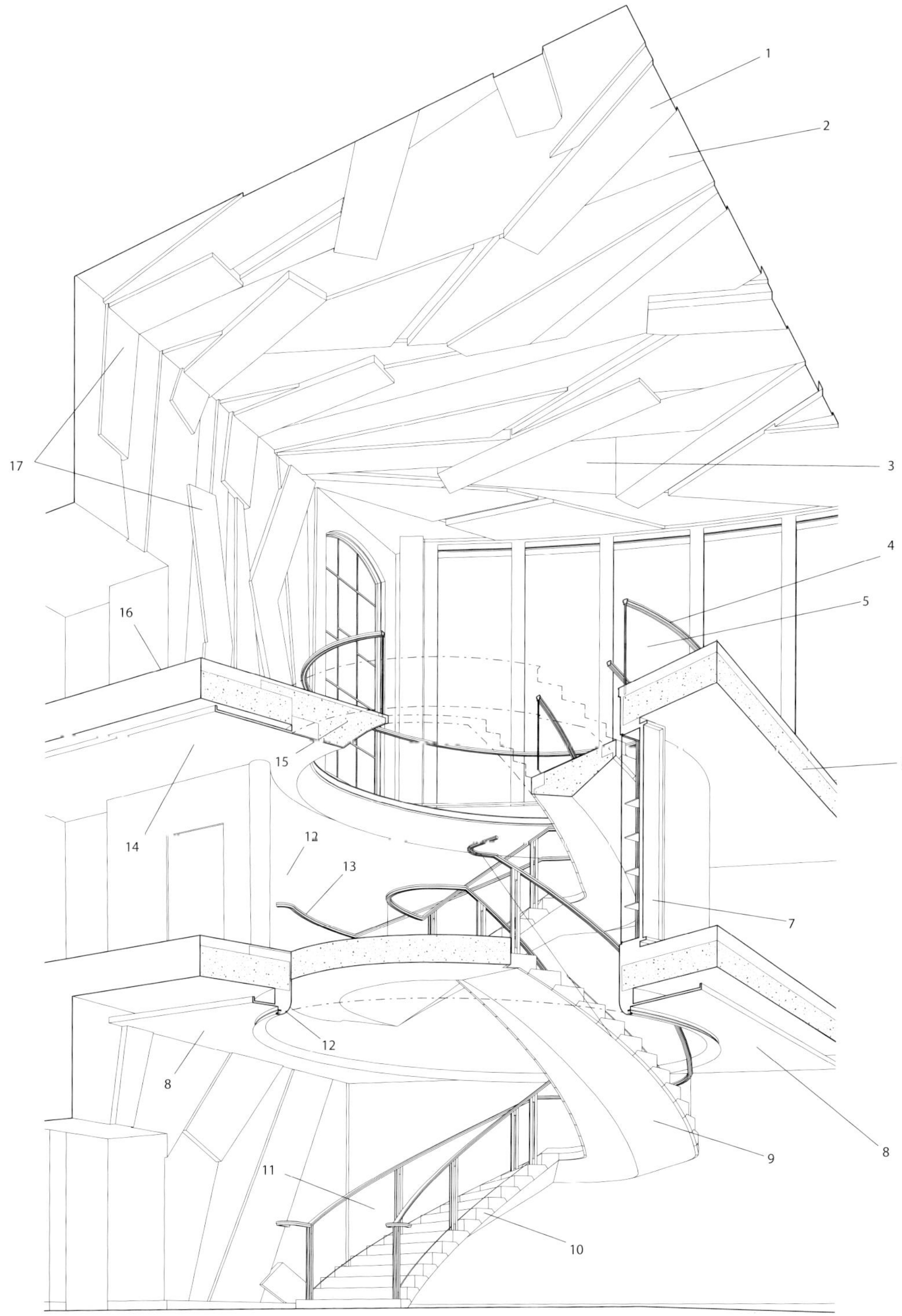

Stair Hall
perspectival section

1 scagliola surface to false ceiling
2 decorative plaster to false ceiling
3 void to skylight
4 curved (metal) handrail
5 cantilevered curved glass parapet, two layers of 12mm clear low-iron glass with 1.5mm clear ionoplast interlayer
6 ground floor in-situ reinforced concrete slab
7 vitrine
8 decoration plaster to ceiling of lower ground floor
9 decorative plaster finish to soffit of stair flight
10 quoined edging Chelmsford Grey granite adhered directly to concrete base
11 curved glass spanning between posts and handrail
12 curved leather panelling
13 handrail support posts without glass
14 suspended plasterboard ceiling
15 cantilevered beams encased in concrete
16 Chelmsford Grey granite flooring slabs
17 scagliola pilasters

The design of the adjoining Court Room, whose windows face out into St Helen's Place, produces a suitably calm atmosphere. The walls are composed of alternating panels of plain and reed-slotted black American walnut – the reeding is for acoustic and air-conditioning purposes. Above the 29-seat European walnut table, made by Luke Hughes, the coved timber ceiling has a central plaster panel, from which hang two fairly simple nineteenth-century cut-glass chandeliers retrieved from the sixth Leathersellers' Hall. The room has a certain formal gravitas, but the prevailing mid-brown surface tones have been accented with three framed Royal Charters, deep red curtains and white leather chairs. The 1950s Wilton carpet and chandeliers were brought from the previous Hall.

On the way down the stairs to the Dining Hall, one passes Leonard Walker's 1937 stained-glass panel depicting Henry VI, and the lower ground floor. One floor lower is the 180m^2 Dining Room, which is slightly more than double-height and creates a triple horizon. The first is formed by the alternating 3.3m-high panels of vertical and horizontal walnut boarding; the second horizon is the continuous 1.3m-deep Company history mural by Victoria Crowe that surmounts the panelling and wraps 40m around the room; and the third is a partly false, backlit clerestory layer. This room recalls the wood-panelled, clerestoried Neville Mariner rehearsal room beneath the northern side of St Martin-in-the-Fields, whose transformation was completed by EPA in 2008.

Parry's characteristic interest in interior horizons is also evident in the thresholds between the Stair Hall and the Reception Room, and between the Reception Room and the Court Room, which have glazed over-panels that effectively divide the rooms into upper and lower portions. The elliptical plan of the staircase also reappears, in the form of an oculus in the southwestern corner of the Dining Hall ceiling, which gives an angled upward view of the church wall.

This desire to make external connections, already obvious in the grandstand view of the church from the Stair Hall, and in the way the entrance canopy tableau adds something unexpected to the otherwise orderly perspective of St Helen's Place, has produced one final Epicurean outcome. Looking north from Great St Helen's or Undershaft the ruddy glow of the ceramic tiles on the south elevation, which backdrops the church, is a delightful affront to the roil of glass, steel and algorithmic vibrations that otherwise engulf St Helen's Place.

It's not too fanciful to imagine that the sheen of the tiles connects the twenty-first-century heat of the kilns that made them with the heat of the eighteenth-century kilns at Wedgwood's Etruria Works in Stoke-on-Trent – a ghostly strand of the Industrial Revolution passing through the bright, manic mills of the Financial Revolution.

above: Dining Hall looking south with the wall of St Helen's Bishopsgate seen beyond.

opposite: Above the panelling, a tapestry fabricated at Dovecot Studios was created by artist Victoria Crowe.

Royal Academy Summer Exhibition

Most of those who attend exhibitions are rarely privy to the curatorial backstories, the rigour applied to the way spaces and surfaces are used.... The selected pieces (mostly drawings, but also some models) focused on the design process itself, as visually anticipated and made possible by the act of drawing.

The room dedicated to architecture took the form of a traditional gallery hang.

Eric Parry's curation and design of the Architecture Room at the 2014 Royal Academy Summer Exhibition was notable in presenting a relatively limited number of models, and in its carefully ordered hang of drawings, three-dimensional objects and video screens. The models, set out on two rectangular tables, were arranged to form particular topographies and contrasts. The hung pieces were positioned to establish horizon lines at about 1.6m (the average height of the human eye) and groupings which, without being precisely symmetrical, conveyed an impression of balance; an approach influenced, no doubt, by Dalibor Vesely's dictum, "symmetry as harmony".

Most of those who attend exhibitions are rarely privy to the curatorial backstories, the rigour applied to the way spaces and surfaces are used to provoke thoughtful or visceral reactions. Parry's appointment as curator, in May 2014, followed an initial discussion with his fellow Royal Academician, the late Richard MacCormac. They agreed that the selection of exhibits would be based on two criteria: that exhibits had to be of outstanding physical or visual quality, and that they would show aspects of architectural processes, rather than completed projects. About 12,000 objects were submitted for consideration, and 140 were selected.

In the case of the models, Parry said: "It had to do more with the quality of the model, than what it represented. The idea of the architectural object, a kind of game of aesthetic judgement, and a knowledge of the authors – like arranging books on a shelf." Parry and the practice faced a very compressed May-to-June design and set-up period, and their approach emphasised the presentation of architecture as a medium of dialogue, which was fundamentally articulated through the drawings that were shown. The selected pieces (mostly drawings, but also some models) focused on the design process itself, as visually anticipated and made possible by the act of drawing.

The exhibition design process began with measured plans for the floor, ceiling and four walls of Gallery VI, supplied by the Royal Academy. They were found to be not entirely accurate; furthermore, a section of one of the elevated picture-rails was missing from the south wall. This imperfection was dealt with in a novel way: one of the RA's art-handlers, who happened to have studied painting, agreed to fill in the gap with a very effective *trompe l'oeil* rail, complete with shadow.

Parry's early sketches for the tables proposed two very different types. One had terraces of shelves, a prism-like form crowned with the representation of a single very large model. The second table was flat and roughly triangular in plan, with an irregular outline designed to fit closely around an asymmetrical arrangement of 24 models.

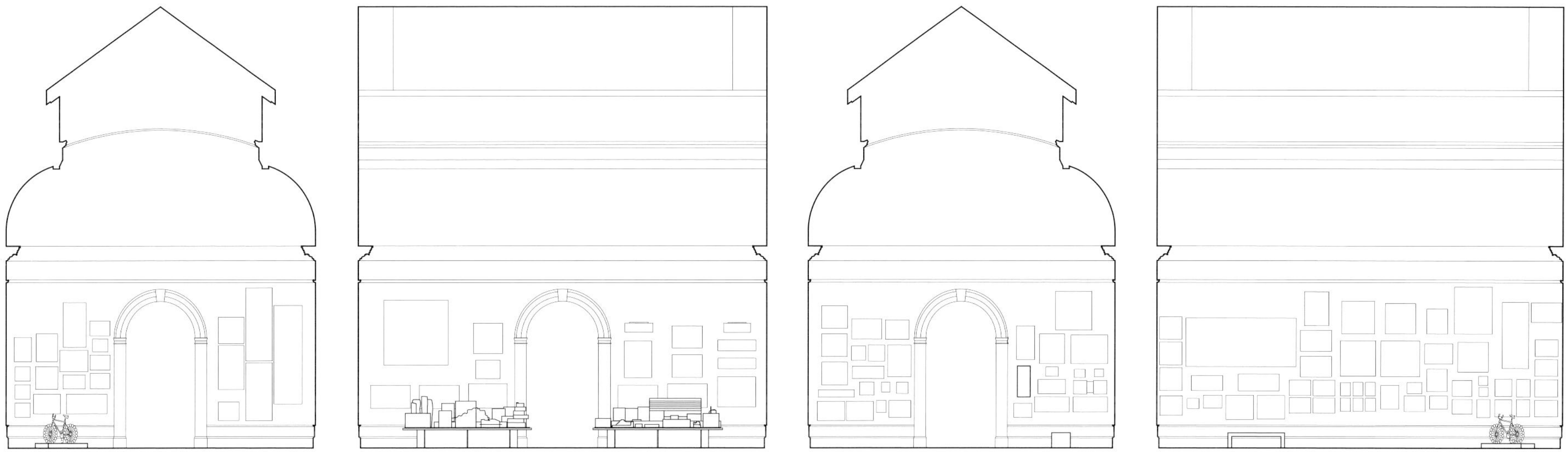

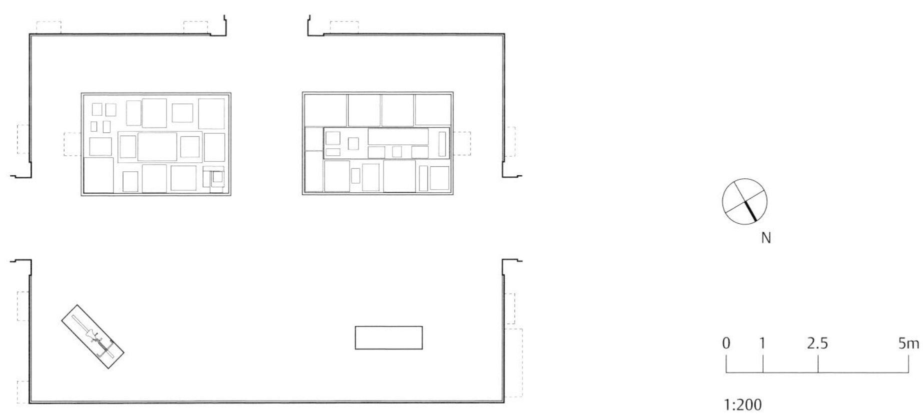
N
0
1
2.5
5m
1:200

But these ideas were superseded, perhaps because the exhibits on the prism table would have disrupted the eye-lines to two of the walls, and it's equally easy to imagine the irregular flat table producing a Manhattan-like salient of overcrowded architectural objects. Ultimately, the tables were set out quite simply. Their rectangular surfaces sat on stands and the height of the stepped edges of the display surfaces aligned with the top of the dado. On each of the tables there was a single plinth covering part of it, and all the plinths were low enough to ensure that the highest models would not interfere with the sightlines to the exhibits on the walls.

The question of how to set out the models and wall pieces was fraught and time-consuming. A process was established: in the mornings models would be set out on the floor of Gallery VI in suggested positions within taped areas the size of the tables; Parry would arrive later, review the layouts, and adjust the selection or positions if necessary.

In arranging the models, the models that had more to say, so to speak, were positioned on the sides of the tables closest to the walls, where exhibition-goers were most likely to pause or gather – and not least in the corners of the room. This precedence was not particularly noticeable, and it was probably more significant that

left: General view of the interior.

opposite: The model stands were designed so that the top of the exhibits on display would coincide with the middle of the screens in the back and establish a comfortable horizon for the viewer.

THE PHILIP AND PAULINE HARRIS GALLERY

the selection of models positioned around the edges of the tables was so effective, vis-à-vis sightlines: one could see the majority of the objects quite clearly, from any side. Parry likened the layout of the models to those in the Model Room at the Soane Museum – "clusters speaking to each other".

The positioning of the wall exhibits was also tested by laying groups of them on the floor and shuffling the pieces. Parry and his collaborators often found themselves working late into the evenings to clarify the configurations, determined to avoid what he described as "incredibly dense salon-type hangings" – though he greatly admires the salon-hangs of specialists such as Gus Cummins RA. "The character and size of each piece is crucial," said Parry. "You start by laying them out on the floor. You think it's right – but, no, not at all!"

The colour of Gallery VI's walls was resolved in what was an homage to the skewed concrete portals created by Eduardo Souto de Moura as his contribution to the Royal Academy's *Sensing Spaces* exhibition, curated by Kate Goodwin, which preceded the 2014 Summer Show. The colour of the concrete under lighting – a very pale grey-blue-green – was used on two walls, and a dark bitter chocolate brown with a subtle greenish tinge on the others; the brown referenced the shadow within Souto de Moura's pieces.

The show was by no means dominated by Royal Academician architects. Fewer than a third of the exhibitors were RAs. They included the late Zaha Hadid, who initially requested a quite substantial area of wall for artworks; her office also submitted a specific hanging-plan which, in one place, would have required drilling a fixing into one of the room's pilasters. This arrangement was not possible, but a number of her models and artworks were gathered in a corner setting, which produced a concentrated impact.

As the majority of the exhibitors were non-RA architects, students and academics, there were some interesting juxtapositions. Among Parry's favourites were Will Alsop's "The Great Northern", a big model which had the qualities of a loose sketch morphed into 3D; Tao DuFour's two pencil, ink and gesso drawings from the project "Colonnofagia and The Dissolution of the Wall" carried out for the Prix the Rome; Paul Koralek's pencil sketches ("exquisitely clear", said Parry); O'Donnell and Tuomey's model of the LSE's Saw Swee Hock Student Centre; and Homa Farjadi's 'Archeologies' (sic) triptych. Bearing in mind the particular pleasure Parry takes in designing virtuosic staircases, it was not surprising to find a photograph of Bonhams' spiral staircase, designed by Lifschutz Davidson Sandilands.

Parry's fascination with palimpsests and materiality must explain the presence of Perry Kulper's drawing, 'David's Island: Strategic Plot',

Detail of the hang dedicated to architecture, as part of the RA Summer Exhibition, curated by Eric Parry and the late Sir Richard MacCormac.

in which the individual figurations, symbols and coloured areas could not be considered as foreground or background items, but only as layers of floating ideas that might or might not coalesce; the artwork was made of Mylar, X-ray image, assorted found imagery, cut paper, foil, transfer letters, transfer film, tape, ink and graphite.

In the same post-William Burroughs' cut-up spirit were videos made by Ron Arad, *Last Train* and *Two Nuns Bike*, the first of which showed the artists Christian Marclay and Antony Gormley scratching lines and circles on sheets of glass using diamond-studded rings. The deliberately uncertain, visually twitchy style of the narrative and imagery failed to prevent Arad's uniquely hooded chapeau from completely dominating the proceedings.

The display tables were not chock-a-block with models, and there was an ample amount of open circulation space; thus, unusual objects did not seem overly imposing. For example, the model of Foster + Partners' "Lunar Habitation" was next to a slightly battered leather case – Rosa Couloute's "Drawing Instruments: My Grandmother's Tool Case". Parry relished the Duchamp quality of the latter, and was also amused by Ron Arad's bizarre "Two Nuns" bicycle, whose wheels are formed with petal-like radii of looped steel ribbons – "there's something performative about it," said Parry. "You think Flann O'Brien could be lurking in the gallery."

O'Brien's ghost might well have been murmuring this line from *The Third Policeman*: "The gross and net result of it is that people who spent most of their natural lives riding iron bicycles over the rocky roadsteads of this parish get their personalities mixed up with the personalities of their bicycle as a result of the interchanging of the atoms of each of them and you would be surprised at the number of people in these parts who are nearly half people and half bicycles."

The author would also have divined Parry's pleasure in including the Cornell academic Peter Ferretto's engraving, 'Abstract Composition 836'. This entirely undramatic, if not sombre grey and black work was positioned at the top corner of one of the hangs as "an act of faith", according to Parry; yet it was the first piece in the show to be sold. And therefore proof of one of Flann O'Brien's dictums: "Strange enlightenments are vouchsafed... to those who seek the higher places."

The Opera Terrace, Covent Garden

Despite the Victorian inspiration, the Opera Terrace structure generates a precisely distinct, contemporary sense of difference – an architectural progression which serves Covent Garden's commercial evolution, and the footfalls of an estimated 44 million visitors a year.

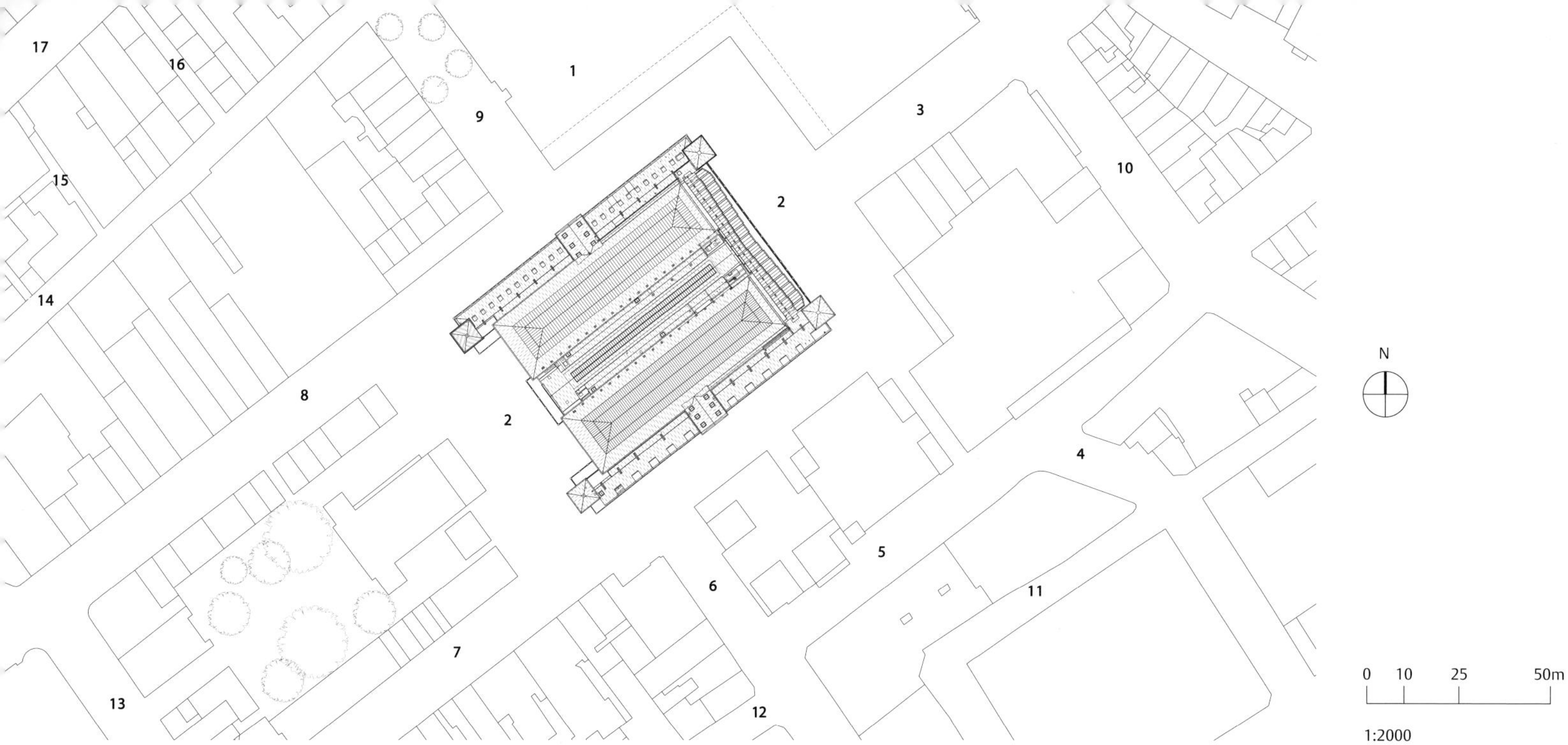

site plan

1 Royal Opera House
2 Covent Garden
3 Russell Street
4 Burleigh Street
5 Tavistock Street
6 Southampton Street
7 Henrietta Street
8 King Street
9 James Street
10 Wellington Street
11 Exeter Street
12 Maiden Lane
13 Bedford Street
14 Floral Street
15 Banbury Court
16 Langley Court
17 Long Acre

The design of the restaurant glasshouse on the elevated east terrace of the Market Building in Covent Garden, London, has a refinement of form, detail, and a lightweight quality that some would immediately characterise as a High Tech cuckoo perched on a relatively stolid Italianate nest. That one-liner is obviously too simplistic, but it highlights the difficulty of suggesting a clear-cut architectural synthesis between Charles Fowler's Grade II* listed 1830 Market Building and the limber, gracefully edgy steel-and-glass structure.

The highly visible intervention was agreed by Westminster City Council planners and Historic England, and survived the equally intense gaze of the Covent Garden Area Trust, which did not exist when the previous – and rather ungainly – Opera Terrace conservatories were erected by a firm of quantity surveyors in the 1980s.

As seen from ground level on the eastern side of the building, the new structure's outline and sloping glass surfaces are not quite shock-of-the-new Modernist architecture: the articulations, and their detailing, are too refined to be considered startling or radical. EPA describe the structure as a delicately pleated contemporary version of a nineteenth-century glass structure – Joseph Paxton's greenhouse at Chatsworth and his vast ridge-and-furrow glass domes at Crystal Palace being the first great uses of cylinder glass and patent plate glass, respectively.

Despite the Victorian inspiration, the Opera Terrace structure generates a precisely distinct, contemporary sense of difference – an architectural progression which serves Covent Garden's commercial evolution, and the footfalls of an estimated 44 million visitors a year. London's historic buildings and settings have been under increasing commercial and touristic pressure since the 1980s, as historic buildings and locales have become consumer backdrops for shoppers and selfie-stickers.

It's particularly evident in Covent Garden, where populist-cum-commercial pressures have been present since the eighteenth century, when the market began to generate substantial amounts of money for the Dukes of Bedford. From 1705, market rights were leased to stallholders for £800 per year, plus one-eighth of their profits. By 1748, there were 335 shops and stands and, physically, the Market resembled a shanty-town.

After the Dissolution of the Monasteries, the land had come into the possession of Henry VIII, until which point it had been a garden belonging to Westminster Abbey. John Russell, the 1st Earl of Bedford, was granted the land in the sixteenth century by the Crown. And from then, until the beginning of the twentieth century,

View from the interior of Covent Garden Market towards the completed restaurant glasshouse over the north east portico.

the Earls and then Dukes of Bedford commanded the development of the area.

The buildings we know today came into being via a Parliamentary Bill for the Improvement and Regulation of Covent Garden Market in 1828. This allowed the sixth Duke of Bedford to raze the existing buildings and led to the construction of three ranges, with a terrace at the east end. The new buildings were erected by William Cubitt, completed in 1830, and by the end of the century the ninth Duke had them roofed.

In 1918, the site was bought by the Covent Garden Estate Company, which later became part of Beecham Estates and Pills Ltd. The history of its subsequent ownership is convoluted, and involved a number of major investors, and at one point the Greater London Council. The owners at the time of the practice's Opera Terrace scheme were Capital & Counties (CapCo).

John Summerson described Covent Garden as "London's first formal open space", and the Market Building as the first of its kind in Britain; and it has caused various controversies through time. In the 1630s, when Inigo Jones designed and built St Paul's Church and the Piazza, the historian and politician Horace Walpole derided the tableau.

"In the arcade there is nothing remarkable; the pilasters are as errant and homely stripes as any plasterer would make," he wrote. "The barn roof over the portico of the church strikes my eyes with as little idea of dignity or beauty as it could do if it covered nothing but a barn. In justice to Inigo, one must own that the defect is not in the architect, but in the order: who ever saw a beautiful Tuscan building? Would the Romans have chosen that order for a temple? Mr Onslow, the late Speaker, told me an anecdote that corroborates my opinion of this building. When the Earl of Bedford sent for Inigo, he told him he wanted a chapel for the parishioners of Covent Garden, but added he would not go to any considerable expense. 'In short,' said he, 'I would have it not much better than a barn.' 'Well, then,' replied Jones, 'you shall have the handsomest barn in England.'"

In 1888, six decades after the completion of Fowler's Central Market Building, *Punch* magazine lampooned it, and the Duke of Bedford, mercilessly: "Mud-Salad Market belongs to his Grace the Duke of Mudford... Vegetable refuse, ankle deep, carpets the pathway in every direction, mixed with mud and rain-water, and trampled into a pulpy slimy muck by thousands of hob-nailed boots... It is not too much to say that Mud-Salad Market is a disgrace to London, a special disgrace to his Grace of Mudford, and about the greatest nuisance ever permitted in a great City of Nuisances."

0 5 10m

1:500

northeast elevation

1 Covent Garden
2 Royal Opera House
3 The Opera Terrace

Covent Garden is no longer a shambolic Victorian stew; it is a stew of another sort. In 2000 Geoffrey Holland, then chairman of the Trust and previously leader of the GLC's development team, offered this waspish comment in a speech: "It has long been agreed that, notwithstanding its commercial and tourist success, several parts of the Piazza area and even, in places, the Market itself had become a visual mess, in danger of coming to resemble parts of Manila or Djakarta."

The design iterations for the glass structure were therefore minutely scrutinised, and the final design demonstrates that in Covent Garden's core area of more than two hectares, the superimposition of a significantly different architectural form on one of London's most famous historic hosts was acceptable if the massing and articulations didn't upstage the fundamental rhythm and composure of the east elevation as a whole.

There have been very few striking architectural interventions in Covent Garden, the most notable exceptions being the temporary Clifton Nurseries structure, and other Postmodernist manipulations in the Comyn Ching Triangle in the 1980s. By comparison, there is no irony or satire in the architecture of the Opera Terrace's glass structure; as a decisively novel attachment to a heritage building, it's easier to align it with the sloping, glazed cowl added by Frederick Gibberd Partnership to the remains of a John Nash building on the Strand in 1978 for its owners, Coutts Bank.

The historic elevation of the Opera Terrace is dominated by three features: a long Tuscan colonnade, four rows deep, in grey granite, supporting the entablature which forms the stone-balustrated Opera Terrace. The colonnade is bookended by two-storey granite and render-faced pavilions. An open-bed pediment containing the arch of a serliana originally supported by pilasters rises from the centre of the terrace, surmounted by RW Sievier's Coade stone sculptures of the Roman flower and fruit deities, Flora and Pomona, and Cupid.

The centres of the granite columns, at about 2.8m, dictated the rhythm of the new glass-and-steel structure, and the widths of the glazing mullions and pleats reference Georgian and Victorian measures. The pediment and sculptures determined the new roofline, which dips down gradually, in glazed steps, from raised shoulder-elements which join the pavilions.

In plan, the façade of the glass structure forms a gently retreating curve, with glazed tri-folding doors – the first of their kind in London. Eric Parry's original proposal was for a smoothly down-curving roofline, but this was rejected because it was deemed to contradict the angular hips of the glass canopies rising above the Market Building. Not that these canopies are particularly remarkable, having been added to the Market Building in 1875 by Cubitt and Co. in the no-nonsense style of the glazed roofs of Victorian train sheds.

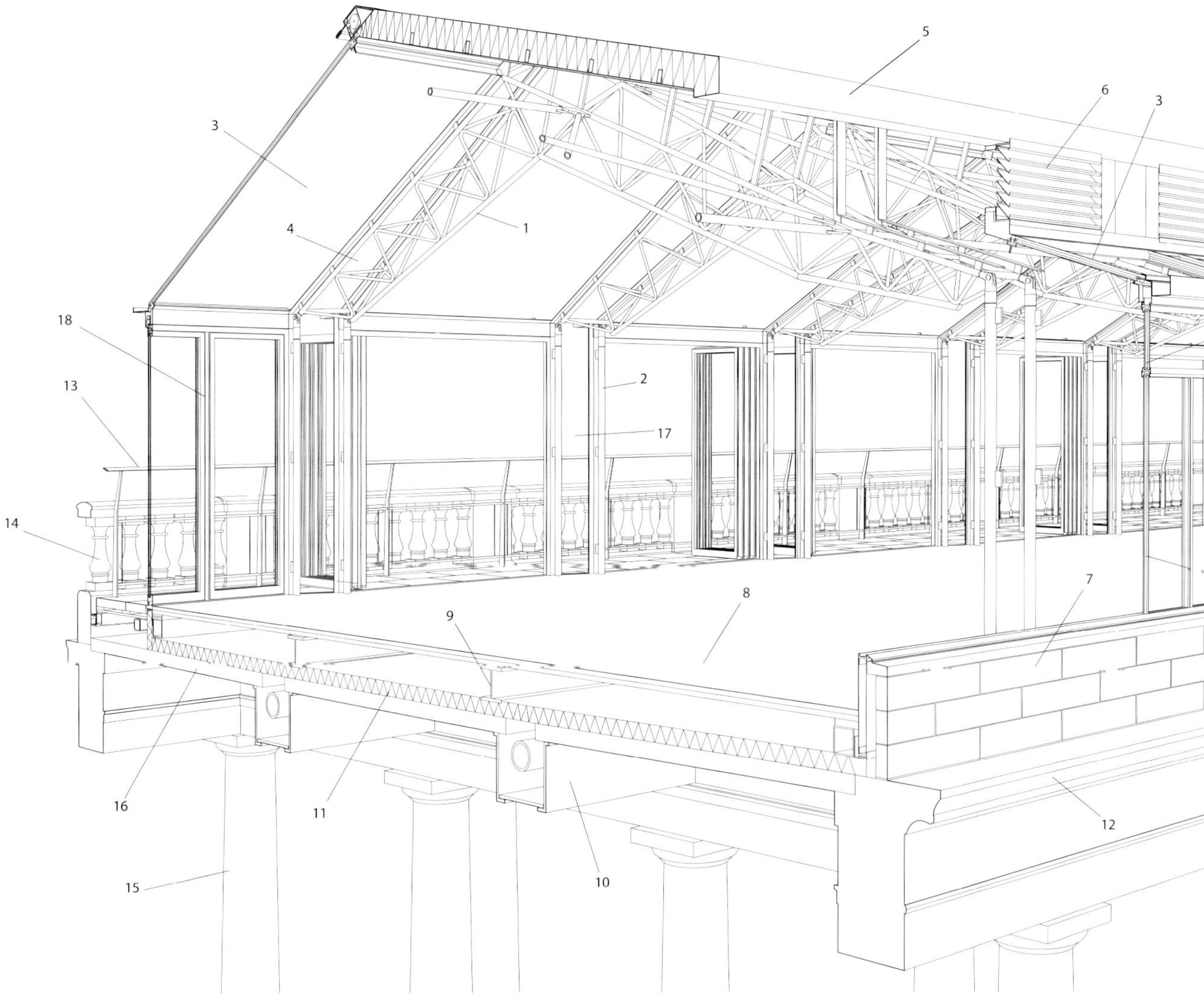

perspectival section

1 duplex stainless-steel trusses with electro-polished bead-blasted finish
2 duplex stainless-steel machined columns with electro-polished bead-blasted finish
3 large-format planar low-iron double-glazed roof panels with solar coating
4 doubly curved low-iron double-glazed roof panels
5 insulated roof panels with walk-on rigidized stainless-steel finish
6 polyester powder-coated painted finish to mechanically operated ventilation louvres
7 new limestone 75mm-thick plinth to match existing stonework
8 floor finish by tenant on new double plywood decking
9 new structural steel raised floor transfer deck with accessible services zone
10 existing hollow cast-iron beams housing new rainwater pipes
11 rigid PIR insulation
12 existing stone cornice
13 new painted mild-steel balustrade with low-iron toughened glass infill panels
14 existing Yorkshire stone bottle balustrades
15 existing solid granite columns
16 existing 125mm-deep stone floor slabs with areas of concrete infill
17 low-iron double-glazed fixed panels
18 hinged sliding low-iron glazed doors with painted mild-steel frames
19 fixed low iron double glazing with painted mild-steel frames and ceramic frit pattern
20 motorised outward-opening low-iron glazing with painted mild-steel frames

opposite: The complete sequence of double-curved glazed connecting panels.

The height descends and retreats to form the al fresco terrace and to emphasise the Coade stone statue of Flora, Pomona and Cupid.

above: Installation of the roof panels on site.

Curved or stepped, the design delivered an important outcome: passers-by below the Opera Terrace, or approaching from Russell Street, now have a clear view of the pediment and Flora and Pomona, a composition that had previously been largely obscured by an architecturally bumptious round-headed conservatory projecting well onto the Opera Terrace from the Serlian arch. The connection between the earlier conservatory structures and the Market Building had also been quite crude; in contrast, the new glass structure has been attached to the back of the terrace adroitly, not least in the resolution of its plan and elevation where the glazing drops down to meet the pavilions.

The structure has doubled the area of the covered restaurant and kitchen space on the Opera Terrace; the latter is in a new rectangular segment which pushes out above Central Avenue from the midsection of the terrace. The practice also replaced the bands of narrow round-headed glazing on the west side of the new structure with deeper rectangular frames, which gives clearer views into the North and South Halls.

Apart from the rounded arch in its pediment, the west side of the original serliana was removed; in its place is a simple arrangement of inter-glazed columns. The two long sides of the new glass structure are therefore more or less transparent from both sides.

The other significant intervention is in the northeast pavilion, which has become the public entrance to the Opera Terrace and now contains a lift-shaft and an almost trademark EPA 'floating' elliptical staircase, which winds around a tapered and discreetly anchored beam. The glass and steel-plate balustrades and handrails chime with the new Opera Terrace structure and its glazed envelope.

Its detailed design is an essay in exposure and concealment. In section, for example, the pleated glass modules form a series of unseen, stainless steel-covered steps on the back side of the roof ridge, which makes room for a services zone to run right across the full width of the structure. A second services and drainage zone lies under the floor, which sits 300mm above the Terrace's original stone slabs and twentieth-century concrete infill panels and beams. The new floor also acts as a structural transfer deck, concentrating loads to the heads of the rows of the original stone columns supporting the terrace.

Internally, the most striking features are the exposed steel lattice trusses, which produce the structure's undulating rhythm. The elliptic-sectioned stainless-steel columns which support them are stylish cross-references to the plan of the staircase. The lattice trusses were configured by EPA and, after the project's engineers sized the individual pieces, remained virtually

left: The entire façade can open to the terrace and the space of Russell Street.

opposite: View of the completed interior after being fitted out by the tenant Sushi Samba and just prior to the opening.

as originally sketched. The stepped fall and rise of the glass envelope, and the curving regression of its façade in plan produce an unusual internal perspective. The practice thinks of the trusses as "more jewellery-like than High Tech", but neither description captures the complex visual sensuality produced by their asymmetries. In a typically subtle move, the gutter section was positioned to create a shadow that takes the gaze away from what Parry describes as "the big structural fascia".

If the new Opera Terrace structure sets a precedent at Covent Garden, it's to do with how a thoroughly contemporary addition demands fastidious attention to formal design and key details. In this case, the rigour hasn't stopped the practice from producing visual delights via the designs of the trusses and the staircase. As a whole, the architecture meets the Special Covent Garden Purposes requirements relating to conservation of listed fabric, and the protection of the special character of Covent Garden.

But, at the time of writing, one can't help imagining Covent Garden in 20 years' time. The locale has already been flooded with multiple branded shops that have made the district's designation as a Speciality Shopping Centre very debatable. There is also the possibility that commercial demands will eventually prompt the creation of additional spaces and structures.

These have threatened Covent Garden as recently as 1999 when, as the Covent Garden Area Trust's past chairman Geoffrey Holland recalled, "architects instructed by the new managing agents produced major new proposals affecting both the building and the surrounding Piazza. It appeared to be presented as a fully developed design concept, a fait-accompli, accompanied by a very expensive model. It amounted to no less than a radical re-branding and visual redefinition of the building. All sorts of gratuitous embellishments were proposed, including kiosks all around the market square, together with extended outside catering areas. Unnecessary architectural alterations and ornamentation were proposed to the building that would have the effect of making it look more like a typical 1990s shopping mall... These proposals may now have gone away, but it illustrates the risk that is constantly posed by dynamic people trying to make their indelible mark on Covent Garden".

He feared that the relationship between commercial profitability and the "constraints of the planning system" is "patently too loose and too coarse a framework to hold on to the special character of an area like this".

The architecture of the new Opera Terrace structure is neither gratuitous, egregiously dynamic, nor the work of vainglorious architects. Only time will tell if its refined, essentially deferential form remains an influential benchmark for the design quality of future changes at Covent Garden.

10 Fenchurch Avenue

Three aspects of the design – the building's substantial and vivid crown of dichroic glazing, its large and open-to-the-sky roof garden, and innovative use of high-resolution LED screens at street level – will make it unique in the City of London.

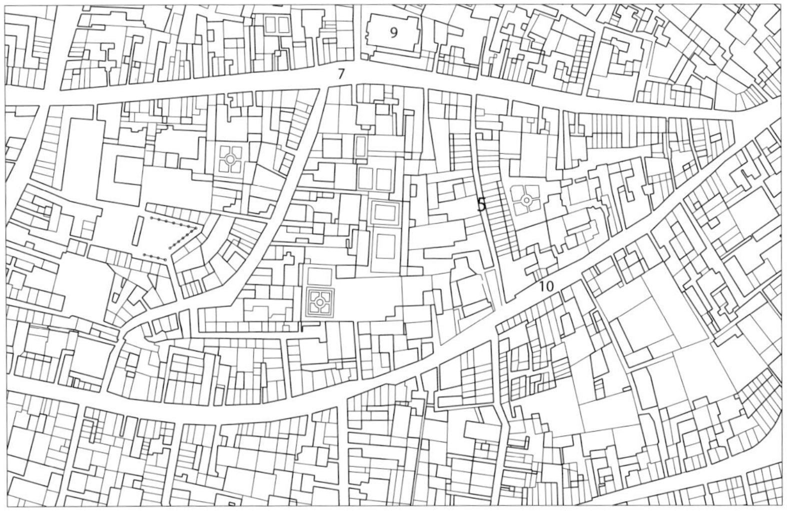

1677

1896

0 25 50 100 200m

1:4000

N

Transformation of the urban grain shown in a sequence of plans based on John Ogilby and William Morgan's *Large and Accurate Map of the City of London* (1677); Ordnance Survey (OS 1896); Corporation of London, *Report of the Improvements and Town Planning... for Post-War reconstruction 1943* (1945); followed by the site plan of Eric Parry Architects' designed 10 Fenchurch Avenue.

To design any building that covers two city blocks obviously presents challenges relating to massing, articulations of plan and elevation, and porosity at ground level. In the City of London's medium-rise sections, it's essential to avoid an over-dominant scheme that would rupture the established character and perspectives of streetscapes whose historic architecture generally takes a rather monumental Victorian or Edwardian form. When these urban conditions are not present – most notably in the heart of the 1980s Broadgate development – unabashedly massive schemes, such as so-called groundscrapers, are deemed acceptable by planners.

By contrast, the mixed-use 10 Fenchurch Avenue building, still under construction as this monograph went to press, confirms the cliché that planning constraints, rather than contextual freedom, tend to produce the most interestingly resolved buildings and spaces. Four aspects of the design – the building's articulation in plan, its substantial and vivid crown of dichroic glazing, its large open-to-the-sky roof garden, and innovative use of high-resolution LED screens internally – will make it unique in the City of London.

The Fenchurch Avenue scheme replaces two blocks, each composed of three compacted buildings of between five and eight storeys. When completed, the new building will add to a metaphor for the evolving architectural physique of the City conjured up by Peter Rees, the Square Mile's chief planning officer until 2014. He referred to 10 Fenchurch Avenue as forming one of the foothills at the southern perimeter of the Eastern Cluster of towers. His take on the design process in relation to the redevelopment of the City since the mid-1990s is instructive.

A Bank of England study in June 2016 noted that more than half the City's growth, serving an additional 85,000 workers by 2027, will be in the Eastern Cluster, and Peter Rees emphasises that it has developed in an ad hoc way. "There was no planning approval for the Cluster," he explains. "It was about finding loopholes in planning constraints." And those loopholes tended to relate to perceived synergies – most obviously, the relationship between tall, densely populated buildings and transport hubs.

Three of the most pressing effects of this densification of the City's core are the increasing amounts of pedestrian traffic moving through the tight mesh of irregularly laid-out streets and passages; the need to provide more retail space; and to reduce congestion caused by delivery vehicles serving the buildings. These situations had an important bearing on the way the scale and porosity of 10 Fenchurch Avenue was dealt with.

1945

2017

sequence of historical plans

1 10 Fenchurch Avenue by Eric Parry Architects
1* Billiter Square
2 Fenchurch Avenue
2* Ironmongers' Hall
3 Lloyd's of London by Rogers Stirk Harbour + Partners
4 Willis Building by Foster + Partners
5 Billiter Street
6 Diamond Tower by Skidmore, Owings & Merrill
7 Leadenhall Street
8 The Leadenhall Building by Rogers Stirk Harbour + Partners
9 St Andrew Undershaft
10 Fenchurch Street

EPA's early-stage design for the scheme, in 2006, proposed a taller building, but the City's planners considered it too high and too Modernist. A revised design in 2008 produced a two-building tableau with a north–south atrium gap through it to accommodate the existing Hogarth Court passage leading to Billiter Square, which together form an ancient right-of-way cutting through the site to connect with the substantial public realm around the Willis Building to the north. The scheme sits on a site which, in the mid-eighteenth century, contained the grandly neoclassicist Ironmongers' Hall, near Billiter Square – "a very handsome, open and airy Place", according to John Strype – and Culver Alley, which was used as a tennis court in the sixteenth century.

The 2008 proposal was approved, but then shelved because of the world financial crash; when the project was resurrected, its redesign had to meet changing market requirements relating to retail space, plant location, the north–south passage through the building, and the roof garden. The revised scheme, which was approved in 2012, has produced a 15-storey building whose 11-storey base segment is clad with engaged, glazed terracotta columns and clear glazing; above this are five more storeys concealed by an envelope of folded, outwardly splayed dichroic glazing – an architectural treatment that is new to the City.

The very top level, which sits above four office floors and an unseen layer of plant across the 14th floor, carries the roof garden landscaped by Latz + Partner. Compared to the original office space in the six buildings across the site, 10 Fenchurch Avenue's 62,762m² of gross office space has increased this volume by 155% and will almost triple the working population across the site to 2,291.

As a contemporary building type, 10 Fenchurch Avenue could be described as an investment silo. But the architecture is an attempt to add something unusual to its physical and commercial heft by bringing together two quite different forms of three-dimensionality, and novel, if not vivacious, uses of colour and reflection.

The design of the 2012 scheme was broadly similar to the 2008 proposal, but had a simpler massing and modelling. "There were still these issues about the bulk of the building in a gently curving streetscape," recalls Rees. "Think of the High in Oxford and the important role of the tree. How could you intervene there without ruining the curve? It's very easy to use a ruler, but that's cheating. I was very concerned about the impact this building was going to have."

The practice's response was to redraw the footprint of the 11-storey base of the building so that it didn't completely cover the site.

Models illustrate an urban discourse with the City planning department over a two-year period.

The new plan has distinct inflections in the elevations facing Fenchurch Street to the south, and Billiter Street to the east. This achieved three things: a reduction in the perceived mass of the building, as seen from the street, and wider areas of pavement. The inflections create more space for pedestrian movement, increasing the pavement widths to a minimum of 3m, and by more than 5m where the inflection angles towards the Hogarth Court retail passage entrance on Fenchurch Street. There is a subtler inflection at the entrance on the north side.

Peter Rees recalls that "we wanted an impressive space contributing to the grain of the city. The previous [proposed] path through the site had a curve in it, so you couldn't see the end. We were looking for something that would provide a degree of reciprocity – for example, off-street servicing to achieve the floorplates, therefore wider at the entrance-points to attract more people in".

The result is a much more distinct main entrance to the building, and a north–south passage which effectively widens Hogarth Court and creates a so-called Banking Hall volume – a substantial two-storey core space, in which walkers can look into the ground-floor retail units facing the passage as they cross between Fenchurch Street and Fenchurch Avenue.

Seen from Fenchurch Street, in particular, the inflected elevations break down the considerable mass of the building effectively and interestingly: the jinking parapet line certainly draws the eye, but not in an overly demanding way. The main inspiration for these inflections, and the sharply modelled corners facing Billiter Street, was Fritz Höger's magnificent Chilehaus in Hamburg, completed in 1924, whose perspectives recall Walter Reimann's sets for the 1920 film *Algol*. The Banking Hall volume at the core of 10 Fenchurch Avenue loosely equates to the Chilehaus's internal hofs, or courtyards.

The design of the top five storeys of 10 Fenchurch Avenue was crucial to the acceptability of the scheme, and subject to intense scrutiny by Rees and his planning team, who suggested that the top segment should take a distinctly different form to the building's base. "We thought the building was uncomfortably high for the site," he recalled. "What was there to compensate for this? A park on the roof, so you could have your site, and open space, plus extra room for pedestrian movement through the City."

But it was not the elevated park, in isolation, that quelled the planners' fundamental concerns about the effect of the unusual bulk of the building on the streetscape. It's the way the elevations of the top four storeys holding up the park cut back at a visually striking angle and come

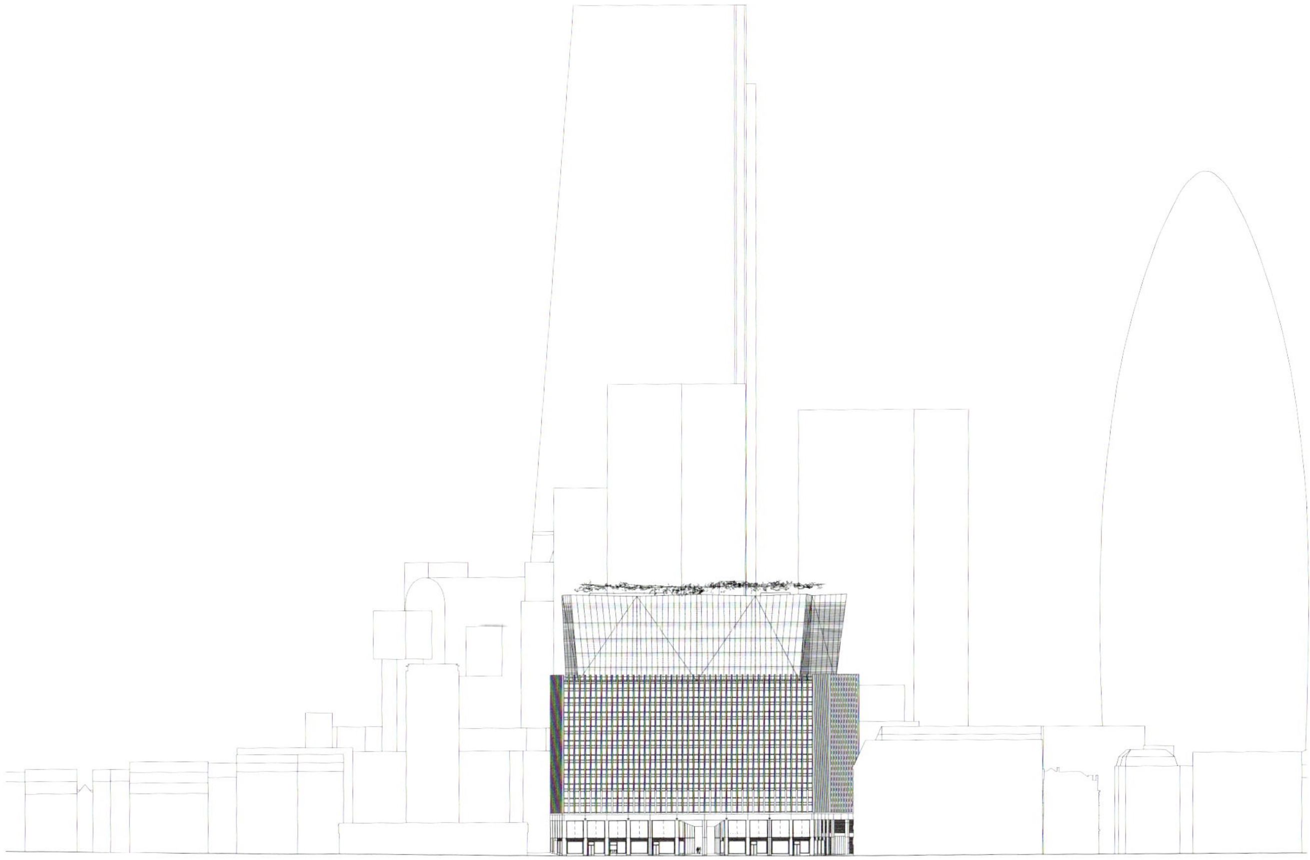

south elevation

1:2000

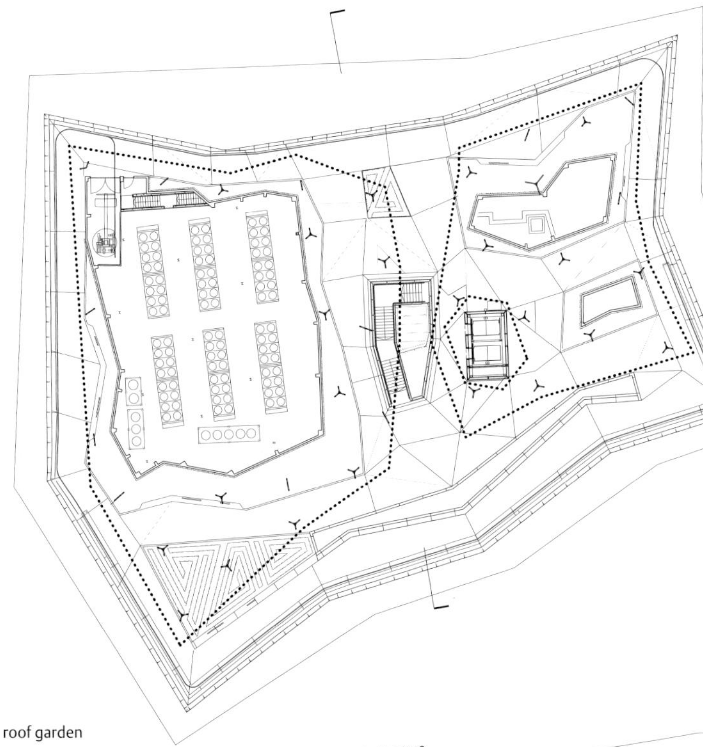

roof garden

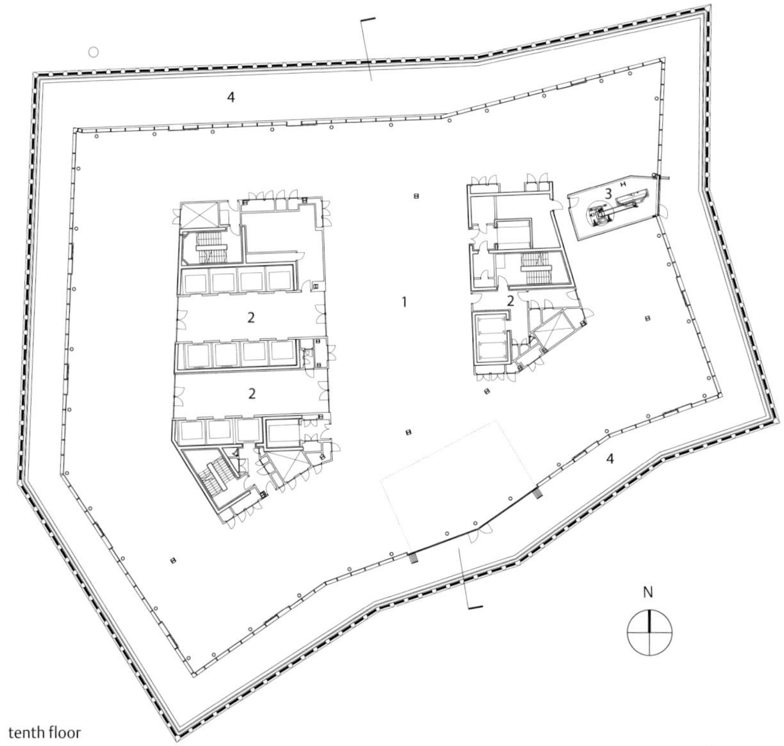

tenth floor

ground floor

mezzanine

1 office
2 lobby
3 building maintenance unit
4 terrace
5 Fenchurch Avenue reception
6 southern reception
7 retail
8 Banking Hall
9 security
10 loading docks
11 management suite
12 switch room
13 generator room

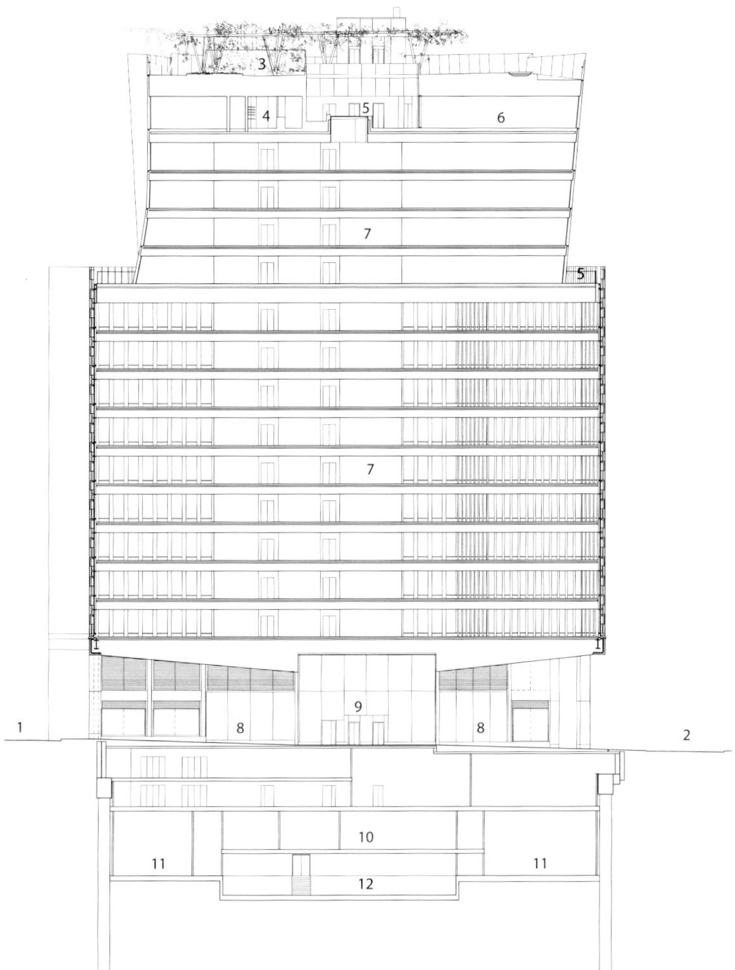

section

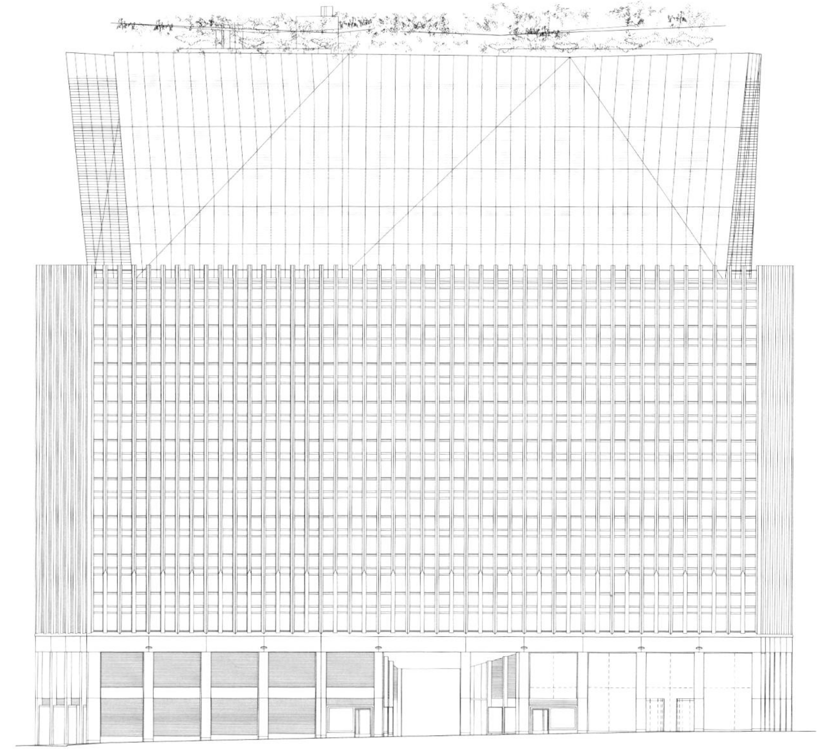

north elevation

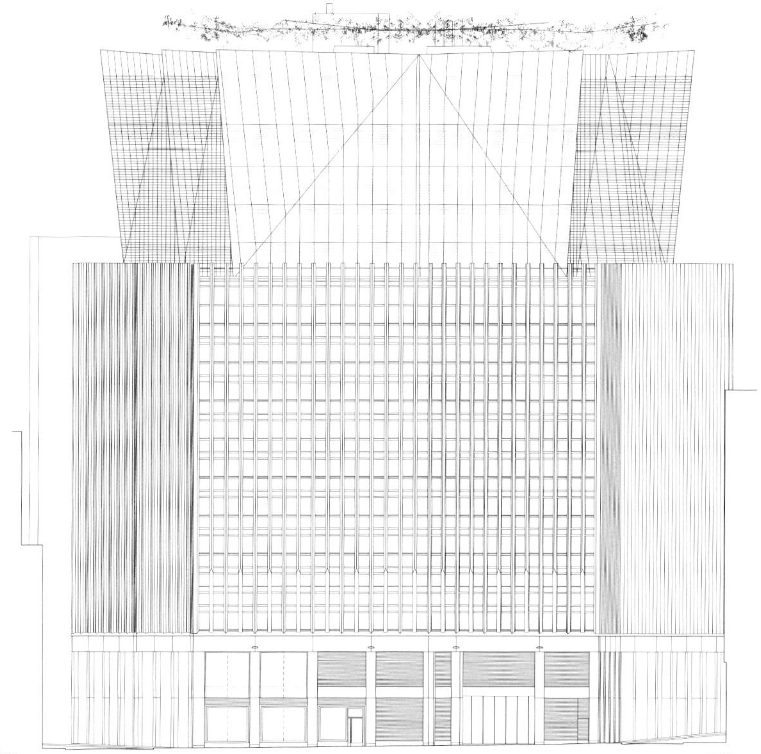

east elevation

1 Fenchurch Avenue
2 Fenchurch Street
3 roof garden
4 kiosk
5 terrace
6 restaurant
7 office
8 ground floor passage
9 atrium
10 basement / mezzanine
11 basement / plant
12 lower basement

0 20m

1:750

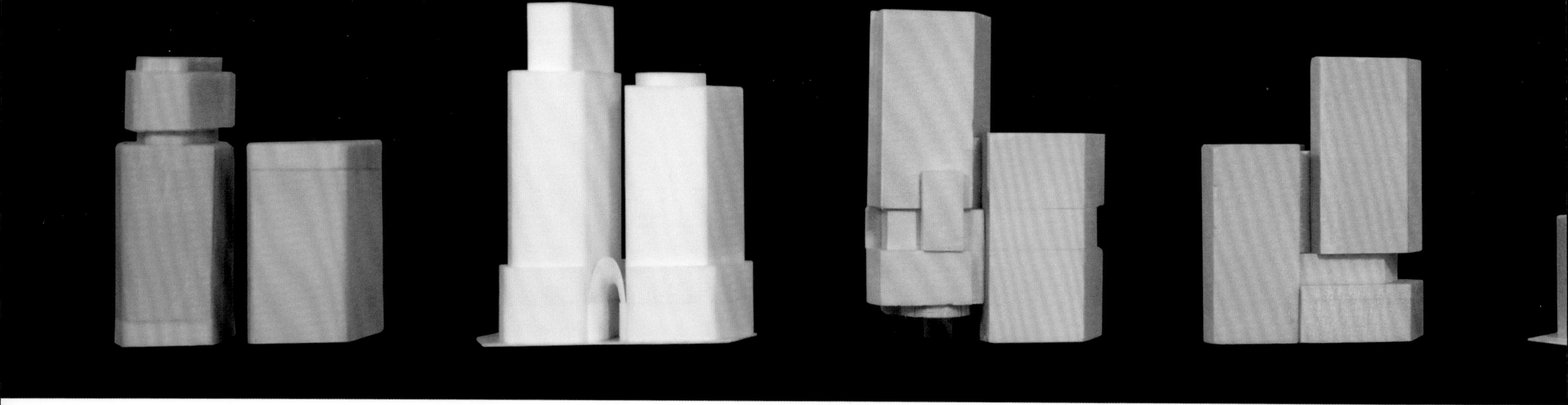

to rest well behind the parapet line of the eleventh storey. Thus, one very big building with three quite different horizon lines: the strongly modelled lintels and columns of the mostly 6m-wide bays of the ground-floor retail volumes, whose frontages were conceived of as vitrines; the geometrically variable notch where the massive, angled sheets of dichroic glass meet the perspectival angles of the parapets; and the differently angled top edges of the glass crown.

The crown is unusual in form and effects. It's encased in a triple-glazed 'climatic' envelope and the surface of the outer layer is treated to produce horizontal stripes of clear and dichroic glass. Looking up from Fenchurch Street or Billiter Street at different times of day, the crown's functional purposes – to clasp a garden above the office floors – is a mystery; it suggests no architectural type, no certainty of weight or degree of transparency; but it does have a playful theatrical quality.

The practice describes the folded glass envelope as a reflective veil, but this is not quite adequate given the range of visual effects the glass produces in different lights. It's tempting to think of the crown as a vast Aalto vase that has been redesigned in the Expressionist manner by Reimann, who also produced the geometric film sets of Robert Wiene's *The Cabinet of Dr Caligari.* The crown is arguably as much an artwork as architecture.

The design of another part of the building's surface – the interface between its structure and the façades of its base from the second to eleventh floors – reveals the practice's long-established concern with the detailing, articulation and sensual qualities of surfaces. The building's steel frame is clad with relatively substantial sand-blasted concrete facings, rather than with a clutter of smaller facings and joints, so that openings can be framed in a clear-cut way. Equal care was taken where the base of the engaged columns meets the profiled cill, which projects beyond the upper edge of the lintel to protect it from drip-marks and weathering.

At the second- and third-storey mezzanine level, the façade carries engaged columns which drop onto a cill of ceramic blocks with a shoe-like profile, which also serves as a cornice to the entablature on the ground floor and protects the lintel above the two-storey retail base. The 'shoes' have a fleeting connection with history: about 130m southwest of Fenchurch Avenue, Rood Lane was, in the sixteenth century, largely occupied by makers of clogs, known then as pattens.

Another surface, the two-storey-high, square soffit of the Bankers Hall at the mid-point of the Hogarth Court passage is as visually surprising as the dichroic crown of the building. The soffit is an 180m^2 high-resolution LED screen, and the intention is to project scenes from the

Sequence of model studies for the massing of 10 Fenchurch Avenue. From the initial approach to the site to the massing, gradually being condensed into one volume, and bringing the passageway to the heart of its urban interior.

rooftop garden – sky, greenery, people – down into the Bankers Hall. The only other significant use of a big civic LED screen in the City of London was as part of Simon Patterson's 2005 public art treatment of Plantation Lane, which runs between Mincing Lane, past St Margaret Pattens, to Rood Lane.

At 10 Fenchurch Avenue, the effect of the screen-cum-soffit is heightened, in both senses, by the fact that the soffits of the two passages leading to the Banking Hall angle down from about 9m high at their street entrance-points, to slightly over 7m just before the 9.1m-high Banking Hall space is reached. Ergo, compression, release, colour visuals overhead; or, as the practice sees it, a twenty-first-century demonstration of Francesco Borromini and Giovanni Maria Bitonto's forced foreshortening of perspective in 1652–3 at the Palazzo Spada, Rome. The proportions of the Banking Hall are historically attuned in other ways – for example, to Soane's Bank of England halls, with something close to Golden Section proportional ratios.

The building's to-floor garden, overlying the plant level, has introduced an oasis to the foothills of the Eastern Cluster, considerably bigger than the planted terraces on the shoulders of the nearby Plantation Place development. Peter Rees offered an interesting aside:

"The plant [in City schemes] has a nasty way of growing at a late stage and popping out of the envelope. The park was a jolly good way of stopping that. A wilful developer and a bad architect will end up with excessive plant on the roof. There were one or two *oohs* and *aahs* in the planning committee about the bulk of the building in the street, but they were very interested in the public space and the landscape on the roof."

Latz's design concept for the garden creates a wide promenade around the perimeter which follows the angles of the inflections in plan, and within it are two types of gardens on a topography composed of low, angular planes. A water feature, individual planting areas and pergolas are angular in plan, and there are greened cubes which conceal the vents of plant chiller units connected to the machinery below.

Rees's remark about the perceived bulk of the building as presented to the planners raises an unexpected perceptual point. EPA's visuals are among the best produced by British architects. For example, the image in the Design and Access Statement, looking westward along Fenchurch Street to the building, would seems to be precisely realistic; so too is the computer-generated view of the north elevation, seen from Fenchurch Avenue.

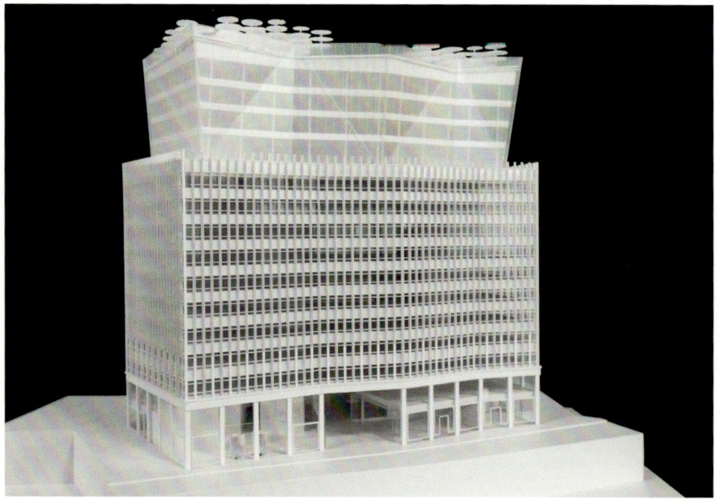

left: Early 1:200 scale model for 10 Fenchurch Avenue from the south.

right: Model for the garden rooftop, Latz + Partner's competition winning concept for an aerial pergola.

opposite: Model of the urban context of 10 Fenchurch Avenue.

However, Rees emphasised, "street views are very difficult to bring off, and models and fly-throughs are not useful. It's difficult to judge buildings in a series of set-piece visuals, and this is an ongoing planning problem". Which suggests that planners and planning committee members, and the architects who present schemes to them, need to be remarkably imaginative to absorb and judge the potential qualities of larger urban schemes in particular.

Even in its unfinished state in 2018, it was clear that the design of 10 Fenchurch Avenue had been a very ambitious exercise in form-making, improvement of urban grain, and greatly increased commercial and retail content; and the perceptual qualities of the building are certainly a first in the City, not least because of planning support. As Peter Rees put it, with his customary brio: "The design was agreed creatively and amicably. I often [in other cases] had the disadvantage of having to sit on my hands, rather than suggest things which might make mediocrity when only awfulness is on offer."

And he added a neat, what-goes-around-comes-around coda. "In 1985, developers would come in and say: 'Retail? That's crazy!' Broadgate was the early exemplar of making mixed-use places a destination, and also No. 1 Poultry, albeit with a much more painful birth, where retail and ground and lower ground were connected. Eric Parry's building is doing the same thing."

The original English Heritage Grade II* listing description of Stirling and Wilford's No. 1 Poultry – which Rees was centrally involved in approving – offered unreserved praise for the architecture's "exemplary urban contextualism in a complex spatial inter-relationship of mixed-use office and retail accommodation, a public right of way, roof garden and restaurant, entrance to the underground station and public house, where the generosity of the public realm is exceptional for a speculative scheme".

If we excise the pub and Underground station, that description parallels 10 Fenchurch Avenue's contribution to the City's fabric. If the architecture is, in two or three ways, surprisingly creative, it was obviously never a mystery to the planner who ushered the scheme into the dichroically refracted light of day.

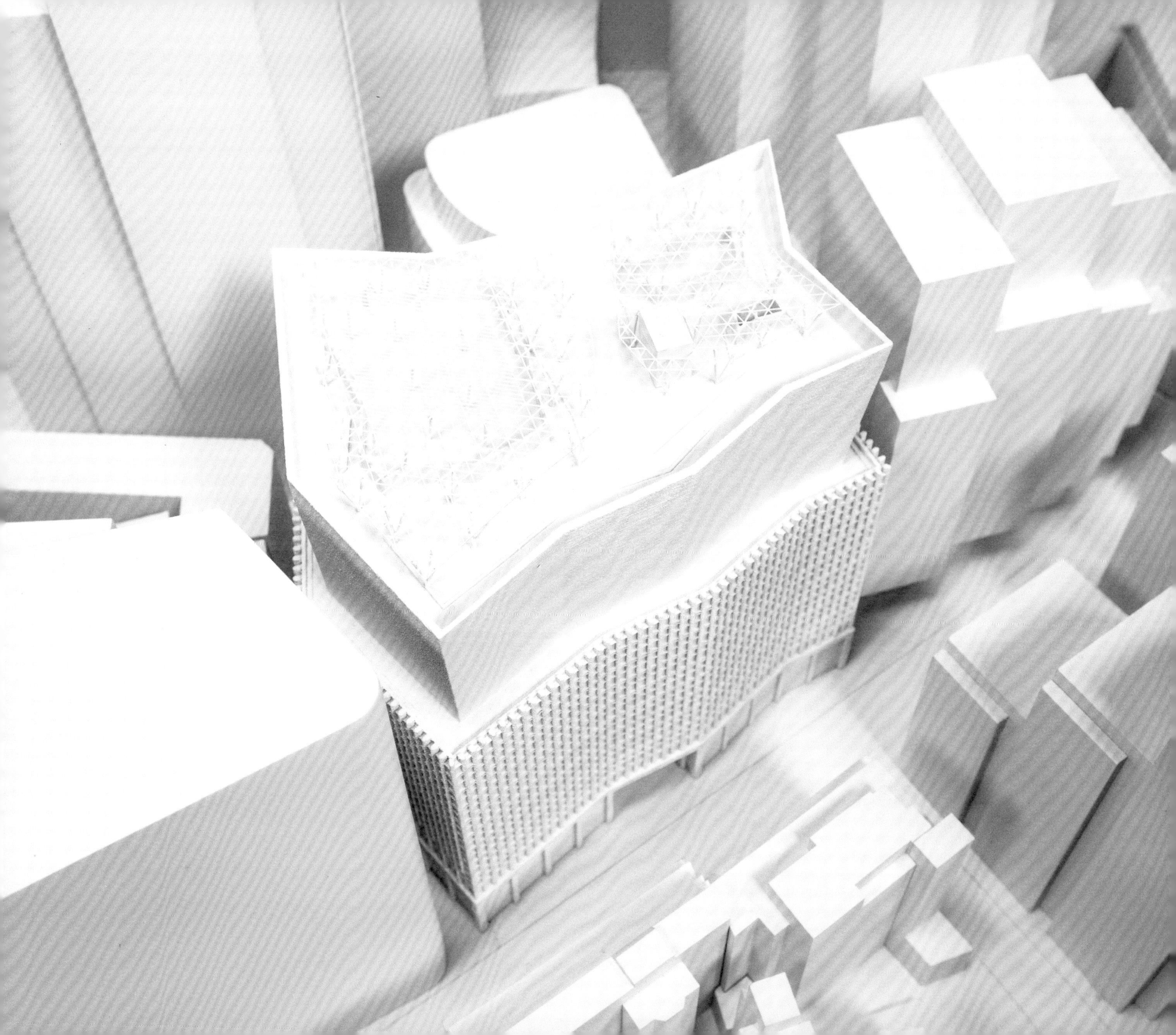

Projects Summary

4 Pancras Square

The development at King's Cross is one of the most significant in London. The site is located to the north of the existing King's Cross railway station, adjacent to St Pancras International on brownfield land formerly used for railway yards and gas containers. The building consists of ten storeys of office above ground, office reception and retail at ground and lower ground floor, with two levels of basement. A Vierendeel frame at the first floor allows the transfer of structure to widely spaced ground-floor pillars that open up the ground floor for the main entrance to the building reception. The façade is in weathering steel punctuated by white glazed ceramic *brise-soleils*. The expressed steel recalls the heroic engineering of the industrial revolution and the railways that enabled the expansion of London. The glazed ceramic was the material that was used in the nineteenth century and in early Modernist architecture in response to the poluted environment of the European cities at the time. The natural patination of the steel absorbs light in contrast to the glazed surface of the ceramic that reflects light.

C: King's Cross Central Ltd Partnership
Employer's Agent: Gardiner & Theobald
SE: AKT II
M&E: Sweco
QS: Gardiner & Theobald
LA: Todd Longstaffe-Gowan
A: EP, RK, RD, MM, JT, TA, MW
Date: 2003–2017

Wells Cathedral School

Our project for Cedars Hall won the RIBA South West Award 2017 and the RIBA South West Building of the Year 2017. This new music facility at Wells Cathedral School, maintains important views to Wells Cathedral as well as across the garden and the grounds. The new building contains a technically excellent recital hall and interconnected flexible spaces for teaching, rehearsing, performing and recording. The recital hall can accommodate an audience of over 400, allowing natural light to fill the space during the day while becoming a lantern in the landscape during the evening. The stage, seating and acoustic wall panels within the hall can be adapted for various layouts with differing acoustic qualities. On the upper floor there are purpose-designed spaces for Woodwind and Percussion, each with glazed observation rooms. An enabling works' project saw the completion of a new sports pavilion and maintenance facility in 2015, which form a family of buildings of similar materials around the grounds. Cedars Hall is linked to Cedars, the Grade II* listed Georgian house and administrative centre of the School.

C: Wells Cathedral School
PM: QSPM
SE: Momentum Consulting Engineers
Acoustic engineer: Gillieron Scott Acoustic Design
M&E: Buro Happold
QS: QSPM Consultants
LA: Land Use Consultants
A: EP, TL*, JM, PBA, CK
Date: 2007-2017

East Village, London

We were commissioned to design one of the residential plots of the 2012 London Olympics Athletes' Village. During the Olympics, one-tenth of the athletes for the whole Games stayed in our buildings. After 2012, the buildings were also adapted to provide a mixed-market and affordable-tenure residential development accommodating 281 units and some retail use. Working within the masterplanning brief, our design response included carefully modulated façades, granting them animation, depth and solidity, as a space of transition to the domestic interior. The generous balconies – featuring strong paintings by Eric Parry – colour the façades. As an urban block, the buildings enclose a large landscaped garden as a distributing space, whose natural light and green treetops are in constant dialogue with the architecture. Now known as East Village, this thriving new place in London enjoys a growing active community.

C: John Sisk & Son and Lendlease
SE: AKT II
M&E: Hilson Moran
QS: Site Engineering Surveys
LA: Applied Landscape Design, Kinnear Landscape Architects, Macfarlane Wilder, Vogt Landschaftsarchitekten
A: EP, NJ, TL, LH, ARM, BD, LB, CK, CLK, KS
Date: 2008–2012

One Eagle Place, Piccadilly

The Crown Estate has given us an extraordinary opportunity to renew an urban block at the very heart of Piccadilly. One Eagle Place, Piccadilly is the Estate's first major project in its extensive St James's portfolio. Straddling two Conservation Areas – Regent Street and St James's – this initiative allowed us to replace three former buildings with both conserved and new façades. The block includes a new building and façade in ceramic, utilising the sculptural and cast qualities of clay and polychromatic glazes. Renowned artist Richard Deacon was invited to undertake the commission of the sculptural cornice that grows out of the body of the building. Also on Jermyn Street, a new building and stone façade is augmented by a vigorous stone sculpture by Stephen Cox at the corner with Eagle Place. While the site itself called for a mixed-use project, this part of our intervention harbours an array of modern retail and work spaces perhaps unsuspected from the street, but discreetly contributing to the rich architectural experience of daily work and shopping within the thriving pace of historic Piccadilly.

C: The Crown Estate
Development Manager: Stanhope plc
SE: Waterman Partnership
M&E: Mecserve
QS: Gardiner & Theobald
A: EP, NJ, MC, LB, CT, GGP, JF, JH, WA, JE
Date: 2008–2013

15 and 20 Jermyn Street

As part of our project for One Eagle Place, we have designed two residential buildings at 15 and 20 Jermyn Street. Within the shell of a monumental 1920s office building at the corner of Lower Regent Street and Jermyn Street, we have created a mix of three-bedroom, two-bedroom and one-bedroom apartments that are fully furnished and decorated for the rental market. With a great location looking over Piccadilly Circus, the airy loft-like spaces of 15 Jermyn Street are a fresh arrival on the London scene. In 20 Jermyn Street, we created behind a retained Edwardian residential façade five lateral apartments for the sales market. The design strategy follows the same pattern as the elegant dress code which is side-by-side with made-to-measure and mass production, of exclusiveness and sober fitness for purpose.

C: The Crown Estate
Development Manager: Stanhope plc
SE: Waterman Partnership
M&E: Mecserve
QS: Gardiner & Theobald
A: EP, NJ, MC*, RC, GGP, JFR, LB, WA, RC, CK
Date: 2008–2015

5–7 St Helen's Place

5–7 St Helen's Place received the RIBA London Award 2017. St Helen's Place is a privately owned road with access through a grand opening with imposing Doric columns. The urban ensemble is faced with Portland stone and topped with mansard roofs. Located in the heart of the City of London, the area is dominated by offices, with supporting retail facilities and other City of London institutions, such as churches and livery headquarters. Our project consisted of rental offices and new fit-for-purpose accommodation for the Leathersellers' Company. The new building incorporates a retained façade to the north, and a new ceramic-clad façade to the south, looking over the old St Helen's Church. The building achieved a BREEAM sustainability rating of 'very good'.

C: The Leathersellers' Company and Great Portland Estates
PM: Brookfield Europe and Gardiner & Theobald
SE: Alan Baxter and Robert Bird Group
Façade engineer: Arup Façades
M&E: Hilson Moran and Partnership Ltd
QS: Aecom
A: EP, RK, MC, RC, CB, SO, RLL, BF
Date: 2009–2015

26 Albemarle Street

26 Albemarle Street houses a handful of the most sought-after apartments in London. With a 23m-wide street frontage opposite the Royal Institution, the building was constructed in 1905 when it was probably intended for residential use, although it was taken for offices until recently. Our proposal included the full retention of the street façade with only minor alterations. The works to the rear façade were more substantial and took into account contemporary requirements such as the provision of outdoor spaces and the enlargement of window areas. The interior design concept was also fully developed by Eric Parry Architects. Each apartment boasts a simple and sophisticated layout that provides a balance between entertaining space and the intimacy of domestic life. The roof was extended to a mansard roof to create a duplex penthouse with large atelier windows onto the street and landscaped terraces to the interior.

C: Albemarle Street Holdings
PM and QS: Jackson Coles
SE: Heyne Tillett Steel
M&E: Peter Deer and Associates
A: EP, RK, MC, TL, LB, WA, KS, RLL
Date: 2010–2014

Brighton College Music School

The new Music School for Brighton College is to the north of Sir George Gilbert Scott's Grade II listed Main School Building, in an area of the campus that had become congested by accretive infill buildings. Our response was to remove the infill and expose the central gable of Scott's principal school range. The Music School – and forthcoming Drama School in Phase 2 – are arrayed either side of the axis set up by Scott's buildings and will be connected by a shared foyer space. The design takes advantage of a 3m level difference between the Scott Building and the playing field, and provides new performance and teaching spaces, plus a new extension to the historic Dining Hall and improved circulation. The new Sarah Abraham Recital Hall looks over the playing fields, with a steeply pitched roof that echoes the gables of the adjacent Scott buildings. The Recital Hall can seat an audience of up to 195, and provides a flexible retractable seating system, integrated stage lighting and a variable acoustic system in the wall linings. Phase 2 is imminent.

C: Brighton College
SE: Momentum Consulting Engineers
Acoustic engineer: Gillieron Scott
M&E: Skelly & Couch
Theatre Consultants: Charcoalblue
QS: Academy Consulting
A: EP, NJ, TL, CH, DL, JM, CHD, LV, GGP, KS, CK, PBA
Date: 2010–2016

The Leathersellers' Hall

The Worshipful Company of Leathersellers at 5–7 St Helen's Place is one of London's oldest livery companies founded by Royal Charter in 1444. Eric Parry Architects were chosen to design the seventh hall following a competitive interview in 2010. The three main rooms are the Court Room, the Reception Room and the Stair Hall. The Court Room, with walls finished in American black walnut, sits a full court of 29. The Reception Room features a clear and indigo drawn glass sculpture by Dale Chihuly. The Stair Hall reuses finely crafted scagliola pilasters, a traditional imitation of marble in pigmented plaster originally from the sixth hall. The stair is a complex spiral ovoid structure in a continuous peel of reinforced concrete. Set into the leather wall are a number of vitrines with artefacts from the Company's rich archive, which can also be found along the entrance and reception rooms. The Dining Hall hosts 120 guests seated in three rows and has a clerestory with views to the church wall above. The artist Victoria Crowe was appointed to design the 42m-long tapestry, whose scale and colour overlies the interior.

C: The Leathersellers' Company
PM: Gardiner & Theobald
SE: Price & Myers
M&E: ChapmanBDSP
A: EP, RK, CB, ASM, RLL
Date: 2010–2016

7–8 St James's Square

At the heart of St James's in London, our design for 8 St James's Square and Apple Tree Yard replaced an over-scaled inter-war office building and incorporates a new basement structure beneath the adjoining building. Our redevelopment provides 65,500ft² of office space around a new private courtyard garden to 7 St James's Square, a fine Listed townhouse designed by Sir Edwin Lutyens in 1911 and now reinstated to a grand townhouse. The completed development is a carefully crafted ensemble of parts that responds to the surrounding urban context. This is especially visible in the massing and treatment of the façades, culminating in the hand-crafted oriel window looking over Apple Tree Yard. The memory of the site is explicitly celebrated with an epigraph to Sir Edwin Lutyens as the place where he laid out his plans for New Delhi. The corner is punctuated by a sculpture in Indian granite, the work of sculptor Stephen Cox, which brings a timeless quality to the everyday of the street.

C: Kish Twelve
PM: GVA Second London Wall
SE: Price & Myers
M&E: Mecserve
QS: Gleeds
A: EP, RK, RD, JSC, EH, ZF, JD
Date: 2010-2015

St John's Waterloo

We were commissioned in 2010 to undertake a feasibility study on the entire site and find how its currently under-used building and churchyard could best be used for the local community. A masterplan included a dramatically improved worship space, better connectivity to the Crypt which will be re-arranged to provide more community uses, plus new below-ground facilities including a double-height Community Hall and Chapel. A Community Café would stand as a pavilion in the Churchyard. This first phase is contained within the existing footprint of the Church and seeks to improve accessibility and use of the Church and Crypt. The intention is return to the Georgian clarity of the entrance sequence and enable a clear line of sight from outside the Church into the east end. We propose a generous entrance area, with a new lift and a stair within a foyer created by a glazed screen under the west gallery. New galleries are proposed in the Church, to mediate natural light and lead the eye to the east end, as well as increase the capacity and afford opportunities for greater choral and theatrical uses of the Church.

C: The Parish of St John with St Andrew Waterloo
SE: Alan Baxter
Acoustic engineer: Gillieron Scott
M&E: Skelly & Couch
QS: Academy Consulting
A: EP, TL, PBA, CD, JM, KS
Date: 2010–ongoing

10 Fenchurch Avenue

10 Fenchurch Avenue is a development at the scale of a city block. Following a transfer of ownership, the initial scheme from 2007 was revised and received approval. It retains three distinct sections: a permeable base with a new public passageway; a main body of nine storeys of high-quality office space; and an upper setback with four office floors with a restaurant and a publicly accessible roof garden above. The specific geometry of the site informed the strong, faceted massing. The vertical, ceramic fins along with a series of horizontal *brise-soleils* provide depth and solar shading. The crystalline form of the upper fully glazed floors reflect the surrounding buildings and sky. The roof garden has a new topography of a gently folding landscape, a water feature and green cubes which enclose the plant facilities below. Encircling its high-level 'wisteria canopy' a continuous perimeter walk gives vistas of the London skyline in all four directions. A LED screen soffit at the centre of the pedestrian passageway will show imagery of the roof garden above.

C: Generali Saxon Land Development Company
PM: Core
SE: Arup
M&E: Waterman Group
QS: Gleeds
LA: Latz + Partner
A: EP, NJ* (2), PBA* (3), CT, CK, DP, PF, SP, CSL, ED, ELP, KS, CD, RL, RD, KS, CD, RK* (1), DL, ARM, SF, NA
Date: 2006–2018

Vicarage Gate House

Vicarage Gate House is at the junction of Vicarage Gate and Palace Garden Terrace. The main entrance to the development reception is from Vicarage Gate, with a broad landscaped courtyard to the rear. The building massing and façade respond to the existing context. The north elevation complements the neighbouring terraces with traditional masonry brickwork; horizontal precast banding, purpose-made punched windows and a zinc mansard at roof level. A ceramic bay with curved windows celebrates the complexity of the building's location. To the east, a stepped terrace provides residents with external spaces. The south elevation consists of brick piers and full-height picture windows. There are bespoke balconies which offer private amenity spaces for each of the apartments. Internally the brief required the apartments to be generously proportioned, planned for ease of living, in line with Code for Sustainable Homes Level 4. Planning consent was granted in February 2013. Practical completion was achieved in April 2016 with tenants taking occupation.

C: Vicarage Gate Limited
PM: Northacre
SE: Conisbee
QS: Hampton
Interior designers: Forme Architecture
Building Service Engineer: Mecserve
A: EP, JO, BD*, AM, AW, EF, ARM, SF
Date: 2011–2016

The Welding Institute

We were commissioned to design the masterplan for Granta Park in the mid-1990s by the then owner The Welding Institute (TWI) in partnership with MEPC. Throughout the subsequent 15 years, the site was transformed from arable farmland to the highly successful science park it is today. Following the recent completion of a restructuring of the ownership of Granta Park, TWI appointed the practice in 2011 to transform their site and create accommodation suited to their growing organisation. This has led to the creation of three new buildings to house amenities, a NSIRC Education Facility and an Engineering Hall including heavy and light engineering laboratories and office space. The design concept has been to develop a building form and material quality which is sympathetic to the quality of its surrounding landscape. In 2015 we were commissioned to create a new landscaped park that links the listed Abington Hall and Repton landscape scheme at its foreground with the new crescent-like pavilion style buildings by a 400m stretch of new beautiful landscaping. The scheme received planning approval in 2015 and is ongoing.

C: The Welding Institute
PM and SE: Glanville Consultants
M&E: Hoare Lea
QS: Aecom
LA: Land Use Consultants/Josephine Morrison
A: EP, NJ, LH, ARM, CT, PF,BL, LB, JIS, DG, KP
Date: 2011–ongoing

Venice Biennale Exhibition

The 13th edition of the Venice Biennale, under the title Common Ground, was directed by David Chipperfield and counted on the participation of a 164 architectural practices from all over the world. Our own work was on show in the exhibition Inhabitable Models and included large-sized models of the façade of One Eagle Place, Piccadilly and Richard Deacon's cornice, as well as wooden models St Martin-in-the-Fields and a model of Shirazeh Houshiary's "East Window".

C: Venice Biennale
A: EP, JIS, RLL
Date: 2012

The Charterhouse

The Charterhouse is a historic complex centred on a fourteenth-century Carthusian Monastery founded by Sir Walter de Manny on what was originally the site for a Black Death burial ground. Following the Dissolution in the sixteenth century, the London Charterhouse became a mansion house and a charitable school, and, in the seventeenth century, an almshouse under the charity of Thomas Sutton. While the Charterhouse School moved to Surrey in the nineteenth century, Sutton's Hospital or almshouse remains today the primary occupant of the site. In 1941, the site was bombed and the extensive damage repaired throughout the 1950s to the designs of Seely and Paget. Recently, the buildings and grounds have been opened to the public to support the almshouse, and in collaboration with Todd Longstaffe-Gowan Landscape Architects, a newly landscaped Charterhouse Square now leads to a public entrance in Chapel Court. Learning and exhibition facilities occupy refurbished rooms around the periphery of the Court.

C: Sutton's Hospital in Charterhouse
PM and QS: Jackson Coles
SE: Alan Baxter Associates
M&E: Venables Associates
LA: Todd Longstaffe-Gowan
Conservation Architect: Richard Griffiths Architects
A: EP, CH, RP, EVP, MW, TW
Date: 2012–2017

1–9 Seymour Street

The site at 1–9 Seymour Street and 6–16 Bryanston Street is owned as a freehold by the Portman Estate. A 1970s building for the Metropolitan Police Authority replaced original Georgian townhouses. It has been recently vacated as part of its consolidation programme within Central London. The site is within the Core Central Activities Zone, the Portman Estate Conservation Area and the Baker Street Quarter Business Improvement District. The project has two aspects: Seymour Street to the north and Bryanston Street to the south.

The Portman Estate aims to redevelop with a mix of residential, retail and office space that with replacement social and community use will provide an improved community asset in their estate.

C: The Portman Estate
PM: GVA Second London Wall
SE: Furness Partnership
QS: Alinea
LA: Garden Makers
A: EP, RK, LH, RC, LM, HT, KS, LB, LMB, RRP, BF, EF
Date: 2012-ongoing

AJ Kiosk

Kiosk was a design event challenging Britain's best architects to create a contemporary kiosk for London. We were one of six architecture studios invited to participate. All six kiosk designs were presented in an exhibition produced with the Building Centre in London and published in a special issue of the *Architects' Journal* dedicated to kiosk design and the use of ceramics in architecture.

C: The Architects' Journal and Turkishceramics
A: EP, AM, EH
Date: 2013-2014

111 Buckingham Palace Road

111 Buckingham Palace Road is part of the Over Site Development (OSD) created in the 1980s near the southwest platforms of Victoria railway station. The large office floors are above the Plaza Shopping Centre. The office entrance is on the east side of Buckingham Palace Road directly south of the Grosvenor Hotel. The office building has a long façade of mirrored glass cladding that returns onto Eccleston Bridge to the south and to the raised service and taxi court to the east side. Our proposal only concerns the ground floor office entrance and its enclosure. The brief is to improve the presence of the office building on Buckingham Palace Road as well as the tenants' and visitors' arrival experience. This is proposed by enlarging the reception and bringing it forward to enclose the forecourt. The site was originally the parcel office for the station with access from the street for vans and a frontage onto the station concourse behind; and the proposed work will increase these back-of-house areas to the line of the new east wall to the reception. The removal of vehicular crossovers will allow improvements to the pavement and quality of public realm.

C: Kennedy Wilson
PM: Burnley Wilson Fish
SE: Price & Myers
M&E: Blyth and Blyth
QS: Burnley Wilson Fish and Gleeds
A: EP, RK, BD, MV, TS
Date: 2013–2016

Cambridge Assessment

We were appointed to design the new headquarters for Cambridge Assessment in 2013, following a limited competition. Established over 150 years ago, Cambridge Assessment operates and manages the University's three exam boards and carries out academic and operational research on assessment in education. The development provides approximately 350,000ft² (NIA) of new office and amenity space for 3000 people with 1325 bicycle spaces. Our vision is an inspiring new group of connected buildings, ranging from four to five storeys in height. These are depth fingers set around raised landscaped podia with a central arrival court and garden. The façades are formed of bands of hand-set brickwork in lime mortar, combined with light-coloured precast concrete elements, and include a visual arts intervention by Vong Phaophanit and Claire Oboussier. A tower is located along the railway, marking the site from the railway and busway approach into Cambridge station. The tower will not compete with the existing taller landmark buildings in Cambridge. The building will be highly sustainable and is targeting a DEC A rating when in occupation.

C: Cambridge Assessment
PM: Turner and Townsend
SE: Ramboll
M&E: Max Fordham
QS: Aecom
LA: Grant Associates
A: EP, NJ, TN, CT, EH, MJ, RP, WW, MV, CL
Date: 2013–2018

29 Great Peter Street

29 Great Peter Street is to the north of Smith Square, and to the east the street leads to the generous and mature landscaped edge of the River Thames and Victoria Tower Gardens. With existing office space on all floors above ground level and amenity spaces in the basement level, our proposal was to change the office spaces to a residential use. The street façades were to be fully retained with only minor repair and refurbishment, and the mansard roof extended and raised to its original height. All dormer windows would be rebuilt to a similar scale and finish. Traditional and reclaimed building materials were to be employed following Conservation Area guidance. Energy consumption and green credentials were to be improved with a target to achieve a BREEAM rating of 'very good'.

C: Aberdeen Asset Management
SE: Curtins Consulting
M&E: ChapmanBDSP
QS: Gardiner & Theobald
A: EP, JS, CK, LM, LB
Date: 2013

14–15 Hanover Square

The Hanover Square site is bound by the world-famous but piecemeal irregular fronts of Oxford Street to the north, Harewood Place to the east and Hanover Square to the south. This historical block, once residential in scale, has been gradually adapted and the original mass and rhythm of the south elevations lost over the last century. Today, floor areas are inefficient and with multiple occupancy, a collection of existing cores, varied floor levels and constrained floor-to-floor heights; and the existing buildings do not lend themselves easily to modern retail and office requirements that form part of the brief. We have developed a feasibility study that aims to retain the best parts of the existing buildings and replace the weaker parts with new interventions in a combination of new and old.

C: M&G
SE: AKT II
M&E: Hilson Moran
QS: Gardiner & Theobald
A: EP, NJ, CB, WW, CRD
Date: 2013

King's College School, Wimbledon – Q Block

Eric Parry Architects won an invited competition in 2013 for the refurbishment and extension of an existing 1960s building for King's College School, Wimbledon. The brief called for a refurbishment of Q Block, the extension of the Dining Hall into the courtyard and the creation of more classrooms on the roof. It was understood the project would need to be phased due to its importance in the day-to-day functioning of the school. We therefore looked at various ways of phasing the works, to enable the school to maintain continuous use of the Dining Hall and minimise disruption to the use of classrooms. The scope also included external works to two adjacent courtyards and new façades onto Wimbledon Common. The extension of the dining room and kitchens was undertaken over the summer of 2015, opening on the first day of the Autumn Term. The Hall was stripped back to reveal RC coffers where bespoke lighting rafts were then placed. The walls were lined with acoustically treated joinery housing cupboards and sliding folding screens to enable the space to be divided for assemblies and evening functions. New servery counters, tables and chairs completed the fit-out.

C: King's College School
SE: Chris Kendall Associates
M&E: Norman Bromley Partnership LLP
QS: Wenham O'Brien Limited
A: EP, TL, DL, CD, MW, JM
Date: 2013–2015

One Liverpool Street

Today the building at One Liverpool Street is between the ongoing infrastructure works, the excavations for the Crossrail project for Liverpool Street Station and the ventilation shaft on the adjacent Blomfield Street site. The existing building looks forlorn and is mostly emptied, but once the works are completed it will directly face the new Liverpool Street Crossrail entrance across a new public space. The joint venture provides the opportunity for the existing building to be demolished and replaced with an office building that through structural engineering solutions can deliver a quality and quantum of Grade A office space not possible on the individual sites. At the heart of the financial district, our proposed office building will provide a more fitting civic backdrop to the proposed new public space and relate to the grand architecture of Liverpool Street station. The site's proximity to the transport hub allows for further densification of commercial uses through animated frontages with both retail and office entrances and the continued improvement of the public realm.

C: Aviva
PM: WT Partnership
SE: Mott MacDonald
M&E: Aecom
QS: Gardiner & Theobald
A: EP, RK, JS, BD, MJ, CK, LM, CD, JFR, DC, JT, SF, GW, ASM, SP, EF, KP, RL, LG, BT
Date: 2013–ongoing

The Opera Terrace, Covent Garden

The Opera Terrace project creates a unique contemporary dining space which celebrates the architecture of the Grade II* Covent Garden Market Building. The site occupies the first-floor terrace facing the opera and areas in the corner pavilions and the north, south and central ranges overlooking the market halls. A conservatory enclosure dating from the 1980s was replaced with a new glass-and-steel structure, designed to reveal the central pediment of the 1820s building with its Coade stone statues of Flora and Pomona by RW Sievier. The roof is made up of insulated double-glazed units and incorporates double-curved panels and external solar blinds. The new electro-polished bead-blasted trusses sit on a steel transfer deck which in turn is supported by the original stone columns and beams. Other interventions include the remodelling of the corner pavilion to create a ground-floor entrance with a new spiral stair and lift, and the infilling of an area in the Central Avenue to create front and back kitchen spaces for the restaurant.

C: Covent Garden London (Capital & Counties Properties plc)
PM: Gardiner & Theobald
SE: Eckersley O'Callaghan
M&E: Skelly & Couch
QS: Turner & Townsend
Conservation Architect: Donald Insall Associates
A: EP, CH, DG, FW, MP, GGP
Date: 2013–2017

Eaton Square

The Eaton Square property is in a Grade II* listed building within the City of Westminster Belgravia Conservation Area, originally built as grand townhouses by Cubitt in the 1830s. Eric Parry Architects have set out to create a contemporary residence with an improved relationship to the rear garden, all the while respecting its architectural heritage. The two levels are connected via an elliptical stair, and collaboration with the lighting designer Ingo Maurer looked to define the image and experience of the approach to the staircase. The proposed alterations to the existing structure involved removing load-bearing walls at lower ground to help create a large family room. The aim was to re-establish the elegance of the original house, whilst simultaneously maximising natural light with an extension that is sympathetic to the existing building.

C: Private Client
SE: Michael Hadi Associates
M&E: Ralph T. King & Associates
QS: Corrigan Gore & Street
LA: Arne Maynard Garden Design
A: EP, CH* (1), SF* (2), TJ, EF, JH, LO, NV
Date: 2013–2018

British School in Rome Summer Exhibition

The British School in Rome Summer Exhibition 2014 counted on the participation of Eric Parry Architects' architectural work with exhibits on display in the British School's entry room. The hanging was designed by Eric Parry, and featured the projects of Finsbury Square and One Eagle Place in particular. With hand drawings by Eric Parry, the exhibition room also included photography by Hélène Binet and Dirk Lindner as well as scale models of Richard Deacon's sculptural work.

C: British School in Rome
A: EP, AM, JP
Date: 2014

Royal Academy Summer Exhibition

The Royal Academy Summer Exhibition 2014 was designed by Eric Parry, and curated by Eric Parry and Richard MacCormac. Held from 9 June to 17 August 2014 in the RA Gallery 6 dedicated to architecture, the exhibition included contemporary architects, artists and scholars. The selected pieces – mostly drawings, but also some models – focused on the design process itself, visually anticipated and made possible by the act of drawing.

C: Royal Academy of Arts
A: EP, JP
Date: 2014

Carlton House Terrace

A refurbishment of a Grade I Listed Regency townhouse off the Mall in Central London into Carmignac Gestion's London headquarters building, reworking of the main stair to the lower ground floor and the introduction of a winter garden at ground floor level. The proposal includes conference and meeting rooms with private and general office spaces, breakout spaces and a sunroom / terrace at roof level. An apartment is proposed at level 2 and a staff / studio room at level 3. The scheme will also house artworks from the Carmignac Foundation.

C: Carmignac
PM and QS: Gardiner & Theobald
SE: The Morton Partnership
M&E: Hoare Lea
A: EP, RK, TS, ASM, EH, MJ, SO, CRD, RLL
Date: 2014–2018

1–3 Grosvenor Square

Following an invited competition, the Lodha Group (a major Indian developer) appointed Eric Parry Architects to lead on the design of their flagship London development at No. 1 Grosvenor Square. With the relocation of a number of diplomatic missions, the scheme reflects the changing nature of the Mayfair area, reverting the site to residential use, and repositions Grosvenor Square as the premiere Mayfair residential square. After detailed consultations with Westminster City Council and The Grosvenor Estate, a strategy of reconstruction has been developed by carefully recording and dismantling the most significant façades. Subsequent reconstruction enables minor adjustments to the building's hierarchy, sensitive contemporary interventions and the provision of basement car parking, residential amenities and enables structural acoustic isolation and enhanced building envelope performance.

C: Lodha Group
Interiors: Yabu Pushelberg
Executive Architect: EPR
Façade Engineer: Arup
SE: AKT II
M&E: Hoare Lea
QS: Arcadis
LA: Chris Blandford Associates
A: EP, RK, MC, JS, JSC, RSW, AR, VG, RLL, KB, KP, AM, MIP, SP, SO, IS, ZP
Date: 2014–ongoing

City Temple Quarter

The site is in a unique location on the historic Holborn Viaduct, currently occupied by two buildings: Morley House, a 1980s mixed-use office, education and retail building; and also City Temple, a Grade II listed church. Our proposal includes the demolition and redevelopment of Morley House into a 191-bedroom hotel with restaurant, bar, spa and conference facilities, and the hotel is targeted at BREEAM 'excellent'. Minor alterations at the lower levels of City Temple will allow us to create office space, and the upper levels are intended for religious and commercial use. This comprises a refurbished church interior and reception, as well as meeting and conference spaces, but also short-term guest accommodation and extended plant areas.

C: MH Viaduct LP
PM: Gardiner & Theobald
SE: Fairhurst GGA
M&E: Hilson Moran
QS: Beadmans LLP
A: EP, RK, GGP, MV, WA, GW, JF
Date: 2014–ongoing

One Chamberlain Square, Paradise Circus, Birmingham

The Masterplan for Paradise was designed by Glenn Howells Architects and received outline planning approval in February 2013. In April 2014, we were invited by the development manager Argent to enter an architectural competition for Building D of the approved masterplan. We won the competition and were appointed to begin design work in September 2014. The building proposal was developed between September 2014 and June 2015 in conjunction with Argent through a rigorous design process and formal pre-application consultations with Birmingham City Council, Historic England and the Design Council.

C: Hermes Investment Management
Development Manager: Argent
PM: Faithful + Gould
SE and M&E: Arup
LA: Grant Associates
A: EP, NJ, LH, ARM, MN, RP, CRD, JIS
Date: 2014–ongoing

Covent Garden Corners

We were asked to carry out a feasibility study to extend the Covent Garden alfresco dining experience into the winter months, providing support to operators who have otherwise to rely on either limited or no internal seating. The aim was to create a structure that customers want to be seen in, but that complements the market buildings and has synergies with the Opera Terrace structure.

C: Covent Garden London (Capital & Counties Properties plc)
SE: Eckersley O'Callaghan
A: EP, CH, CT, FW, EF
Date: 2015

St James's Market

The area formerly covered by the historic St James's Market is integral to the Crown Estate's regeneration plans for St James's. As part of the Crown's long-term strategy, key urban blocks were selected between Haymarket and Regent Street for mixed-use (retail and offices). Our submission included site research elements covering the whole of St James's and in particular the old Market and the pre-existing Royal Opera House and its arcade. In response to the nature of the site and the requirements of the brief regarding porosity to reconnect the site to its chief surroundings, a crossing was suggested, which would take the form of a double-height arcade, continuing Nash's Royal Opera Arcade to a new urban interior, eventually connecting Haymarket to Regent Street with bespoke retail on the lower floors and offices on the upper floors.

C: The Crown Estate
A: EP, RK, NJ, CT*, SO, AM, JIS, EF, DC
Date: 2015

30 St James's Square

30 St James's Square is formed by two interconnected office buildings of 21 and 22 Pall Mall, set within the St James's Conservation Area of Westminster. The proposal for 30 St James's Square comprises the retention of the existing basement, with a new core and structure constructed behind a retained façade, extended one storey to provide six storeys above ground, with a new mansard roof concealing a roof plant room. The building includes six floors of speculative office accommodation, above the office entrance and retail on the ground floor.

The design of 30 St James's Square has been driven by principles of sustainable design in order to reduce energy consumption in occupation and to provide a comfortable and healthy environment for its users. The building is on target to achieve a BREEAM 'excellent' rating and will deliver a BREEAM 'very good' rating as a minimum.

C: British Grolux
Development Manager: Hanover Cube
SE: Price & Myers
M&E: KJ Tait Engineers
QS: Quantem Consulting LLP
A: EP, RD, MM, RP, JT, FW, WA
Date: 2015–ongoing

Byzantium Project

Our proposed refurbishment, extension and renewal of Dolphin Square is to provide additional residential accommodation on the main building, tennis court site and westerly access road. It includes opening up the central square as a public facility by selective demolition of existing facilities and the provision of new leisure, community and retail accommodation to include improved landscaping and public realm with a new entrance and face to Chichester Street.

C: Westbrook Partners
PM: Radcliffe Construction
SE: Heyne Tillett Steel
M&E: Thornton Reynolds
LA: Todd Longstaffe-Gowan
A: EP, NJ, RD, GGP, KB, IS, JT, MV, CRD, RP, WA, MM, WW
Date: 2015–ongoing

Chelsea Barracks

We won the competition for phase 4 of the Chelsea Barracks site, with a high-end residential proposal including car parking, spa and sports centre. Our design consists of three new apartment buildings around a private court, and an additional area of soft landscaping. Built in stone, the façades are evocative of the British architectural legacy and its classical references, calling upon the collaboration of a visual artist in the long stone entablature that will punctuate the architecture with a new work of public art.

C: Chelsea Barracks (4) GP LLP
PM: WYG
SE: Arup
M&E: Hoare Lea
QS: Gleeds
LA: Gustafson Porter
A: EP, RK, NJ, MC, TP, ARM, CB, DL, AR, MJ, SH, AM, BL, CLK, GW, JM, JIS, KB, VG, MIP, MP, MV, RRP, SP, TA, AW, LG, MLP, EA, AG, BT
Date: 2015–ongoing

1 Undershaft

A detail planning application was submitted to the City of London in January 2016 for the 73-storey development at 1 Undershaft in the City of London. At 289.94m tall, it will rise to a height of 304.94m AOD (Above Ordnance Datum), crowning the new cluster of planned skyscrapers in the Square Mile. The building will provide approximately 90,000m^2 of office space. The offset design of the core and the rigidity provided by the unique external bracing means floor space has been maximised, providing much needed flexible, quality office accommodation for businesses in the City of London. A new larger public square will be created at the base of the tower. The elevated office reception lobby means that the public will be able to walk freely beneath the skyscraper. Retail space will be created in the lower level retail gallery, with new restaurants, cafés and shops accessed from the public square. At the top of the building will be the UK's highest public viewing gallery, served by dedicated lifts. A public restaurant will be located on the level beneath the viewing gallery.

C: Aroland Holdings Ltd and Perennial and Wilmar International Ltd
SE: WSP
Vertical transportation: WSP
Fire enginnering: WSP
QS: Aecom
A: EP, NJ, TP, SH, TN, JIS, JSC, WW CD, MN, ED
Date: 2015–ongoing

Great Ormond Street Hospital

Our proposal was part of a shortlisted competitive dialogue process with GOSH to develop phase 4 of their masterplan. Phase 4 would replace outdated facilities on part of the hospital's Central London site, supporting its clinical teams in delivering world-class paediatric care and research. GOSH is one of the world's leading children's hospitals with the broadest range of dedicated children's healthcare specialists under one roof in the UK. The hospital sees more than 268,000 patients every year from around the world. The building would become the new 'front door' for the organisation and an architectural expression of its guiding principle: The Child First and Always. The client's vision for the development was shaped by a comprehensive review of the GOSH masterplan and engagement with GOSH staff, patients and families.

C: Carillion
A: EP, LH, PBA, FW, JIS, DP, ED
Date: 2016

Marylebone Lane Hotel

Our proposal is to remove the existing 1970s brutalist car park in Marylebone Lane and build a high-end boutique hotel of 206 rooms. The new hotel will have two basement levels with business and fitness facilities, as well as a café, bar and signature restaurant on the ground level, fostering the improvement of the public realm. There are nine levels of accommodation above, including a members' lounge with a small pool on level 9. The concrete frame structure accommodates for arrangement of the 2.6m-clear ceiling height guestrooms around the perimeter and the central light well. The exterior is to be clad in extruded faience panels with horizontal blue banding, continuing onto the sculptural roof.

C: Shiva Hotels
PM: Buro Four
SE: Manhire Associates
M&E: Elementa Consulting
QS: Gardiner & Theobald
A: EP, NJ, CB, EF, KB, EVP, KP
Date: 2016–ongoing

Staff List

The order of initials reflects design responsibility; * marks project team leader. Where this was passed on between designs (1) and construction (2) the * is followed by the respective figure.

References for Design Team:

C	Client
PM	Project Manager
SE	Structural Engineer
M&E	Mechanical Engineering Consultant
QS	Quantity Surveyor
LA	Landscape Architect
A	EPA Team

EP Eric Parry
BA Hons (Newcastle), MA (Cantab), MA (RCA), AADipl, Hon DA (Bath), RIBA, RA
founded the practice in 1983

RK Robert Kennett
MA (Cantab), DipArch (Cantab), RIBA
worked at EPA from 1989 to the present
appointed director in 1997

NJ Nick Jackson
BA Hons (Cantab), MA (Cantab), DipArch (Cantab), RIBA
worked at EPA from 1990 to 2018
appointed director in 1997

JO Julian Ogiwara
BA Hons (UEL), DipArch (UEL), RIBA
worked at EPA from 2000 to the present
appointed associate in 2007
appointed director in 2010

MC Merit Claussen
Textile designer, Architect RIBA
worked at EPA from 1999 to 2016
appointed associate in 2007
appointed associate director in 2010

RD Robert Dawson
BA Hons (Birmingham), DipArch (Oxford Brookes), ARB
worked at EPA from 2006 to the present
appointed associate in 2010
appointed associate director in 2016

LH Lee Higson
BA Hons (Leeds), DipArch (London Met), RIBA
worked at EPA from 2006 to the present
appointed associate in 2007
appointed associate director in 2010

TL Tim Lynch
BA Hons (Newcastle), DipArch (Mackintosh), RIBA
worked at EPA from 2004 to 2017
appointed associate in 2007
appointed associate director in 2010

TP Tanya Parkin
BSc Hons (QUB), DipArch DipBRS (OBU), RIBA
worked at EPA from 2001 to the present
appointed associate in 2006
appointed associate director in 2016

JS Justin Sayer
BA (Oxon), BSc (East London), DipArch (UCL, DBA), RIBA
worked at EPA from 1996 to the present
appointed associate in 2003
appointed associate director in 2007

PBA Paul Barke-Asuni
BArch, MA (Princeton), ARB
worked at EPA from 2011 to the present
appointed associate in 2014

CB Christopher Burton
MA Hons (Mackintosh), DipArch (Mackintosh), ARB
worked at EPA from 2004 to the present
appointed associate in 2010

RC Ros Cohen
BA Hons (Cantab), MA (Cantab), DipArch (UEL), Architect ARB
worked at EPA from 1998 to 2001 and 2003 to the present
appointed associate in 2010

BD Brendan Durkin
BA Hons (Kingston), DipArch (London Metropolitan), ARB
worked at EPA from 2006 to the present
appointed associate in 2014

SF Sofia Ferreira
BA (Hons), DipArch, ARB
worked at EPA from 2006 to the present
appointed associate in 2017

SH Sven Heimann
Dipl.-Ing., MArch, ARB
worked at EPA from 2014 to the present
appointed associate in 2017

CH Christine Humphreys
BSc distinction (McGill), BSc (Arch) (McGill), PostGradDip Painting (CSSD), RIBA
worked at EPA from 2006 to 2017
appointed associate in 2008

DL Damien Lee
BSc Hons, DipArch, ARB
worked at EPA from 2006 to the present
appointed associate in 2014

ARM Anil Mistry
BA (Hons), DipArch, MArch, ARB
worked at EPA from 2006 to the present
appointed associate in 2014

TN Takayuki Nakajima
Arch (UBA, CPAU)
worked at EPA from 2013 to the present
appointed associate in 2017

GGP Guy Parkinson
BA (Hons), DipArch, ARB
worked at EPA from 2007 to the present
appointed associate in 2014

JSC Jonathan Schöning
BA, DipArch (Mackintosh), Architect ARB
worked at EPA from 2011 to the present
appointed associate in 2017

CT Claudia Tschunko
Dipl.-Ing. Arch. (Stuttgart), Architect ARB
worked at EPA from 2007 to 2018
appointed associate in 2010

Architectural staff

AC	Abigail Connor
AG	Aura Gnerucci
AM	Aya Maeda
AR	Alex Rider
ARM	Anil Mistry
ASM	Asher Meltzer
AO	Andrius Ovsiukas
AW	Alexander Watt
BD	Brendan Durkin
BF	Brian Fitzgerald
BL	Brenda Leonard
BT	Benedek Takács
CB	Christopher Burton
CD	Christopher Drummond
CH	Christine Humphreys
CHD	Christopher Daniels
CK	Catharin Knuth
CL	Carl Laffan
CLK	Cecilie Kjeldsen
CRD	Charles Debelle
CSL	Chloe Spiby-Loh
CT	Claudia Tschunko
DC	Damien Clayton
DG	Derek Gibbons
DL	Damien Lee
DP	David Pérez
EA	Eduardo Argüelles
ED	Edward Dyhouse
EF	Eliot Foy
EH	Eimear Hanratty
ELP	Emily Posey
EP	Eric Parry
EVP	Eva Pospechova
FW	Fei Wu
GGP	Guy Parkinson
GW	Gary Watkin
HT	Hannah Tourell
IS	Iulia Statica
JD	James Davies
JE	Jeff Essen
JF	Jamie Flynn
JFR	Jeremy Foster
JH	Joshua Harskamp
JIS	Jiehwoo Seung
JM	James McNeill
JO	Julian Ogiwara
JP	José de Paiva
JS	Justin Sayer
JSC	Jonathan Schöning
JT	Jessica Tettelaar
KB	Kenet Bakamovic
KP	Katharina Parsons
KS	Krystin Schwendel Smith
LAF	Lyn Ang Ferrari
LB	Lewis Benmore
LG	Louise Godfrey
LH	Lee Higson
LM	Lee McKinley
LMB	Lisa Basu
LV	Lan Van
MC	Merit Claussen
MIP	Melissa Patterson
MJ	Michelle Jeremiah
MLP	Macushla Peek
MM	Mike McMahon
MN	Markus Nurkkala
MP	Michael Perkins
MV	Michael Vale
MW	Matthew Wells
NJ	Nick Jackson
PBA	Paul Barke-Asuni
PF	Paul Fielding
RC	Ros Cohen
RD	Robert Dawson
RK	Robert Kennett
RL	Rebecca Lim
RLL	Roo Lam Lau
RP	Richard Prest
RRP	Ruby Penny
RSW	Rupert Willard
SF	Sofia Ferreira
SH	Sven Heimann
SO	Sarah Oxley
SP	Sara del Piñal
TA	Thomas Atkinson
TJH	TJ Hartnett
TL	Tim Lynch
TN	Takayuki Nakajima
TP	Tanya Parkin
TS	Tom Sweet
TW	Thomas Windley
VG	Valentina Grittini
WA	William Aitken
WW	William Wang
ZF	Ze'ev Feigis
ZP	Zoe Panayi

Non-architectural staff

Anthony McGoldrick
Craig Lochhead
Christy Fry
Duncan Macdonald
Emma Tracey
Fiona Henry
Jake Bailey
Jin Georgiou
Joanne Gold
Joshua King
Natalia Vonta
Rebecca Macdonald
Roma McCook
Russell Watson
Zoe Atherton

Photo Credits

Cover: DL

4–5. DL

Introduction

6. Private collection
15. DL

Timely and Enduring Architecture

14. DL
17. DL
18. DL
19. DL
21. DL
23. DL

4 Pancras Square

28. DL
35. GS
36. DL
37. DL
38. DL
39. DL
40. DL
41. DL

One Eagle Place

42. DL
46. DL
47. DL
49. DL
50. DL
51. DL
52. DL
53. DL
54. DL
55. DL

7–8 St James's Square

56. DL
61. GS
62. DL
64. DL
65. DL
68. DL
69. DL

East Village

70. MO
73. JH
76. JH
79. JH

The Charterhouse

80. DL
84. EPA
85. EPA
87. DL
89. DL
90. DL
91. DL

The Welding Institute

92. DL
95. DL
97. DL
98. DL
99. DL
100. DL
101. DL
102. DL
103. DL

Wells Cathedral School

104. DL
109. DL
111. DL
114. DL
115. DL
118. DL
119. DL

Brighton College Music School

120. HB
124. EPA
125. EPA
127. HB
130. GS
132. HB
133. HB
134. DS
135. HB

The Leathersellers' Hall

136. DL
138. DL
140. DL
141. DL
144. DL
145. DL
146. DL
147. DL
148. DL
150. DL
151. DL

Royal Academy Summer Exhibition

152. NK
154. NK
156. NK
157. NK
158. NK (detail)

The Opera Terrace, Covent Garden

160. GS
163. GS
166. GS
167. GS
168. GS
169. GS

10 Fenchurch Avenue

170. AP
174. EPA
178–179. SA
180. SA
181. SA

Photographers

AP Andrew Putler
DS David Shearing
DL Dirk Lindner
EPA Eric Parry Architects
GS Grant Smith
HB Hélène Binet
JH James Harris
MO Mike O'Dwyer
NK Nick Kane
SA Sam Ainsworth

Acknowledgements

Volume 4 opens with the completion of 4 Pancras Square in 2017, fourteen years after the concept charrette in 2003. Like a vintage wine, it has improved with age whilst maintaining the original tectonic and material ideas. The volume closes with the history of the design development of 10 Fenchurch Avenue which, as we go to print, is being fitted out ready for occupation in 2019 and the completed project will be described in *Volume 5* which is itself being planned.

For Joseph Rykwert to write an Introduction, which he carried out with great care and judgement, was beyond my wildest hopes. We are deeply indebted to Joseph for interrupting his own work to do so, particularly with the sadness of Dalibor Vesely's passing, who had written the introductions for *Volumes 1*, *2* and *3*.

Jay Merrick accepted the task of writing about the projects together with his 'Timely and Enduring Architecture' essay. It has been a great pleasure to accompany Jay on visits to all the projects he has written about and which he has set into such a broad and erudite perspective. It has been a great pleasure to stand back as an outsider so to speak and be surprised and challenged by his analysis and understanding.

I hope that the enjoyment of the physical art of making is evident at many scales from the landscape and building of The Welding Institute or 10 Fenchurch Avenue to the close crafting of metal structures at The Charterhouse and The Opera Terrace. This is only possible through the sending of the translation from drawings and models to workshops of great craftsmanship. Our deep thanks are due to the dedication of those at either end of the process.

In making explicit the layers of construction, Graham Bizley's projective drawings have added to our collection in Volume 3. In corrections and critical review of the drawings and captions, many members of the office have helped particularly, Tim Lynch, Robert Dawson, Paul Barke-Asuni, Christopher Burton, Brendan Durkin, Christine Humphreys, Derek Gibbons, Damien Lee, Anil Mistry, Takayuki Nakajima, Guy Parkinson, Jonathan Schöning, Claudia Tschunko, James McNeill, Katharina Parsons, Mike Mc Mahon.

José de Paiva has been responsible for the whole endeavour and has been ably assisted in the graphic design of Volume 4 by Daniel Benneworth-Gray. Our graphics team, headed by Russell Watson and including Roma McCook and Uzma Waheed have been responsible for the reconstruction and correction of *Volume 3*.

Our growing portfolio of excellent architectural photography has been created by Dirk Lindner, Grant Smith, Hélène Binet, Nick Kane, Andrew Putler, David Shearing, James Harris, Mike O'Dwyer, and Sam Ainsworth.

One addition to the range of work is the interior design of more civic buildings than dwellings; this is particularly evident in the Livery Company headquarters for The Leathersellers, where a wonderful range of crafting is evident from glass to leather, and we wish to thank all those involved in such an ambitious and rewarding journey of discovery and innovation.

Artifice Press Limited
298 Regents Park Road
London N3 2SZ

t. +44 (0) 20 8371 4000
office@artificeonline.com
www.artificeonline.com

Designed by Daniel Benneworth-Gray for Eric Parry Architects
www.danielgray.com

British Library Cataloguing-in-Publication Data.
A CIP record for this book is available from the British Library.

ISBN 978 1 911339 31 1

Artifice Press is an environmentally responsible company.
Eric Parry Architects Volume 4 is printed on sustainably sourced paper.

Printed in Italy by Faenza Printing Industries S.p.A.

Also available:

Eric Parry Architects Volume 1
ISBN 978 1 906155 62 9

Eric Parry Architects Volume 2
ISBN 978 1 906155 25 4

Eric Parry Architects Volume 1 & 2 Box Set
ISBN 978 1 906155 63 6

Eric Parry Architects Volume 3
ISBN 978 1 908967 03 9

Eric Parry Architects Volume 3 & 4 Box Set
ISBN 978 1 911339 32 8

Artifice